CANCEL WARS

Cancel Wars

HOW UNIVERSITIES CAN FOSTER
FREE SPEECH, PROMOTE INCLUSION,
AND RENEW DEMOCRACY

Sigal R. Ben-Porath

The University of Chicago Press CHICAGO AND LONDON

The University of Chicago Press, Chicago 60637
The University of Chicago Press, Ltd., London
© 2023 by The University of Chicago
Published 2023
Printed in the United States of America

32 31 30 29 28 27 26 25 24 23   1 2 3 4 5

ISBN-13: 978-0-226-82378-2 (cloth)
ISBN-13: 978-0-226-82380-5 (paper)
ISBN-13: 978-0-226-82379-9 (e-book)
DOI: https://doi.org/10.7208/chicago/9780226823799.001.0001

Library of Congress Cataloging-in-Publication Data

Names: Ben-Porath, Sigal R., 1967– author.
Title: Cancel wars : how universities can foster free speech, promote
    inclusion, and renew democracy / Sigal R. Ben-Porath.
Description: Chicago : University of Chicago Press, 2023. | Includes
    bibliographical references and index.
Identifiers: LCCN 2022018908 | ISBN 9780226823782 (cloth) |
    ISBN 9780226823805 (paperback) | ISBN 9780226823799 (ebook)
Subjects: LCSH: Academic freedom—United States. | Freedom of
    speech—United States. | Education, Higher—Political aspects—
    United States. | Democracy—United States. | Polarization (Social
    sciences)—United States. | Politics and culture—United States—
    History—21st century. | BISAC: EDUCATION / Philosophy, Theory
    & Social Aspects | POLITICAL SCIENCE / Political Ideologies /
    Conservatism & Liberalism
Classification: LCC LC72.2 .B464 2023 | DDC 378.1/2130973—dc23/
    eng/20220608
LC record available at https://lccn.loc.gov/2022018908

♾ This paper meets the requirements of ANSI/NISO Z39.48-1992
(Permanence of Paper).

TO MY SISTER, MAYA RADAY

Contents

Introduction

Can colleges and universities help heal a backsliding democracy? Some see these institutions as culprits in the demise of democracy and point to students' sensitivities or professors' ideologies as reasons to lose faith in their contributions. I suggest instead that higher education in all its variety, from the Ivy League to community colleges, is well situated and ready to take on the challenges democracy currently faces. This book considers the struggles over the boundaries of speech in order to make the case for the active role that institutions of higher education can take in bridging political divides and helping reverse the process of democratic decline. Colleges are laboratories in which democracy is learned, practiced, and enhanced. As students, instructors, and leaders in higher education pursue and disseminate knowledge—and work to create inclusive and engaged learning communities—they seed democratic habits and practices. It is necessary to focus on the boundaries of speech on campus because of both the nature of work in higher education, where so much of the work involves speech, and the current state of democracy.

We can understand and begin to address some of the most pressing challenges to democracy by paying careful attention to struggles over truth and to disagreements over belonging and inclusion. These controversies have taken center stage at many college campuses in recent years, especially in debates over the regulation and protection of speech on campus. I argue that the challenges of campus speech are the result of contestations over broader societal fractures concerning truth and inclusion and that campuses need to, in most cases, address these challenges through efforts to engage across differences rather than as breaches to be corrected through regulation or punishment.

The boundaries of acceptable expression on a campus should be set by the mission of the institution, by the call to search for truth through shared work, and through the inclusion of diverse perspectives and voices in the process of inquiry.[1] If a form of expression excludes some people on campus, it is the institution's responsibility to correct the outcomes of that speech. In the vast majority of cases, this does not mean censorship, firing, or "canceling" but rather other types of action taken by the institution to ensure that equity and continued dialogue are both preserved. In this way, speech remains robust while inclusion is reaffirmed and sustained. This is a modified version of the "more speech" response encouraged by Justice Louis Brandeis:[2] it seeks to not simply encourage more speech but also to place the burden of expressing, supporting, and sometimes sponsoring more and better speech on the institution as part of its educational and democratic role.

College campuses have become flashpoints in the current culture war. In this book, I argue that the escalating struggles over "cancel culture," "safe spaces," and free speech on campus are a manifestation of broader democratic erosion in the United States. I take a closer look at how these tensions play out to illuminate a path toward revitalizing American democracy. In what follows, I consider the gray areas of permissible speech, taking a close look at their sources and offering solutions to the tensions they create. I situate open expression on campus within the broader polarization occurring in the political sphere to show that the fight over the future of democracy takes place in two battlegrounds: one revolving around truth, how to identify it, and how it is distorted; and the other around inclusion, exclusion, and "cancellation" from the public sphere. Taken together, tensions around truth and inclusion reshape the civic culture of contemporary democracies. Colleges and universities, along with K–12 schools, are among the main arenas where these battles are fought, and they hold a key to surmounting the current democratic impasse.

Chapter 1 begins with an assessment of the role of contested speech and of struggles over the boundaries of speech in the current polarized environment and the process of democratic erosion that is already underway. I discuss the growing polarization in American society (among other democracies) and situate contestations over acceptable speech—particularly at educational institutions—within this polarized context. Polarization is evident in ideological views, (in)action by elected officials and party elites, and a public debate that is growing ever more heated. This process accelerates the decline of trust in educational and other institutions. Significantly, it exacerbates the decline in civic and social trust, increasing citizens' suspicion of those who do not share their ideological views, which in turn justifies their being labeled as dishonest, threatening, or deserving of censorship or censure. The decline in civic and social trust accelerates as political ideologies grow to coincide with other social identities, creating overlapping fissures in society. Which views can legitimately be heard in public, and which are harmful, treasonous, deceitful, or libelous? The struggle over the boundaries of speech pushes some, especially among the younger generation, to question the value of protecting free speech. Thus, the very ideas of open expression and speech protection become polarizing, complicating the possibility of having a discussion across diverse experiences and views. Polarization and the isolation that it breeds push individuals and communities further apart. This process expresses tensions as old as the republic itself, which continue to fester across racial lines; the tension takes on new forms in the virtual public spheres in which much of today's political debate takes place. These old and new threads set the stage for a debate over the boundaries of what might be said, what views are legitimate, and what expression is protected in a democracy.

In chapter 2, I consider the challenges to maintaining a shared foundation of knowledge, as well as its importance. A common understanding of the process of developing and disseminating knowledge—and coming to agreements on key facets of reality—are necessary for a sustainable democracy. The primary challenges to this shared foundation are polarization and mistrust. I start by making the case for a shared epistemic foundation, and I consider three avenues for outlining its boundaries: distinguishing between fact and opinion, identifying experts who can help identify claims that are true, and selecting proper sources of information. None of these prove to be sufficient tools for delineating the boundaries of a reliable shared epistemology, on account of both politically motivated reasoning and willful ignorance. The final section of this chapter positions truth, expertise, and reliable sources of information within the work of academic institutions and envisions the shared construction of knowledge as a solution to truth decay. Building epistemic networks, which is possible through the long-term engagement among campus members typical of higher education institutions, makes expanding and disseminating knowledge possible and can help rekindle the civic trust that is necessary for revitalizing democracy.

In chapter 3, I address the evolving ways in which claims about harm shape conversations and give rise to concerns over "canceling" and silencing, and how these claims subsequently frame forms of membership in social and institutional settings. Increasingly, American society and many of the communities within it clash over the boundaries of membership: the value of diversity, the significance of inclusion, and the "cancellation" and exclusion of people and views. The sensibilities of the increasingly diverse community on campus, and the growing recognition of diversity more broadly, give rise to urgent demands to prevent hurtful speech. To what extent should such demands be accommodated? Some have derisively termed the calls to scrub the conversation of hurtful words, exclusionary assumptions, and uncivil practices "cancel culture." Understanding this "cancel culture" requires an evaluation of the harms that speech can cause and what claims of harm can and cannot do. I illustrate the changing landscape of permissible speech and its consequences through current struggles over using bigoted, hurtful language in classrooms and other public spaces and offer criteria for how to respond to such uses. These criteria acknowledge that the call for creating a more welcoming and inclusive climate on college campuses, on social media platforms, and in democratic debate sometimes clashes with the legal protections for speech that require protection of diverse views, even noxious ones. A focus on the boundaries of acceptable speech, and on the disproportionate impact that hate speech has on marginalized groups, sheds light on possible responses to these tensions.

What is the source of the apparent generational change in attitudes toward speech? Democratic attitudes begin to take shape at a young age and are often seeded through children's engagement with the most significant institution in which they take part, schools. While the sources of democratic backsliding are varied, some can be traced to limited opportunities for civic growth, including a scarcity of open discussion of diverse views. In chapter 4, I consider the ways in which democratic habits, and especially a commitment to an open exchange of ideas, are shaped in school. The development of these habits is achievable but challenged by various factors, including politically motivated efforts to limit students' and teachers' speech. The courts have continuously eroded speech protections for students over the past decades, thus allowing schools to maintain a more controlled environment. Further, schools reflect the communities in which they operate and are locally controlled in ways that increasingly reflect polarized social and political visions. I consider practices available to schools for addressing the erosion of democratic protections for speech, particularly through programs of media literacy that help students sift through the information and misinformation that they encounter, and devoting time to discussion in class, so that children learn to listen to diverse views and perspectives and to consider their own in light of open dialogue with others.

Those high school graduates who end up going to college are often less than prepared for the type of open exchange in which colleges take pride. Chapter 5 offers policy suggestions and practical guidance for addressing contemporary speech challenges faced by higher education institutions. Extending the framework of inclusive freedom developed in my earlier work, this chapter provides a pathway for revitalizing democracy through practices that express a commitment to speech and inclusion on college campuses. I look closely at campus settings where the boundaries of speech are negotiated, including classrooms, residences, student organizations, and university boards. I consider the complex reality of negotiating the boundaries of speech and illustrate ways for students, instructors, and administrators to anchor democratic practice in a commitment to truth and inclusion.

This book is the result of my work with college students, activists, faculty, and administrators at many institutions. In aiming to help craft policies and practices that reflect an equal commitment to open expression and inclusion, I have had the benefit of engaging with countless individuals at many institutions in the United States, Canada, and Europe and of observing the ways in which democratic erosion reverberates in the current clashes over campus speech practices. Some of these clashes are the result of generational differences in views on democracy, speech, and inclusion, while others arise from attempts to accrue political power. The higher education sector cannot ignore or duck these pressures, nor can it maintain a reactive approach. This book considers struggles over free speech as a way to clarify the place of higher education in the current democratic moment, and it offers a path for taking on these struggles as part of the effort to renew democracy.

1 · A Polarized Democracy

POLARIZATION OVER FREE SPEECH

An instructor for the popular Gov 50: Data course in the Department of Government at Harvard was exposed as a blogger posting controversial views pseudonymously. He invited a conservative guest speaker to present his views about innate differences that distinguish races, classes, and genders, claiming that Harvard students need to be exposed to more right-wing views. Student sleuths identified the instructor as posting perspectives online in opposition to affirmative action and questioning the suitability of Black and low-income students to attend selective colleges. They demanded that the college dismiss him.[1]

· · ·

Ours is an era marked by growing polarization, overlapping social fissures, and a rise in social and civic mistrust. Young people, depicted as unable to properly participate in open political exchange, are frequently blamed for generating or accelerating these trends. Periodic lamentations about "kids these days" are increasingly focused on contestations about the boundaries of speech. With a decline in trust and a growing sense of alienation among those who hold different views or attest to different experiences, it becomes harder for them to give people on the other side the benefit of the doubt, the grace that comes from assuming good intentions. It is easier to assume that a person on the other side of a social or political divide is lying, or is intentionally speaking in hurtful ways, which makes them an appropriate target for social rejection and punishment.[2] It is commonly suggested, especially by conservative commentators, that young people are attempting to "cancel" or silence those with whom they disagree. In response, others suggest that "cancel culture" is nothing but a myth, a construct made up for political gain, or that it is in fact a practice commonplace across the political spectrum, rather than describing just one side.

Scholars such as Alexander Meiklejohn hold that the democratic interest in both individual and institutional speech stems from the epistemic (or knowledge-related) importance of free speech to self-government.[3] Still, much of the effort in the past few decades to maintain and expand the boundaries of acceptable speech—at least what has been visible to the public though key Supreme Court cases—has been focused on protecting hateful forms of expression. In prior decades, notably the 1960s, struggles over what could be expressed in public focused on protecting political opposition, dissent, and protest; today, jurisprudence, legislative efforts, and public debates significantly focus on the permissibility of expressing racist, anti-LGBTQ, and anti-immigrant perspectives. For some advocates of free speech, the development is jarring: "College students used to demand the right to free speech. Now they demand the freedom from speech they find upsetting."[4] The impact of these debates on individuals and communities is direct and influences the relationship within and across diverse communities. If the questions that were common in earlier decades were, for example, "Can a student wear an anti-war armband to school?" and "Can students and other activists block roads when they protest?" common questions now are "Must a professor use a student's pronouns?" and "Is it ever permissible to mention slurs in class?" (see chapter 3 for discussions of these and other issues). The contours of the discussion about speech and the stances toward speech are changing both across ideologies and across generations.

Young people observe these efforts to protect hateful and exclusive expression in the public sphere, and some become suspicious of the very idea of protecting free speech. The case of the Harvard instructor that opened this chapter demonstrates this tension: the instructor's goal was to push for a wider variety of views, which he suggested were not sufficiently available to students. He pointed to the dearth of conservative and right-leaning views, a commonly raised concern among critics of higher education. The perspective he was looking to introduce, though, was one students found abhorrent, and they subsequently identified him as holding those views himself. In this incident and in similar ones, striving to expand the types of views presented in a college classroom is depicted by one side as a struggle for free expression and diversity of views and by the other side as permitting the infiltration of hateful, bigoted, or exclusive views. The decision to relieve the instructor of his teaching and advising duties might satisfy the latter, but it does little to quell the cultural clash over the boundaries of acceptable speech. The students were taking a stance against what they saw as positions that are both harmful and inappropriate for a college classroom; their stance in turn was depicted as an instance of "cancel culture," a framing that aims to delegitimize their efforts.

Generational and ideological differences in the level of support for freedom of speech have become one of the core polarizing issues in American public culture in recent years. If, in the 1960s, freedom of speech, assembly, protest, and petition were largely progressive causes, where the young demanded to be heard, as the twenty-first century unfolds, the defenders of the right to speak freely are heard more loudly in conservative circles. In surveys, some young people express doubt about the importance of protecting free speech and a willingness to censor speech that might be harmful, such as racist or otherwise bigoted speakers and statements.[5]

Thus, we see a growing suspicion of the democratic relevance of free speech and a sense among some, including young people in particular and especially those on the progressive side of the map, that fighting to protect open expression ends up serving reactionary political goals. Significantly, and despite years of politicized tensions around the matter, a recent poll showed that over 80 percent of respondents identified free speech as a value that is extremely or very important to them and 76 percent saw "working together toward the common good" as similarly important.[6]

It is important for democracy that freedom of speech be recognized as a core value and practiced as such. Freedom of speech is a key aspect of democracy and a primary tool for ensuring the lively public debate necessary for political representation and freedom of thought. Without it, the silencing of dissent, the oppression of minority views, and the imposition of a uniformity of ideas and views become real concerns. The centrality of protecting free speech in a democracy is a central discussion in legal and political scholarship. The democratic commitment to free speech reflects the core democratic assumption of equal dignity and worth: by protecting the right of all to speak, a society establishes the equal human and civic worth of all its members and the presupposition that they are all agents, actors, and individuals who have the potential to contribute to the common good. In educational institutions, free speech is protected for other reasons and can therefore have different boundaries, and this distinction animates this book. But the struggle over the boundaries of speech in democracy reverberates on campuses, and it needs to be addressed there. As Ronald Daniels notes, "institutions of higher education can neither be indifferent nor passive in the face of democratic backsliding."[7] Moving beyond the moral panic of "cancel culture" and away from attempts to cast blame can enable a clear-eyed look at the current state of democracy and of free speech within it.

Protections for open expression are in many ways vital to democracy, and they are vital in even more ways to the mission of higher education. To rekindle within the younger generation the belief that free speech matters and is in fact a democratic value worth protecting, colleges should serve as spaces where free speech is explicitly cultivated as a value—namely, where students are not just expected to practice it and to benefit from it but are also introduced in direct ways to its centrality in college life and democratic practice. Colleges and universities should also ensure that the speech protections they enact align with the broadest possible democratic goals. As Daniels rightly notes, "what we have seen play out on campuses in the past several years is not yet a crisis but rather a steady, unremitting beat of frustration at the state of speech whose remedy will require more than a referee."[8] Indeed, colleges and universities will need to not simply express a commitment to open expression and delineate its boundaries but also take an active role in defining these boundaries and alleviating the unequal burdens created by protected speech on campus.

Inclusive freedom provides a framework for fulfilling the promise of free speech in higher education, as well as in other institutional contexts that support and enact democratic values.[9] On college campuses, inclusive freedom aims to make free speech tangible by sustaining broad boundaries for permissible expression and ensuring that all members of the community can benefit from them. To ensure that free speech benefits everyone, a higher education institution (like other institutions) needs to take a close look at who pays the price for free speech. This means ensuring legal and democratic protections for speech and attending to the burdens that they create: if some members of the community are hurt, silenced, or pushed out by permissible speech, the institution needs to take as its responsibility the assertion of their belonging and the enacting of policies that reflect their equal standing. The institution thus takes it upon itself to maintain an environment in which all can effectively speak and participate.

In a political climate that is polarized and hostile, it might be hard to let cool heads prevail; in this context, freedom of speech has sometimes been interpreted and applied in ways that serve politically expedient goals that undermine democratic principles. Some partisan legislation expresses support of free speech but interprets it in a way that promotes partisan goals, elevating some ideological stances while silencing others. For example, in some states, protests on college campuses can lead to suspension for participating students.[10] In others, taking part in a demonstration in which someone else caused property damage—say, broke store windows—can land demonstrators who did not contribute to the damage in any direct way in prison for up to fifteen years.[11] Some state legislators aim to ban specific subjects and even words from college and K-12 school curricula.[12] One Arkansas bill states that "No events or activities should group students based on ethnicity, race, religion, gender, or social class."[13] All these legislative efforts, along with cases such as *Masterpiece Cakeshop*[14] and *Meriwether*,[15] use speech protection as a tool to allow the powerful— business owners and corporations, professors and employers, police and administrators—to silence and censor those under their authority, especially those who aim to dissent or are members of minority groups. No wonder, then, that some who support democratic values are becoming disenchanted with free speech as a principle and as a practical tool for ensuring an equal and free democratic public sphere. When the concept, and legal principle, of free speech is wielded as a tool of exclusion, some citizens who care about democratic equality will begin to question its value. As I argue throughout this book, this reaction should not be readily understood as marking a turn against democracy and toward authoritarianism but rather as an effort to ensure that all members have access to the same speech (and other) protections. While this critique of free speech sometimes goes too far, the values underlying this response to the current struggles over speech need to be understood in this political context. The political context of polarization is key to understanding these struggles, and it is central for sustaining institutional contexts (such as colleges) and a public sphere where both the principle and the reality of equal freedom are possible.[16]

POLARIZATION AND IDENTITY

In recent years, political polarization, and especially a mistrust toward counter-partisans, has been growing in the United States.[17] On the eve of the 2020 elections, Americans of different political ideologies expressed their fear for the vitality and stability of American democracy as a top concern.[18] While the mistrust Americans feel about those on the other side of the ideological divide must have contributed significantly to these concerns, with accusations of socialism on the one side pitted against accusations of fascism on the other, it is evident that confidence in the stability of democratic institutions, including elections themselves, is eroding and that Americans are looking for ways to fortify their democratic institutions and culture. The American civic fabric is pulled in many directions, to the point of fraying.

Polarization, or significant distances between views, values, and beliefs in society, is common in various domains and does not necessarily challenge the social cohesion required for a functioning democracy. For example, diverse religious groups live side by side peacefully, even as they espouse significantly different values and views about proper ways to live. These significant differences do not necessarily create negative public (or private) consequences, so long as these groups are able to peacefully manage the public and shared aspects of their lives. This peaceful coexistence can be maintained through legal or constitutional boundaries, or through policies and practices that allow religious communities to maintain some protection for their own forms of practice while participating in other domains to the extent that they choose. Even religious communities that are sorted into separate neighborhoods or towns, or separate schools and other institutions, can participate in public life and avoid the negative consequences—bias, disengagement, etc.—that might result from isolation.

However, in the political domain, the growing differences between groups have produced various negative consequences.[19] As Danielle Allen notes, "Social or economic loss becomes political when citizens believe themselves disadvantaged by a collective decision. Regardless of whether their beliefs are reasonable, they will be registered in negative emotions like anger, resentment, disappointment, and despair. These bring with them psychological stress for the individuals and, worse still for the polity, they sow the seeds of distrust."[20] When these feelings of stress and distrust are widespread, and when they manifest in a context of overlapping splits among different social groups—or what Liliana Mason calls "mega identities"[21]—they give rise to the kind of polarization, sorting, divergence, and extremism that have been widely discussed in recent years, both in scholarship and in the public debate. Negative attitudes about democracy are rising in the United States and in many other liberal democracies, indicating that rising support for authoritarian populism continues to be a significant trend.[22]

Some of these negative attitudes can be attributed to the very perception, possibly exaggerated, that political parties and political camps are exceedingly polarized.[23] Polarization undermines social solidarity, cohesion, or functioning when the (perception of) distance between polarized groups correlates with partisan antipathy[24] or, more broadly, negative attitudes toward people who hold different or opposite opinions. As Mason has shown, even when attitudes toward policy are not significantly distinct, polarization may increase on account of a strengthening of political identities, as has occurred in the United States in recent years.[25] Cass Sunstein documents this process empirically in his description of "group polarization"—the process that causes sorted and relatively homogeneous groups to embrace a more radical view of their original beliefs.[26] Kevin Vallier has argued that "social and political distrust and partisan divergence are mutually reinforcing"[27]—that is, divergence, or the distance between ideological positions, and social and political distrust create a feedback loop. The more we feel like the adherents to another ideology are distinct from us in significant and deep ways, the more we tend to judge them as unfit to share decision-making power and unworthy of our good faith; this process of distancing and suspicion feeds polarization and undermines trust in the principles of liberal democracy.[28] Ideological and geographic distance alone do not undermine civic ties, but once groups are ossified into positions of rivalry, they have already begun to spin away from each other. Then antipathy and a sense of alienation develop—a sense that members of the other group are not just distant but different in normatively and civically significant ways. This antipathy is entrenched and strengthened through exposure to ideological media that feeds on fear and mistrust, which in turn enhances them.[29] Reduced trust feeds its own escalation: as a result of this process of distancing, alienation, and erosion of trust, groups find themselves in a position that offers limited incentives or a reduced capacity to act together for shared or common goals. These belligerent forms of partisan polarization can erode the commitment to democratic principles—and to democracy itself.[30]

A key concern for democracies is thus not so much policy differences but citizens' attitudes toward those who have different ideological identifications—or in other words, the reduction in social trust. As Vallier argues, "social trust is that trust which each member of a society has that other members of her society will generally follow publicly recognized moral rules."[31] Civic mistrust is significantly more concerning than mistrust of governmental institutions, as Allen notes, "citizens' distrust not of government but of each other leads the way to democratic disintegration."[32] It is clearly healthy for citizens to avoid blindly trusting governmental institutions, to maintain a critical stance toward elected officials, and to demand transparency and accountability. But this stance can become corrosive when it turns into a position that undermines the standing of political and public institutions altogether, and even more so when it generates mistrust toward the opposing ideological camp. It is a short step from mistrust of public institutions and members of an out-group to support for restrictions on speech by counter-partisans who are seen as untrustworthy and whose words are suspected of being inauthentic, misleading, and intended to cause real harm.

Trust in fellow citizens, as well as trust in our power to hold institutions accountable to our needs and interests, is key to the functioning and sustainability of democracy. A major way to respond to concerns about the erosion of trust, as noted by Robert Putnam and many others, is the threading of the civic fabric through local ties and interpersonal as well as institutional connections.[33] Allen clarifies that "the key to generating trust is, above all else, an ability to prove that one governs one's life by equitable, not rivalrous, self-interest."[34] Extreme partisanship, which drives the political sphere to focus on mere power and undermines the feasibility of collaboration (or its perceived electoral incentives), is detrimental to generating trust. More alarmingly, this process can lead to polarization and mistrust around facts and about the institutions and standards that are used to help sort out core facets of a shared epistemology. In chapter 2, I discuss the politicization of knowledge in more detail; first, I take a closer look at the evolving phenomenon of social mistrust.

CIVIC TRUST AND MISTRUST

Political polarization in the United States has become part of a process of social grouping in which differences in income and wealth, race and ethnic identity,[35] religious affiliation and religiosity,[36] and other identity features are increasingly tangled up with individuals' political identity and together constitute the conditions for a geographic and social distancing between social groups. Sorting into like-minded associations, groups, and geographic locations reduces interactions with and generates negative feelings toward those on the outside of one's group, thus exacerbating the process of polarization. Groups are identified in terms of their political affiliation, understood not so much as a matter of policy views but of social identity, incorporating geography (region, or divides between urban, suburban, and rural), level of education, ethnicity, and other identifiers. Some sorting processes occur through the simple aggregation of free personal choices, but others are coordinated or even induced by policies meant to keep different groups separate (more on this in the section "The Racial Thread" later in this chapter).[37] Taken together, sorting erodes the connections across social groups and strains trust across divides.

The continuing rise of sorting as a trend in the United States highlights the significance of social contexts where people from diverse backgrounds, ideologies, and identities spend time together. Institutions of higher education are one such significant context, and they are discussed throughout this book as important locations for building civic trust. However, these institutions are ultimately limited contexts: less than half of each age cohort attends college, and the higher education sector is significantly stratified, especially by class. Education level aligns not only with levels of civic participation but also with various aspects of identity. These overlapping fissures in society divide the country into two—sides, views, attitudes, values, and goals—and the division is reinforced and continues to expand.

Educational attainment is not the only culprit suggested to be responsible for sorting, polarization, and mistrust. Nolan McCarthy et al. suggest that polarization tracks income inequality and related social issues.[38] Others have shown how communities are separated ideologically and geographically.[39] Regardless of the causes of the overlapping divides, their social impact is intensifying and becoming harder to bridge.[40] The further away social groups are—in terms of geographic location, information sources, or ideological positioning—the harder it is to cultivate trust across these divides. Psychological polarization—negative assumptions about the virtues and values of the opposing group's identity—results not only from these divides online and in the real world but also from overlapping, calcifying social identities and the ways these identities lead us to interpret others' motives and views.[41] These real, virtual, and psychological distances generate the conditions for polarization as a social and political phenomenon. Polarization continuously erodes trust and, at the same time, feeds truth decay by creating insulated communities where only one set of narratives or perspectives can thrive. This negative feedback loop is evident in recent surveys[42] that document the distances between Democratic and Republican priorities and policy preferences. While some personal and community values are documented in these surveys as shared across much of the population—including the importance of being healthy, honest, and hardworking—party identification guided many respondents to voice starkly different values, policy preferences, and assessments of how well the country was doing.[43]

Polarization is the distance between views, a collective epistemic practice: it denotes the distribution of beliefs across a group and suggests a missing or diminished center in the distribution. Nancy Rosenblum notes that when attached to the description of a political party, "extremism signals deviation less from some putative political center and more from the ethics of partisanship."[44] When understood as social phenomena, though, polarization and extremism differ in key ways, though both are social processes that contribute to the erosion of democracy. Accordingly, the struggle against polarization and the more insidious effects of the movement of groups away and apart from each other shares some features with more coordinated efforts to limit extremist radicalization. Like polarization, radicalization is the process of coming to accept an ideology that pits "us" versus "them" in ways that justify alienation, mistrust, and sometimes violence.[45]

Polarization is evident not primarily in values or policy views but in how citizens think and feel about each other, and about their shared institutions. The focus on the personal character of people aligned with an opposing ideology in political discourse does not allow for factual or policy-related discussion and instead creates or flames mistrust and disdain. Using resentment and offense, shaming, or sanctimony creates a toxic discourse. Relational aspects seem to remain the core issue: while distrust and alienation intensify among divergent ideological camps, positions on democratic norms and practices remain relatively stable despite the rise of affective polarization. While some extremist ideologues are evidently willing to disrupt and even attempt to dismantle democratic institutions, most citizens' views about democratic institutions seem unchanged by affective polarization.[46] Still, these processes are recognized as a significant threat to political stability. Leading researchers describe these processes as the "superordinate construct of political sectarianism" and warn that "political sectarianism cripples a nation's ability to confront challenges."[47] To understand why citizens turn away from each other and from institutions they used to trust, we need to turn to both social psychology—the study of relations among groups in a society—and to epistemology—the study of the knowledge we have. I suggest that both perspectives are essential for analyzing the rise in polarization and the erosion of trust, and both will be equally essential in overcoming this process. To cultivate civic trust in ways that can help a society overcome the effects of a years-long process of polarization, it is necessary that people learn to recognize not simply that they share some views, as is evident, but also that they have shared interests, that even self-interest requires sharing resources, and that overcoming social tensions and even conflict demands practicing methods of acknowledging conflict and looking to resolve conflict in amicable ways with the long term in mind.

The cultivation of social and civic trust is key to overcoming extreme polarization and establishing a sustainable democracy; a commitment to a clear and inclusive vision of free speech is a core aspect in this effort. To come closer to realizing this vision from where American society (and some other democratic societies) is today, diverse aspects of mistrust need to be considered, including cognitive aspects that are important for developing a shared understanding of facts as well as social and relational aspects that will be necessary as we learn to listen to one another and build trust. This involves institutional dimensions too, as institutions—schools, government offices, private and public associations—often mediate the way we relate to each other. To address the current challenges that polarization poses, a broad view is necessary, and I attempt to take this broad view in regard to the challenges posed by polarization over speech, and the struggle over speech in the democratic public sphere and on college campuses.

Psychologically speaking, trust requires some level of vulnerability, and that is less likely to be exhibited in contexts of significant and overlapping fissures, when individuals feel that they do not share enough with those who are not a part of their group. In Annette Baier's seminal work on trust, she observes, "When I trust another, I depend on her good will toward me." She continues, "Where one depends on another's good will, one is necessarily vulnerable to the limits of that good will."[48] To trust another person, and to some extent to trust an institution, demands accepting some sense of vulnerability, because trust is necessarily interlaced with the possibility of harm. In Baier's model, an analysis of trust is based on an understanding of what is entrusted: "Thus, there will be an answer not just to the question, whom do you trust? but to the question, What do you trust to them? What good is it that they are in a position to take from you, or to injure?"[49] Accepting an inherent vulnerability to others who can intentionally or inadvertently cause us harm is an inevitable aspect of social life. It is one that both requires social trust and can escalate insularity within smaller and more cohesive in-groups when it proves unreciprocated or unwarranted. The hardening of mistrust and identification with the in-group becomes hard to overcome when the connection is based on a sense of belonging strengthened by a shared epistemology. Opposing groups that do not share the same understanding of reality would prioritize their belonging to their identity group over a critical analysis of the sense of reality that binds them together.[50]

Epistemologically or cognitively speaking, when different groups' views of reality are significantly bifurcated, and when the information they have and the places where they seek information are divergent, trust evaporates. In the aftermath of the failed insurrection on January 6, 2021, a Trump supporter lamented, "On the news, they keep saying now that they shouldn't have said that [Vice President] Pence can stop the certification, that was just a big lie . . . They didn't say that before . . . Maybe some of the other news stations that I don't trust, but the ones that I do, that's not what they were saying."[51] The crumbling of a shared civic epistemic foundation—the erosion of a shared set of truths and facts, a shared understanding of reality—is a major contributor to the reduction of trust in each other and in shared institutions.

Eroding levels of political trust are evident in perspectives on scientific institutions and might also be implicated in a growing public uncertainty about scientific recommendations and positions. Rising levels of doubt about vaccines, the safety of genetically modified crops, and guidance about COVID-19 prevention are cause for significant public concern. A reduction in trust can in some cases be attributed to limited media or scientific literacy, possibly in relation to changing guidance and positions that cause confusion. But the struggle over mask mandates and similar mitigation measures reveals another cause of the growing mistrust of science: the politicization of scientific institutions, such as the FDA, CDC, and even local health officials. It is easy, and reasonable, to lament the process of politicization, which results in phenomena such as reduced adherence to vaccination guidelines and virus mitigation protocols. It is important to recognize that this process is not exclusively the result of citizens choosing to reject scientific knowledge; it is also another reflection of the polarized public sphere, which colors individuals' positions, beliefs, and attitudes to match their polarized ideological affiliations. If an institution is seen as politicized, political actors—voters included—treat it as belonging either within or outside their political group rather than as a source of expertise that stands outside the political fray and offers guidance on matters of objective truth.

This process is not generated solely by interested parties—including political parties acting out of vested interests in maintaining power—but also by the role that science and other types of expertise play in political decision-making. As Sophia Rosenfeld notes, that decision-making is done by scientific and other experts at all is in itself a democratic choice, challenging the vision of popular knowledge and aggregative "general will."[52]

Institutions play a key role not only in generating democratic trust but also in mediating social trust. Trust is necessary for communities to thrive and is essential for the stability of democratic civic culture and of democratic institutions. Democratic institutions rely on a basic level of trust from those they serve and those who elect and erect them. As Allen notes, "the development of practices for generating trust among citizens should supplement, not replace, efforts to maintain allegiance to democratic institutions."[53] Absent at least some limited trust, even if accompanied by a healthy level of critical judgment (or a reasonably low dose of cynicism), democratic institutions would be unable to provide services, collect taxes, engage with constituents, or guide and sustain collective action.[54]

Democratic civic culture similarly depends on at least a shallow level of trust in one's fellow citizens, neighbors, and compatriots. The shared use of public goods and the shared interests in elections and the functioning of local and national institutions are built on an assumption of communal and reciprocal trust. For a citizen to trust the outcome of an election, they need to trust other voters to act legally and honorably, even if they disagree on matters of policy and political affiliation, and they need to trust poll watchers, county officials, ballot counters, and many others who shepherd along the complex process. It would make sense for them to demand transparency or call for procedural changes to strengthen the process, but it would still be necessary for all citizens to trust that decisions are being implemented in good faith and followed by all. Thus, trust in institutions and trust in fellow citizens, while distinct, are not independent of each other.

Accordingly, the public and coordinated effort to sow mistrust in the results of the 2020 elections targeted citizens, poll watchers, election officials, elected officials, and even every level of the courts. Any who noted that there was no evidence of fraud or other issues that could have affected the results were deemed untrustworthy. Such mistrust is not unique to the context of elections, although it might be most dramatically evident when their results are put into question. The year 2021 saw a rise in mistrust of school boards and education officials, from teachers to librarians, indicating an erosion in the trust some citizens are willing to afford this shared institution. Even in local and mundane contexts, like using a public park, each of us has to assume that sharing sports fields, swings, and paths with others is safe—we need to trust each other to use shared and public goods fairly.

Political polarization, declining social trust, and the rise of extremism have all been a part of American democracy for a long time, perhaps since its inception. Social mistrust is evident in the relations, and the animosity, among racial groups in the United States and especially between white and Black Americans, as well as between recent immigrants and established citizens. In the next section, I briefly trace some of these situations to show the how long standing the features of polarization and mistrust in American society are. At the same time, some aspects of the current social dynamic are new, related to the proliferation of virtual means of connecting and sharing information. A short look at this newer public sphere will illustrate the compounding challenges that exacerbate social fractures, as well as some new opportunities to bridge them.

Has It Ever Been This Bad? Yes: The Racial Thread

Civic trust has long benefited some citizens and not others. In particular, Black Americans and other visible minorities have often been treated as unworthy of even the most basic trust. The experiences of Black and African Americans, followed around in stores, ignored by taxi drivers, and targeted by police, demonstrate how insular trust can be and how it is commonly confined within communities to the exclusion of those seen as outsiders. As was evident in the widely circulated incident of the white woman who called the police on a Black birdwatcher who had asked her to leash her dog—and countless similar incidents—trust cannot be reasonably expected to cross racial lines in contemporary America.[55] Trust among members of an in-group is more common in communities consisting of a single racial group, but it is often lacking across racial groups, a situation that might exacerbate civic and political mistrust across ideological lines.

Racial distance, distrust, and animosity can not only illustrate but can also illuminate the issues of mistrust and civic fracture.[56] It can be argued that polarization is rooted in racial distrust or prejudice. Some historians suggest that the Republican Party began its rightward move and its ideological consolidation in response to civil rights legislation of the 1950s and 1960s.[57] A large part of the development of the two ideological camps' differences in policy and attitude can be understood as a series of movements toward and away from a multiracial democracy. The negative attitudes these camps harbor toward each other are sometimes seen as a reflection of racial animosity or as the rejection of an idealized vision of racial harmony. Such a rejection of this idealized vision may be the result of an exasperated resignation to the unlikelihood of its materializing—or it may be evidence of an embrace of a different, antithetical vision.

Harm and truth, the two lenses through which this work considers speech and the current state of democracy, can similarly be assessed in a racial context. Speech protections are questioned by students and other young people as insensitive to the harm speech can cause to minorities. The debate over the boundaries of expression returns again and again to the use of racial slurs, especially in class. The debate over the intersection of speech, truth, and academic inquiry centers on disagreements over what is self-evident, what is already known and requires no further investigation, and what, on the other hand, can be reconsidered, questioned, or revisited. The current iteration of this struggle came to the public's attention with Charles Murray's 2017 visit to Middlebury College and the forceful claim by some students and faculty that his views on "race science"—views that suggest a natural hierarchy of intelligence by race—go beyond the permissible boundaries of discussion. Other related, dubious tropes about race are significant factors in the struggle over the limits of free and fruitful inquiry. The place of race, and especially anti-Black racism, in the current discussion of free speech fuels a line of argument that sees free speech protections as inherently racist.[58]

Thus, in some sense, race is at the core of this work. It is central to the questions raised here, and the discussion often returns to matters of racial inequality, racial diversity, and the place of race in depictions of truth and harm in the academic enterprise. Inasmuch as tensions around race underlie at least in part the process of democratic erosion, race is also a core aspect of the current struggle over the boundaries of speech. The (im)permissibility of restricting expressions of racism and bigotry, the acceptability of "race science" in academic discussion, the use of racial slurs in classrooms—these related matters are key in the struggle over open expression.

Much as the social and political perceptions of racial diversity animate a large part of the struggle over the boundaries of acceptable speech, a key aspect of the work to revitalize democracy is continuous conversation in diverse contexts like colleges and universities. This is not possible absent broad diversity, along racial and other lines, that many colleges seek to construct and integrate into their work. The degree of diversity colleges have is itself the result of decades-long struggles over affirmative action, access, and equality of opportunity illuminating the centrality of the makeup of student populations (and faculty) to the ability of higher education to fulfill its democratic mission. Diversity, particularly racial diversity in the United States, is part of the aspirational democratic infrastructure: learning to live with one another as free and equal members of society and learning what we can expect to achieve in diverse institutional and social contexts are vital to the strengthening of democratic habits and capacities. Recognizing the core tenets of democracy, and especially the necessity of acknowledging the equal standing of all members, and developing the ability to converse across differences, is a process that takes trust, time, and care. Colleges can and sometimes do provide the space to do that, and K–12 schools can be supported in doing the same.

Has It Ever Been This Bad? No: Virtual Democracy

Social media is no longer new, and it is no longer solely about communication: it is a set of institutions that plays an important role in shaping society, society's self-perception, and its shared decision-making processes. The centrality of virtual interaction in our shared lives, and particularly in our civic and political lives, was presented in its early stages as having great democratic promise. Techno-utopianism celebrated the reduction of barriers to interaction and opportunities to engage with multiple, diverse, distant others—these developments seemed like a true leap in the democratizing of the public sphere. The rise of corporate power and the waves of hatred that have risen in the virtual domain have soured many on this promise, leading some to hold a dystopian view of information technology. Virtual connections indeed create new challenges: information bubbles, where users are exposed to partial and biased news and data, and echo chambers, where users share their views only with those who already agree with them, harden the walls of the epistemic niches.[59] Within these walls, extremist ideas are rewarded and promoted, thus expanding their reach.[60] At the same time that a user's knowledge is limited by the niches they choose, their exposure to diverse others—diverse in belief, ideology, background, or various other attributes of identity—is significantly limited. Some influential scholars suggest that similar processes afflict traditional media and trace much of our current polarization to the rise of right-wing newspapers and TV shows and the propaganda such outlets disseminated, later spreading to social media platforms.[61] Sealed off from diverse ideas and counterevidence, users are repeatedly, continually exposed to the same perspective, often in escalating forms. But the easy access many users have to posting their views, including fraudulent and hateful ones, creates a unique challenge from which traditional media does not suffer.[62] Truth and inclusion are both undermined in this environment as hatred and disinformation reverberate and expand their reach. An unregulated online public sphere seems untenable for a sustainable democracy.[63]

The place and meaning of speech protections in this context are hotly debated. With some scholars adhering to a perception of a stable—or expanding—set of freedoms carved out over centuries that must be preserved and others suggesting that the advent of social media makes the First Amendment and its protection of speech obsolete, guidance about the boundaries of speech in the information age continues to evolve.[64]

Recent efforts to counter some of the destructive effects of misinformation on polarization and democratic stability have mostly focused on regulation. Attempts to revoke or rewrite Section 230 of the Communications Decency Act, which protects social media companies from liability for content posted on their platforms, have become a bipartisan rallying cry, even as the implementation of reforms stalls. Companies have taken it on themselves to clamp down on lies and hatred (as well as some criminal and other types of content) on their platforms, from taking down graphic videos to shutting down bot accounts and accounts that circulate fraudulent and incendiary content, most famously the Twitter accounts belonging to former president Trump and some of his high-profile supporters.

Top-down responses to the anti-democratic pressures generated by the ubiquity of social media communication are a helpful tool in combating disinformation, hatred, and related anti-democratic influences. It is important, as other democracies have recognized, to find the right balance between protecting speech on the one hand, and slowing the spread of misinformation and hate speech on the other hand. Doing so can also limit the power of private, democratically unaccountable media companies. But regulatory efforts cannot suffice. Some platforms have begun to recognize that they also need to harness the perspectives of their users in addressing these concerns, both through the ability to report abuse by other users with a reasonable expectation that the platform will follow up and by "upvoting" or expressing their views on the credibility of other users. Of course, these too can be used in bad faith, which can in turn create new mobs and new rifts among those who view or interpret reality in particular ways. But there are no shortcuts to revitalizing democratic culture, and the opportunity for users—and citizens—to speak to each other about issues that matter to them cannot be circumvented, even as the virtual forums in which such exchange happens need to be continuously reshaped in response to new challenges.[65]

Civic media, or social media committed to civic practices, can supplement and coincide with other social media uses such as entertainment, connection to friends and family, and news consumption. Ethan Zuckerman suggests a framework for rebuilding civic trust through participatory civics and platforms that enable greater voice, involvement, and organizing power and that are conducive to expanding speech and collective voice.[66] Along the same lines, Jennifer Forestal argues for the establishment and maintenance of digital publics in which citizens can encounter a variety of views and find shared interests and ways to engage around them. She demonstrates how such alternatives are more democratic and more effective for countering hatred and misinformation than top-down regulation, gatekeeping, or censorship.[67]

Democracy depends on such opportunities to participate, and it also depends on a shared epistemic foundation, a foundation of facts, sources, and shared practices of assessing and sharing them across our differences. It depends on attitudes that allow members of the political community to have enough trust one another that they can negotiate their differences in good faith. The following chapter considers the crumbling foundations of knowledge and offers some ways to shore them up.

2 · Scientific Truth, Partisan Facts, and Knowledge We Can Share

I came to a small college town to help resolve tensions over an invitation extended to a speaker who some students saw as anti-gay, but the professor who joined me for coffee when I arrived had barely heard of the case. He was thinking about telescopes. In his astronomy class, the students had refused to hear about the potential findings of a new telescope that was being built because the construction took place on Native Hawaiian land.[1] The professor was exasperated. "I am introducing them to knowledge about the cosmos!" he exclaimed. "I don't know anything about land rights. I could not teach my class."

· · ·

Science class is not exempt from the current culture clashes on campus, and scientific facts, along with harmful statements, are often interpreted through lenses of values and ideology. Disagreements over facts, truth, knowledge, and evidence all animate clashes on college campuses, which have become key battlegrounds in the culture wars. While campus speech struggles are not new, the terrain has been shifting, and recent challenges on campuses are typical of the current hyper-partisan and polarized political sphere. Both inside and beyond the classroom, charges of censorship, demands for civility and adherence to unspoken rules, debates about the legitimacy of protests, and concerns about silencing proliferate. College campuses, long seen as labs for democracy, now serve as flashpoints in a social struggle over the future of democracy. The current struggle over "cancel culture" reflects the tensions over the boundaries of expression, raising questions about who should be allowed to speak, where they can speak, and what they should never say.

Many of these clashes can be resolved through open dialogue, which might have helped the astronomy professor mentioned above. Setting classroom norms and preparing for the possibility of controversy can sometimes help, even when one is unaware of what struggles could potentially arise in a specific class (more on that in chapter 5). But creating the conditions for such dialogue first requires recognizing that the development and dissemination of knowledge occurs within social and political contexts. Truth, and in particular the path leading to knowledge and reliable information, is a cornerstone of a democratic public sphere. A shared epistemology—not necessarily shared knowledge but an agreement on how knowledge can be recognized, tested, and agreed on—is necessary for shared governance. To negotiate policy, a society (or its representatives) must agree on facts, on the reality of the circumstances. What President Obama has recently called "an epistemological crisis" is upon us: in 2020, nearly 80 percent of American adults agreed that partisans cannot agree with each other on basic facts.[2]

To act as democratic citizens and share responsibility for our governing institutions, we need to share a basic view of reality from which we can debate our desired policies and actions. This vision is complicated by the fact that one of the core features differentiating democracy from other forms of governance is that in democracies, individuals are invited and allowed to make up their own minds and share their diverse views. Although democratic citizens are free to make up their own minds, fully divergent sets of facts, starkly different views of the reality in which we live, and divisions into epistemic niches all make democracy untenable. If we cannot agree on facts such as who won an election, whether climate change is the result of human actions, or whether there is unjustified disparity in the opportunities afforded to all racial groups in society, how are we to make policy and to be governed as a nation? In order to live together, to make decisions that will influence how we live, to coordinate and guide shared and public aspects of our lives, we need to have a basic common understanding of reality and agree on how knowledge can be identified, tested, and accepted.[3] Even if this goal remains elusive, democratic sustainability requires that we aspire for it rather than let it slip away.

Unlike subjects of authoritarian regimes, democratic citizens are not compelled to adhere to views sanctioned from above that aim to coordinate private and public stances and action. As Hannah Arendt notes, totalitarianism depends on a shared—and fabricated—representation of the world. She says,

> Before they seize power and establish a world according to their doctrines, totalitarian movements conjure up a lying world of consistency which is more adequate to the needs of the human mind than reality itself; in which, through sheer imagination, uprooted masses can feel at home and are spared the never-ending shocks which real life and real experiences deal to human beings and their expectations.[4]

Authoritarians weave half-truths, near-truths, and simple lies in the service of the preservation of their own power. A widely believed fabricated reality is necessary for the survival of an authoritarian regime, and believing in it is often a condition for the personal survival of the regime's citizens, since challenging the reality presented to them is a subversive political action.

Democracies, by contrast, permit diverse perspectives to flourish. While recently some strong arguments have been made for regulating lies in the public sphere, the "marketplace of ideas" still permits wrong and misleading concepts to proliferate.[5] Democracies accept not only multiple preferences, perspectives, and visions but also various representations of reality—religious, secular, science-based, or otherwise—as well as misleading and untruthful ones. While authoritarians and their regimes posit themselves as the arbiters of truth, in a democracy, it is broadly assumed that knowledge evolves with human experience and exploration and that, therefore, there is no one authority that should be able to determine, control, or regulate it. Citizens are trusted to have not only the ability to discern and make judgments for themselves but also the responsibility to determine their own perceptions and, subsequently, their preferences. After having been taught the basic skills that provide access to knowledge in the course of one's education, the onus of selecting and assessing sources of knowledge and information falls to the individual.

This idealized view of the democratic public sphere—and the capacity of democratic citizens to make their own judgments—does not tell the whole messy story of how citizens think and operate. A tension often arises between the freedom to think independently and the democratic need for fact-based coordinated action, and this tension often manifests in disagreements over what perceptions and views individuals may legitimately express in the public sphere. Clashes over speech protections abound in recent years: Is it permissible to lie on social media? Should platforms warn their users about misinformation posted by other users? And on campus, should climate deniers be invited to speak? What about Holocaust deniers? These conflicts over the permissibility of counterfactual and deceptive speech illustrate the struggle over the boundaries of truth—and therefore the boundaries of what claims can publicly be expressed as true.

While much careful attention has been paid to lies, and particularly the place of lies in politics and the lies told by elected officials,[6] I focus not on how official lies break down our shared perception of reality but rather on the effect of that breakdown on our shared perception—and I offer a preliminary sketch of how to build it. This chapter shines a light on the caveats to and limitations on the broad claim that democratic citizens should be expected to make up their own minds. I argue for the need for shared epistemic foundations and that this need in turns necessitates that we agree on institutions—universities among them—that have the authority to disseminate accepted knowledge and adjudicate disagreements, including when these contestations result from political polarization.

COMMON SENSE AND WHERE TO FIND IT

Bruno Latour argues that "no attested knowledge can stand on its own . . . Facts remain robust only when they are supported by a common culture, by institutions that can be trusted, by a more or less decent public life, by more or less reliable media."[7] Shared foundational knowledge and shared institutions are necessary features for democratic civic culture, and, in a way, they serve a purpose similar to that of shared language—they allow citizens, wherever they might come from, to communicate and consider their diverse goals for projects of common interest. Like a shared language, they require tools for mediated communication, which adds another wrinkle because these mechanisms need to be trusted as honest and fair. As Rosenfeld suggests, the Enlightenment was characterized by a rejection of inherited principles of epistemology and a new sense that to be true and reliable, knowledge must be collective, arrived at through conversation, and cherished as a shared, or common, sense of the world.[8]

Polarization pushes citizens into epistemic niches, or toward informational insulation, where they can share knowledge and views with others similar to themselves without being challenged. Recent studies have offered a nuanced taxonomy of the different ways in which limited exposure to information comes about, differentiating the more organic development of information bubbles, which result from the tendency to associate with others who share one's (overlapping set of) identities, from echo chambers, which are produced by the active rejection of critical sources of information.[9] I return to the significance of this distinction later in the chapter in a discussion of willful ignorance. For now, I use the term *epistemic niches* to encompass those conditions that find individuals relying on ideologically homogenous sources of information and reasoning.

Epistemic niches contribute to the rise of extremism, as is evident in the rising popularity of conspiracy theories and alternative realities—especially those promoted via online groups and forums. The accessibility and convenience of epistemic niches generate forms of misinformation that spill into the public sphere, where they endanger the functioning of democracy and generally make it hard for citizens to find ways to share knowledge in such a way that they are able to act on it for the purpose of the common good. In some sense, the embrace of pluralism as a value stands in the way of developing a shared foundation of knowledge. Similarly, critically assessing and revising accepted wisdom is inherent to both democratic accountability and the scientific endeavor. Questioning institutions and individuals that hold power and those that generate or establish knowledge are basic facets of democratic practice. How, then, can we distinguish between acceptable democratic and scientific processes of establishing and revising knowledge from conspiratorial, anti-democratic ones that erode democracy, shared understanding, and common sense? In the sections below, I briefly consider three traditional criteria for delineating acceptable common sense and knowledge with three key questions: First, *what* types of statements does knowledge consist of? I include in this the effort to distinguish facts (or statements that can be evaluated for their truth value) from nonfacts (or views, beliefs, and other statements that are not open to the same type of evaluation); the purpose of this distinction is to allow all to embrace the former before they debate the latter. Second, *who* gets to determine the truth value of statements, and how do we identify experts and center public debate on their findings? And third, *where* does our information come from, and are these sources reliable?

I suggest that all three criteria for discerning reliable knowledge are contested and insufficient as conclusive tools to address the current epistemic disarray. Then I present an argument that an understanding of politically motivated reasoning is vital to understanding why we cannot agree on these basic matters. At the end of the chapter, I sketch the role of college campuses in anchoring a civic approach that is developed in the rest of this book, one that incorporates a nuanced understanding of facts, expertise, and sources.

What Can We Know? Facts and Views

The discussion of BMI (Body Mass Index) was already heated in the public health class, where some students felt that the measure responds to cultural and even aesthetic preferences rather than strictly to matters of health. The instructor insisted that maintaining a "normal" reading, rather than an "overweight" one, was an important aspect of patient care and that medical professionals should absolutely discuss it with their patients. Of course, this must be done with attention to cultural differences, he seemed to agree. For instance, immigrants tend to gain weight when moving to the US. "Tell Mexicans to stop eating so many burritos!" he suggested. "They should watch their weight more. There are enough obese people here." Many students in class felt that the instructor was insensitive both to immigrants and to people with different body sizes.[10]

• • •

Democracies should be open to diverse opinions, views, preferences, and ideologies; all of these would ideally rely on a shared view of facts that would be accepted as a shared foundation. On this shared foundation, we can develop our own preferences and visions and express our values and priorities. For example, we might agree on a shared set of facts about the economy—describing markets, money, transactions, and the like—and disagree about economic goals and priorities. We might agree on a shared set of facts about immigrants and immigration, for example, and still debate the appropriate processes and the pace of migration desirable for the country.

The ability to distinguish facts from views is often recognized as essential for realizing this vision—and as key to basic civic literacy— but this ability remains elusive. Both young adults[11] and adults[12] continually demonstrate failure to distinguish facts from views and, as a result, are easily swayed by opinions presented as facts or remain skeptical about substantiated claims. Relatedly, some demands to restrict speech pertain to lies and misinformation (even as those are generally protected categories of speech in the public sphere, and to a lesser extent in academe); it is sometimes suggested that hate-based and bigoted views belong in the same category of speech as these falsehoods and that they should not be protected.[13] The public health professor's views about migration and weight are related to his scholarly work, which makes it difficult to parse out the specific point at which facts end and views begin in his speech.

The long-standing democratic hope of separating facts from views for the purpose of creating a shared foundation of knowledge crumbles under scrutiny: references to facts and to views are often inseparable. Some still aspire, in the tradition of liberal education, to focus on fact-driven pursuits, such as science, history, and reading. In this vein, John Stuart Mill calls for instruction on matters rooted in value commitments or based in visions and views, such as religion or politics, to be factual ("certain people believe x") rather than persuasive ("you should believe x"):

> To prevent the State from exercising, through these arrangements, an improper influence over opinion, the knowledge required for passing an examination (beyond the merely instrumental parts of knowledge, such as languages and their use) should, even in the higher class of examinations, be confined to facts and positive science exclusively. The examinations on religion, politics, or other disputed topics, should not turn on the truth or falsehood of opinions, but on the matter of fact that such and such an opinion is held, on such grounds, by such authors, or schools, or churches.[14]

With the additional centuries of democratic experience since Mill's time, it seems patently impossible to neatly achieve an agreed-upon, sharp distinction between "facts and positive science" on the one hand and "religion, politics, or other disputed topics" on the other, or more broadly to distinguish between what is verifiable, knowable, and agreed-upon and what is a matter of personal views and values. Scientific facts are not as universally accepted as Mill would have them be, and they are subject to ongoing internal challenges from within disciplines, in addition to political challenges on topics ranging from climate change to vaccination programs. On the other hand, views and values are not as flimsy as some, like Mill, might suggest they are: for true believers, religious edicts are no less factual than any scientific theory or finding, and political views can provide a significant foundation for how we perceive the world (for better or worse). The lines differentiating political views from scientific ones are also sometimes hard to draw, and, importantly, facts alone do not serve to generate agreement across differences.[15]

These contestations do not suggest that knowledge is relative or that the concept of truth is no longer a useful device as some have argued.[16] Rather, they demonstrate that making a simple distinction between facts and views does not readily help us articulate the boundaries of a possible shared epistemology; nor do they help us clearly define the boundaries of acceptable speech in matters of scientific dispute or political discussion that seek to rely on true facts. The astronomy professor in the anecdote that opened this chapter had no sense that the data he was sharing—reliable as it was—was disputed because of how it was obtained. In other cases, statements are made about purported or true facts as a way of advancing a political agenda. The distinction between facts and views, while sometimes important, does not hold up as a clear indicator of the contents of a possible shared set of facts or understanding of reality.

If we cannot distinguish facts from views, reality from opinion, how can we have enough of a shared understanding of the world to act in concert? Or to debate our differences in earnest? These challenges point to a need to first agree on the scope of the factual basis we might share and the evidentiary basis that can help us substantiate facts. One way to resolve this challenge is by turning to experts in relevant fields, a process that raises its own challenges, as I discuss next.

Who Can Tell? Expert Opinion about Facts

The dean was uncertain how to react to the list of speakers for an event at her school. One of the speakers, a well-known professor, had widely discussed his views on the benefits of carbon emissions. His challenge to the consensus of his fellow scientists regarding the human impact on the global climate had made him into an outspoken public figure associated with the political right. Now a member of the department had put him on the list of invitees for the school's event. The dean wanted to know: Should he be there? Is there a reason, or a way, to object?

·   ·   ·

During the 2020 presidential campaign, then-candidate Joe Biden repeatedly made a promise: "I will listen to the experts." In outlining his planned response to the challenges faced by the nation, from the COVID-19 pandemic to climate change, Biden was hoping to reassure voters by suggesting that his policies would be based on expert knowledge, on science, on truth. In stark contradiction to the policies of his predecessor, who regularly shunned his administration's scientific experts and pressured them to prioritize his own political aims, Biden offered a plan that he claimed would be science-based, guided by truth and evidence, and effective.

It seems emblematic of our polarized time that this type of technocratic statement would be seen as partisan. But the politicization of sources of knowledge is anything but new. The reign of experts, the ideal that imagines the democratic state as being led by those with the most official knowledge or degrees, is challenged by a view of popular and populist knowledge based on the freedom to make decisions according to one's values or preferences. This populist rejection of expertise is evidenced in everything from the demand to make vaccines optional to denunciations of the "deep state" and its bureaucratic, self-important civil servants. Experts are portrayed not as people working to deliver the best knowledge available but rather as agents of a technocracy, and hence they are repugnant to the populist view of "true democracy." As Muirhead and Rosenblum demonstrate in their assessment of conspiracism, "specialized knowledge is essential to democracy," but it also challenges democracy by raising "the specter of rule by experts."[17]

This "specter" is complicated when expertise itself is challenged. The dean who worries about the controversial professor's appearance at the school event should not intervene in the decision to invite the speaker, though she might use the opportunity to consider more deliberate and deliberative processes that would seek more input from peers and the community when selecting who to invite. But even after a list of speakers has been approved, it would be important to contextualize a presentation that offers views that fall outside the scientific mainstream, possibly through a panel discussion or a public interview (more on that in chapter 5, under "The Blessing of a Contrarian View"). The difficulty in identifying and agreeing on reliable, accurate sources of information intensifies the epistemic anarchy that has characterized American democratic public life for decades, or longer.[18] Despite the country's long history of anti-intellectualism, there are aspects of the current condition that have escalated to a new level. As Tom Nichols notes, "the emergence of a positive *hostility* to . . . knowledge . . . is new in American culture, and it represents the aggressive replacement of expert views or established knowledge with the insistence that every opinion on any matter is as good as every other."[19] Gil Eyal underscores that even the use of the term *expertise* "communicates the new and urgent need to find accepted ways of adjudicating whose claim is legitimate, when the old definitions and exclusions no longer work."[20] The inherently hierarchical notion of "the expert" is anathema to visions of epistemic equality, and to the vision of accessible knowledge popularized in the information age. But were we to relinquish this notion, we might fast discover how valuable learning and investing one's time and effort in deeply understanding something really is; such a move would flatten the difference between devoting years to solving a question and googling it, and, in its most extreme form, would give all claims and statements, regardless of source or evidence, the same force and weight. Further complicating the matter are prejudiced views about who can be recognized as an expert on a subject: historically, women and racial minorities were rarely seen as experts, and even when they speak on issues pertaining to their own experience, members of these groups are written off as subjective and thus unreliable (more on that in the section on inclusion and moral injury, below).

This vision of knowledge as fully democratized, where there is no hierarchy of statements or those who make them, is at least in part responsible for some far-fetched "critiques" of acceptable knowledge, and visions propagated by the likes of the Flat Earth Society and QAnon.[21] That obviously will not do in matters of science, but it also will not do in the arena of policy, and in democracy more broadly. The challenge and danger of a fractured epistemological basis became evident, and not for the first time, after the 2020 elections, when many citizens followed President Trump's lead in making various fantastical claims about fraud, insisting that the results of the elections were not what election officials, the courts, and the Electoral College had all certified. In 1967, Noam Chomsky forcefully stated that it is "the responsibility of intellectuals to speak truth and to expose lies."[22] Chomsky's "intellectuals" were mostly the academics, or experts, of that time who had leisure and public recognition in enough quantity that they were afforded a perch from which they could speak publicly. But Chomsky's demand to speak truth and expose lies was ideological at the time he was prodding his peers to speak up, and remains so today. Cleanly distinguishing fact from belief when speaking truth to power is consistently difficult.

It is often insufficient to use expertise as the sole determinant of the boundaries of a shared epistemology. Despite the utility of debates about evidentiary standards and the scope of expertise, which are inherent to the scientific process, these debates expose the weakness of technocracy as a means for achieving broad consensus about facts.

Thus, the ability to discern truth from mistakes and lies is clearly necessary for democracy to survive and to function. Neither a fully democratized epistemology nor rule by experts seems to fit well with the current public discourse—or with the flow of information discussed in the next section. Next, I identify additional complications raised by sources of information that are currently available to all.

Where Can We Find Out?

In the days after the 2016 elections, the two college newspapers regularly published on campus—one long standing, one newer and conservative-leaning—both discussed the responses of students to the election results. While one conducted interviews and offered analysis of the stance the new administration might take on student loans, the other focused on the shocked responses of progressive students. The paper's lead headline reported that the campus "responded to Clinton loss with cancelled classes and coloring [art therapy]." Some students took offense to their depiction in the story and demanded that the newspaper be shut down or otherwise punished.

· · ·

For some traditional liberal thinkers, historical and contemporary, the quest for truth is situated within a set of institutions that are committed to truth-seeking, particularly higher education, the news media, and scientific organizations.[23] According to this view, our current epistemic condition can only be remedied through a recommitment to communities that provide structure, standards, and mechanisms for ensuring the quality of findings and validation of the empirical reliability of the knowledge produced. While this view has much in common with the one presented in this book, it fails to account for civic culture: it does not acknowledge the need to develop and sustain trust in these institutions nor the necessity that these institutions earn this trust through responsiveness to the critiques raised against them. Let me briefly consider the limits of this pure institutional approach before clarifying its limitations and their remedies in the subsequent sections.

Extremism and factionalism pervade both the media landscape and the public sphere,[24] and as these phenomena expand and deepen, they create new challenges to the norms and practices of democracy. The contemporary media landscape, from the abundance of partisan news to the sparsely regulated social media platforms, further complicates the development of a shared epistemic foundation. It is no wonder that even a college campus finds itself supporting more than one student newspaper, and that these papers sometimes clash—though administrators should not intervene in such disputes. But any notion that "a single language, a single grammar, a single learning method, or a single repository like a world library will lead to universal knowledge" is an old and always fleeting dream.[25] Aspiring to a single, shared source of knowledge and information relatedly and similarly fails to recognize the diverse interests, communities, and preferences of citizens. A pluralistic society that supports multiple and diverse information sources—different types of schools and colleges, many media sources (instead of the authoritarian's singular voice), platforms in which people can voice their views—should not be seen as a problem for democratic stability, unless the sources, when taken together, create a fractured view of reality. The information echo chambers that many citizens inhabit do not cause polarization, but as they align with the other fissures in society, they can enhance, amplify, and widen social differences.

Early on, the internet generated a great deal of optimism. It was expected to democratize knowledge, to develop a fully accessible, virtual repository of knowledge, and to generate more equitable opportunities to engage. None of these expectations have fully materialized. It is hard today to envision, and even harder to support, a marketplace that replicates virtual platforms where many "sellers" are anonymous and inauthentic, and where motivated disinformation is common and often prioritized by the algorithms over more valid content and interactions. Instead of offering the potential diversity of views and serendipity of encounters that could be expected of an ideal version of a traditional newspaper or news program, online purveyors of news often lead their users to increasingly stark ideological content. Worse still, exposure to falsehoods on social media platforms seems to incubate belief in blatantly false news stories, even when the stories are explicitly labeled untrustworthy.[26] That platform users have the ability to insulate themselves from conflicting views, or to dismiss information that contradicts their views, strengthens partisanship and reduces acceptance across difference.[27]

I do not mean to dismiss the importance or the potential of this medium, but I want to simply note that, like other historic developments in the dissemination of knowledge, the virtual sphere remains bound to human nature and social practices and, as such, cannot single-handedly resolve concerns about epistemic hierarchies or fractures. Today, it is increasingly recognized that the boundaries of speech on online (social media and other) platforms need to be negotiated and demarcated as they are in any other context in which information is exchanged. In choosing whom to listen to, individuals rely on existing levels of trust, community connections, and affiliations, and they therefore express their preferences through their choices rather than letting their selections shape their preferences. The ascent of online journalism and social media platforms calls for a period of adjustment to this mode of information consumption and requires the development of new tools for discerning fact from opinion and fiction. Regulation of social media platforms and the introduction of digital public spheres[28] can help limit users' exposure to lies and expand users' exposure to substantiated facts—key for the strengthening of our shared epistemic foundations. Evidently, rules and norms for regulating the presentation and spread of news and information have to mature and evolve in the context of social media platforms, just as they had to evolve in prior eras that saw a rapid rise of new types of media.[29]

The array of available sources and contexts for exchanging views is thus both an opportunity for and a challenge to democracy; it impedes the possibility that people can rely on a clear and common assessment of sources of information as a way of restoring a shared epistemic foundation. One of the challenges posed by populist-driven polarization today is that it is propelled by skepticism about "elitist" purveyors of knowledge, from science to the media to educational institutions. Thus, these established authorities cannot in and of themselves generate a consensual basis of knowledge.

As I have aimed to show, the crumbling epistemic foundation of a polarized society cannot be restored solely by differentiating true facts from views, by identifying reliable experts to consult, or by turning to shared sources of information. The main issue seems not to stem only from the information or its purveyors but also from the consumers— that is, from the ways that citizens select, judge, and endorse the information available to them. Even if a shared understanding of knowledge were possible and available, it would not become the mechanism that would resolve polarization on its own. The incentives to reject inconvenient knowledge are all around us, and are incentivized by current forms of access to information. Individuals choose what to know based not only on available sources of information—which can already be biased—but also on their values and preferences.

I next consider politically motivated reasoning as a key source for the current epistemic strain, and then offer the shared creation of knowledge as a way to develop civic trust and reconstitute the basis of a shared epistemic foundation.

POLITICALLY MOTIVATED REASONING AND WILLFUL IGNORANCE

When a fellow citizen shares a preposterous belief—that there is a child trafficking ring operating out of the basement of a pizza shop, that COVID-19 is a "hoax," or that a secret cabal of lizards controls the government—it seems easy to dismiss their claim as insincere.

Surely, they cannot truly believe that. But in the social and political domains, values and ideology sometimes determine knowledge, and our political alignments mediate our willingness to challenge falsehoods.[30] Rather than the rationalist ideal in which a person finds out facts as best they can and then develops their own political analysis and subsequent policy preferences, the process is often reversed, or at best muddled: starting with political values and preferences, individuals seek knowledge (true or otherwise) that will support their views. Politically motivated reasoning is driven not by evidence or even belief but by political aims; in a polarized public sphere and a fragmented media environment, partisans choose sources of information that fit with their beliefs and values. They are then strengthened in their beliefs by the information these sources provide. It is important to note that even when the information provided is false, it is not merely supported by its motivated recipient but seems to be sincerely believed.[31] During the COVID-19 pandemic, many Republicans (and some others) rejected the reality of the pandemic, the need to wear masks, and the importance of mitigation and vaccination campaigns, even though such rejections posed an immediate risk to their lives.[32] Clearly their beliefs were more than performative.

A politically motivated belief, even when far-fetched, is often authentic; it is fortified by ideological affiliation and therefore cannot easily be corrected with evidence to the contrary. Partisanship can give rise to a willful decision to believe that which is wished to be true or that which best serves one's political aims. Being shown evidence to the contrary does little to dissuade the true believer of politically motivated falsehoods, as the believer's evidentiary practices are ideological rather than factual. One's belief might be based on lies or fantasy, but uncovering the truth does not always mean that this truth will now be readily known or accepted as truth. In the political context, polarization is a barrier that may stand between knowable truth and the acquisition of knowledge about it: truth is often rejected because of competing epistemic, social, and ideological stances.

Willful ignorance is a type of motivated reasoning that takes an active stance against available contradictory information. This process can be starkly observed in the realm of racial politics. Charles Mills notably identified these barriers in his discussion of racial epistemological differences, specifically what he terms "white ignorance." Mills describes an active social epistemology that insists on remaining ignorant of the plight of racial minorities in American society. He writes of "an ignorance that resists . . . an ignorance that fights back . . . an ignorance that is active, dynamic, that refuses to go quietly."[33] Some of this rationalizing effort is expended by white Americans to maintain double ignorance—both failing to know the extent to which Black Americans are discriminated against in the contexts of work, criminal justice, and beyond and maintaining a blind spot for what they do not know.[34] Kristie Dotson has termed a related, broader phenomenon "pernicious ignorance," describing it as "any reliable ignorance that, in a given context, harms another person (or set of persons)."[35] For marginalized people, having others refuse to hear one's testimony about one's own experiences on the basis of an assumed unreliability is a common experience. Women who report harassment are often met with responses that claim they are making up stories, are too emotional, are imagining things, or fail to understand humor. In many visits I've made to campuses, I have observed racial and ethnic minority students trying to voice their sense of rejection, silencing, or daily humiliation, only to be dismissed as being overly sensitive or demanding, despite decades of evidence that back up their claims.[36] These are forms of pernicious—pervasive and harmful—ignorance, manifest in a refusal to accept testimony from affected individuals and groups. These are forms of willful ignorance, since evidence is readily available both as testimony offered and in the broader form of a wealth of long-standing research on the matter.

As Clarissa Hayward notes, willful ignorance has been recognized as an important analytic element in a number of fields, and it "involves the attempt to avoid liability (law) or a subjective sense of guilt (psychology) or the cognizance of one's moral culpability (philosophy) through the refusal to know some unsettling, and typically compromising, truth."[37] It has become clear from recent studies that politically motivated reasoning shares a similar defiant streak and can be found in many areas of public debate that go well beyond racial politics, including basic scientific statements.[38] Dan Kahan et al. show the power of politically motivated reasoning to not only influence analysis but also to alter the interpretation of reality in the minds of observers.[39] Their study participants reported observing inappropriate and illegal conduct in videos documenting protests at far higher rates when they were informed that the protest was for a cause they did not support. Like the other phenomena discussed here, politically motivated reasoning is not new but is accelerating in this polarized time.[40] This acceleration is especially happening in areas that are subject to new or renewed politicization, such as vaccine hesitancy, vaccine conspiracies, and the safety of GMO food consumption. Socially acceptable conspiratorial beliefs such as these grow to become "self-sealing," meaning that they are impervious to evidence or proof that runs contrary to what they believe—in response to such evidence, those who believe will simply develop explanations for how it fits into their conspiracy narratives.[41]

Much of this assessment of knowledge and ignorance is rooted in the relatively new domain of group epistemology, or the understanding that our knowledge—our personal view of what constitutes true and reliable facts—does not usually develop in solitude but rather through relationships and as part of our affiliation with groups, especially identity groups.[42]

The spread of politicization informs Elizabeth Anderson's concerns over what she calls "Double-Down Dogmatism," the tendency of an individual to dismiss evidence that runs counter to a misguided belief and to further fortify that belief in response.[43] An insistence that true facts presented by experts or by testimony are not true but rather are hoaxes, lies, or mistakes is characteristic of political debate. This type of rejection leads to the development of echo chambers, both online and in direct interpersonal interactions. As Kathleen Hall Jamieson and Joseph Cappella note, those who inhabit an echo chamber distrust those outside of it and work to systematically isolate themselves and those who share their beliefs from outside epistemic sources.[44] In differentiating echo chambers from information bubbles, C. Thi Nguyen focuses on the former's intentional rejection of contradictory information when it is presented or becomes available and the centrality of mistrust in this rejection. As he notes, contrary to the more organic development of information bubbles, an echo chamber depends on more than mere participation in a partisan, limited, or one-sided context, and like Anderson's dogmatism and Mills's willful ignorance, it requires active discrediting of alternative (truthful) information. An echo chamber is an "epistemic community which creates significant disparity of trust between members and non-members . . . by excluding non-members through epistemic discrediting . . . [and] general agreement with some core set of beliefs is a prerequisite for membership."[45]

During the pandemic, the rejection of COVID-19 as nothing more than the common cold is demonstrative of the type of dogmatism espoused by those maintaining "membership" in their echo chambers. These matters go beyond policy disagreements over the appropriate response to the pandemic, some of which can be based on reasonable value and policy differences: Should responses at the federal, state, or county level take precedence? When should schools be closed? What is the appropriate capacity for indoor dining establishments, if it should be permitted at all? What is the limit of the state's power to mandate these steps? Or the use of masks in public spaces versus just recommending their use and leaving the decision in individuals' hands? Double-Down Dogmatism, or willful ignorance, is based on disputes about the facts that provide the foundations for such policy disagreement. Is the virus real, or is it a hoax? Have hundreds of thousands of Americans died from COVID-19, or have the numbers been conjured up to advance a political agenda? Are doctors diagnosing the illness, or are they pretending to do so to earn more money, as the then president suggested at some of the rallies he held before the 2020 elections? The differences in how people answer these questions go beyond values and preferences and are rooted in divergent views of reality, some of which contain truly confounding yet widespread beliefs.[46] And while some such statements might be motivated by the personal interests of those making them, the people who believe them—and double down on them even in the face of competing evidence—are motivated by political reasoning and by identity group affiliation and connections rather than personal interest. As Christopher Achen and Larry Bartels note:

> For the voters who identify with a party, partisanship pulls together conceptually nearly every aspect of electoral politics. Once inside the conceptual framework, the voter finds herself inhabiting a relatively coherent universe. Her preferred candidates, her political opinions, and even her view of the facts will all tend to go together nicely. The arguments of the "other side," if they get any attention at all, will seem obviously dismissible . . . It will feel like she's thinking.[47]

Politically fortified beliefs lead to politically motivated action, from voting to selecting information sources to protests; the actions people take then serve to strengthen their commitment to their beliefs.

The importance of these insights for our understanding of truth and truth-seeking, and more broadly for the effort to reconstitute a shared epistemic foundation, is in the recognition that a presentation of fact, even with relevant evidence, is often insufficient for the fact to take hold. When motivated to believe otherwise, individuals let evidence fall by the wayside, sometimes recommitting themselves to the belief that was just exposed as misguided.[48]

It is somewhat comforting to note that continued exposure to evidence does often end up eroding the misguided beliefs borne of partisan, politically motivated reasoning, both when it comes to epistemic bubbles and even for those who inhabit echo chambers.[49] While the threshold for when that point of erosion is finally reached can be rather high, that it does happen at all suggests both that there is a point to continuing public debate and exposing people to facts, even when it might seem futile, and that educational preparation (of the types discussed in chapter 4) can improve an individual's susceptibility to evidence, thus lowering their personal threshold. Even if this change is not the case for committed partisans—and especially those who are spreading inaccuracies they firmly believe in or from which they stand to gain—Lee McIntyre notes that while the speakers who declare their belief in a factual inaccuracy may be too far gone, they have an audience that can still be brought back from the brink of willful ignorance.[50]

Exposure to facts, especially when exposure occurs in a consistent and substantive manner, can help in the process of countering intentional lies and casual or misguided inaccuracies, overcoming politically motivated reasoning, and clarifying a muddied public debate infused with the unsubstantiated narratives of political partisans. However, exposure to truth alone is not always sufficient. Sometimes an individual's motivation to believe lies is too strong and persists (or even gets stronger) despite others' best efforts at persuasion.[51] Even as McIntyre tells us of the hopeful decision by the BBC "to stop giving equal airtime to climate deniers" and how the media stopped telling "'both sides of the story' on vaccines and autism once there was a measles outbreak in fourteen states in 2015,"[52] the fact remains that both climate denialism and vaccine conspiracies still continued to occupy a prominent place in the public debate.

Hence, even with changes that likely include the regulation of social media platforms and the centering of expertise in public policy-making, it still seems that regulating away lies, misinformation, and politically motivated willful ignorance will remain impossible. The demand for fake information that confirms existing biases keeps the work of "race scientists" alive no matter how often their work is debunked. For another example, climate denialism is propped up not only by big business interests but also by the preferences of workers in certain fields, such as the fracking, oil, and automotive industries, that could be negatively affected by a move to green energy production, as well as by consumers who find these industries' products convenient. These bolster those who subscribe to the political ideology that favors unregulated markets to reject the scientific consensus on climate.

The realities of politically motivated reasoning, including willful ignorance and Double-Down Dogmatism, require that we address the civic vulnerabilities that sustain cycles of mis- and disinformation production and consumption. These psychological tendencies are rooted in political and civic life and have a profound impact on them; the best response that we can provide is civic—that is, not focused solely on the regulation of information or the tweaking of particular individual's values and views.[53] The response needs to take place at least in part within accessible and local contexts, and colleges, as institutions that are charged with developing and disseminating knowledge, are well positioned to play a key role in it.

Civic culture is stressed by increased epistemic fracturing, and since this fracturing is a result of the intersection of personal preferences and our media landscape, it seems necessary to create, support, and expand new contexts that allow civic ties to form and mature. I agree with Anderson that a Dewey-style democratic civic culture is the antidote we need for this condition.[54] While Anderson focuses on mechanisms such as "deliberative polling" and other cross-group interactions that can help citizens overcome both animosity and disinformation, I see educational institutions as key to the resolution of democratic erosion, particularly as it relates to the loss of shared foundations of knowledge. These foundations are necessary for a healthy democracy, but as we have seen, they cannot come solely from experts, from shared sources, or from an aggregation of our perspectives; they cannot be established alone or be bestowed to the public by elites. A shared epistemic foundation will have to be constructed as a civic endeavor. Schools and higher education institutions can play a key role in this process.

Truth and new knowledge cannot be made easily accessible and shared in an environment that is suspicious of out-group partisans, in which good-faith dialogue is not supported, and where the norms of conversation and the boundaries of speech are disputed. For more people to share a belief in facts, and thus to move on and away from politically motivated reasoning and willful ignorance of reality, local and persistent connections across divides need to be forged. Clearly, policy and normative differences can persist, but the initial setting of the common ground on which we can all stand requires, at minimum, the development of basic civic trust in both one another and in shared institutions. Those institutions include governing and serving institutions, as well as those that are tasked with searching for, identifying, verifying, and amending knowledge. The development of trust in institutions that can help generate and sustain a shared epistemic foundation can be supported by political disruption, engagement with others, and, through these, developing the habits of civic exchange and friendship. I say more about all of these in the final chapter.

FINDING TRUTH ON CAMPUS

What this era of truth decay is missing, as I have argued, is not merely intellectual virtue or better sources of information but rather more trust in the knowledge we do have and more practice in sharing the same epistemic domains. Communities that include people from diverse backgrounds, identities, and ideologies who work together toward the same goals are key to reigniting the democratic capacity to overcome differences and to make an honest effort to address shared concerns. As Michael Lynch notes, "democracies must place special value on those institutions and practices that help us to reliably *pursue* the truth,"[55] and universities, along with news media and other knowledge seeking institutions, are well suited to do that.

Higher education institutions are tasked with seeking truth, expanding the boundaries of available knowledge, and making it accessible to others through teaching and publishing. At the same time, higher education is expected to play an economic, social, and civic role, sorting young people and training them to take on diverse roles in the market and in society in a fair and equitable way. Both missions generate debate about the boundaries of acceptable speech, and these debates expose the social predicaments of our time. Clashes over acceptable speech are illustrative of the polarization around open expression. The sense of marginalization and vulnerability reported by those whose belonging is questioned because of their identities and the sense of silencing reported by those whose political ideologies are vilified represent an erosion of trust in one another's good faith. These senses also represent an erosion of trust that their institutions will protect them, include their voices, and reassure them that they belong on campus. This is not to equate the experience of racial or sexual minorities with that of ideological minorities: after all, ideology, as distinct from identity features, is a choice, and it should not be safe from questioning, reflection, and revision. But it is notable that the experience of feeling under attack permeates the discussion; an institution can reduce the intensity of this feeling by enacting institutional changes, beginning with taking responsibility for its democratic role. Such changes will not resolve the core differences between views or their impacts but can minimize the incentives to be ever more radical and vocal in public, as well as reduce the costs of membership for marginalized individuals in an institution that values open expression.

I delineate in the following pages a path toward developing a shared view on campus, based on a reliance on facts, experts, and reliable sources, and also on shared work that can help students and others overcome the politically motivated tendency to reject available knowledge. This type of learning can serve the development of a shared epistemic foundation within a campus community and, subsequently, can contribute to shared understanding in the broader democratic community.

Colleges and universities are not simply one among the institutions that make up civil society and thus can help a shared epistemology to take hold. Rather, they are part of a web of institutions that share in the search for knowledge and, along with traditional media, public research and scientific organizations, and K–12 schools, serve the mission of expanding the boundaries of knowledge available to society. As we have seen, colleges have not been exempt from political polarization; they are implicated in the culture wars and sometimes find themselves in the crosshairs.

Students, both residents and commuters, often encounter their campuses as the most ethnically, economically, religiously diverse spaces they occupy. Though campuses are often not as diverse as the broader communities in which they are situated in terms of race, socioeconomic status, and ideology, they are often more diverse than elementary and secondary schools, neighborhoods, and other contexts where students spend their time. College students tend to spend a few years with the same few cohorts and within the same contact groups, allowing them to develop long-lasting ties with people from diverse backgrounds. Such long-term connections help an individual develop a sense of affiliation, trust, and shared interests. Those can contribute to the open mind necessary for both the cultivation of knowledge and the development of a sense of shared civic fate, which promote the possibility of a shared epistemic foundation.[56]

In this unique social environment, higher education institutions attend to knowledge: they are charged with expanding the boundaries of our understanding; with discerning truth from inaccuracies, mistakes, and lies; and with disseminating true knowledge to their students for the benefit of society. These roles have various uses, some intrinsic—like attempting to satisfy a basic search for answers—and some instrumental—like preparing students for jobs and sorting them by their interests.[57]

Given the core role of knowledge in their mission, higher education institutions are well positioned in their diversity to help build a shared epistemic foundation through their research and teaching functions. But today their position is challenged by the weakened valuation of science and expertise and by the challenges raised against universities as arbiters of truth as a result of the politicization of both higher education and free speech itself. Colleges—and the attainment of education in general—have become politicized in recent years, as views on higher education track other fissures in society.[58] At a time when the "reign of experts" is under attack by populists and elite institutions, such as the media, the civil service, or the judiciary, are questioned about their suitability as arbiters of truth and decried as insufficiently attentive to the voice of "the people," higher education is caught in the struggle over the viability of standards for measuring truth. The erosion of truth and the erosion of democracy thus go hand in hand, as the crumbling epistemic foundation destabilizes institutions and undermines trust in elections, the news media, and the justice system.

This process is further enhanced by the increasingly politicized view of speech protections. Political calls for such protections have become typical of conservative political actors who routinely condemn what they depict as silencing, censorship, and "cancel culture." As

Joan Scott has argued, this weaponized version of the constitutional and jurisprudential protections for free speech operates as a vehicle for expanding the space for conservative visions on college campuses.[59] Once speech protections shift from being a democratic civic commitment to a tool in the arsenal of political actors who seek to increase their own power, the notion of a marketplace of ideas becomes even harder to realize. Moreover, the regulation of academic speech and the delineation of its boundaries through disciplinary practices (or the use of tools based in academic disciplines) become embroiled in the political brawl. Free inquiry in its best form, a foundational practice of the university, is an ideal that underlies the production and dissemination of knowledge. It is based on the assumption that to advance beyond what we as a society and individuals already know, we must assume that there is much to be learned; we must be able to freely try out new ideas and new avenues for investigation that could enable us to uncover, realize, or better understand answers to scientific and social questions.

For free inquiry, knowledge is closely related to expertise. Disciplinary tools, developed to assess and advance specific types of knowledge, are used to distinguish reliable, valuable, accurate hypotheses and evidence from everything else—mistakes, fraud, inaccuracies, failed attempts to attain proof. The core mission of higher education, and the key reason for universities to exist as institutions tasked with serving the public, is their unique capacity to produce and disseminate knowledge. Accordingly, they rely on strict measures of knowledge of truth—as identified by experts and assessed using clear, transparent tools—to perform their role. Truth and knowledge, for this purpose, are developed by experts, in domains that are kept behind a set of gatekeeping mechanisms. While these gatekeeping mechanisms, and the definition of expertise, can and are being contested regularly in academe, clear criteria and boundaries remain key over time, and thus they maintain the central position of facts, experts, and reliable sources to the academic endeavor. These criteria are insufficient for contemporary democratic society, where they are contested and politicized. However, the institutional practices of academic institutions can allow them to reestablish their standing as vital to a shared foundation of knowledge. To do so, they need to ensure that they can serve as "bastions of fact in democracies," in Daniels's words; doing so depends on universities taking responsibility for enacting and communicating their commitment to truth: "It is time for us, too, to 'show our work.'"[60]

In the academic context, obtaining, expanding, testing, and establishing true knowledge is a shared endeavor, taken up within specific disciplines, and based on shared views about what constitutes evidence or proof. In the broader democratic context, such a shared endeavor can help mend epistemic and perceptual fractures, in that it is built on trust and helps broadcast this trust through its network of participants. This network is established in classrooms, labs, and similar learning contexts, but it is deepened and expanded through the civic work of college campuses.

Higher education institutions serve as civic labs, where young people are invited to develop their values and beliefs and to learn to act in coordination with others to organize, mobilize, and promote various social and civic causes. Prioritizing local and interpersonal contexts has been the focus of much of the literature since Putnam's seminal work on the erosion of voluntary association and democratic culture and, conversely, on trust, well-being, and social welfare increasing together with a rise in local connections and sustained positive interactions.[61] As Allen argues and illustrates in *Talking to Strangers*, "our best taught habit of citizenship is 'don't talk to strangers' . . . [and] precisely this habit allows us to ignore how strangers bring us benefit."[62] The civic role of colleges aligns with the democratic necessities of reestablishing connections with strangers and generating trust, as Allen persuasively argues for. To learn to voice their views, to hear others' perspectives, to reconsider their own beliefs and social preferences, and to organize with others to promote shared goals, young people, including students, should be encouraged to engage in a sustained conversation with a diverse array of others and different beliefs. Structured and sustained exchanges in the context of college, both in and out of the classroom, and within the (debated, evolving, but still present) boundaries of acceptable expression and a shared civic and epistemic mission, can fulfill the promise of free expression in the academic context.

On first blush, this might sound similar to the domain of inquiry that typifies the core mission of searching for knowledge. Free inquiry, like civic development, requires maintaining open and broad domains of investigation, which allow participants to explore heterodox, marginal, and countervailing ideas. How else would the boundaries of knowledge be expanded and new knowledge develop? How else would individuals consider the breadth of ideas, beliefs, and values that they might subscribe to? How else might a person be awakened from their dogmatic slumber, whether it be political or epistemological? These two roles, civic development and truth-seeking, seem to be distinct in a number of ways and, notably for the current discussion, might denote competing visions of the boundaries of permissible expression (or free speech): in the context of building shared epistemic foundations, it is notable that both roles seem to require different levels of tolerance to claims on or beyond the boundaries of truth. The truth-seeking role seems to tolerate a broad range of perspectives and hypotheses, along with adherence to evidentiary standards. This is important in that it raises heterodox ideas, questions presumptions and common views, and advances knowledge through critical consideration of beliefs as well as truth-seeking practices. The presentation of ideas and arguments is, however, bounded by disciplinary rules and practices, ones that organize the search for knowledge and the dissemination of evidence. At the same time, the civic and social role of the academic endeavor seems to depend on an openness to diverse people and perspectives, and it allows for a more relaxed interpretation of the boundaries of views that one is allowed to assert and advance on campus. However, to make sure that these voices are heard and considered in a respectful manner, the civic mission requires limits on ideas that are exclusionary, undermine the dignitary safety of members of the community, or challenge members' belonging to the learning community on account of their social identities or immutable characteristics.

In an ideal world, in which all were acting in good faith, prioritizing truth-seeking would call for clear rules about how one searches for knowledge and a broad openness to most content that fits within procedural rules, and prioritizing the civic and social mission of higher education, which includes teaching and other forms of disseminating knowledge, would call for clear rules for the construction of a learning community and would allow for more circumspection about certain types of heterodox content, especially those that might alienate some of the participants in the community. Devoid of considerations of power and politics, these two goals could give rise to tensions between the civic demand to avoid hurtful statements and the truth-seeking demand to entertain unpopular views regardless of their social impact. Many traditional liberal scholars who lament pressure from progressive students to limit bigoted or other hurtful content, perceive this as the core tension in the debate. But the current polarized state of politics further complicates the matter: truth-seeking is sometimes used as a guise for misinformation, as in the call by bizarre conspiracy theorists to "do your own research" rather than trust experts or the media. Truth-seeking is also sometimes used as a cloak to allow repetition of bigoted views in the form of "just asking questions" about long-debunked theories about racial hierarchies; a commitment to inclusion can go so far as to endorse lived experiences and essentialized identities as superior, or even exclusive, sources of knowledge.

I suggest that our present tensions revolve around questions of trust and mistrust, and that within the current polarized context, promoting the truth-seeking and civic missions of higher education through a *shared search for truth* is the main way out of this conundrum. Academic truth-seeking is best understood as a shared and communicative endeavor, or as Catherine Elgin puts it, "Reasons thus provide answers to an audience's (often implicit) question: why should we think that? In effect, a provider of reasons is saying: these are the factors that weigh with me; they should also weigh with you."[63] This process is not merely persuasive in nature but also expressive and relational, and sometimes communal. Given that inquiry and the search for knowledge depend on evidentiary practices, disciplinary conventions are often a part of the truth-seeking process—in other words, researchers in a given discipline discuss and negotiate what are open and closed questions in their area of research, what qualifies as evidence, what statements within their field of research are legible, interesting, provocative, or meaningful.[64] The boundaries of acceptable expression evolve through ongoing negotiation among experts in a field in consideration of what is already known, what remains to be understood, and what interventions in the conversation are productive.

In the civic domain—outside the content of the syllabus or the work in the lab—and within the realm of relationships, exchanges of views and beliefs, and expressions of commitment, the boundaries are different. Such exchanges take place both within the classroom and beyond it in the work of civic associations, clubs, and social interactions. The goal of these exchanges is distinct from that of exchanges that occur in the service of inquiry and knowledge production: they do not work merely to inform, to deliver knowledge, or to construct knowledge through a shared investigation, but rather they aim to present and voice views, shape views, or attempt to persuade others to share a perspective or a vision. Civic exchanges rely on the protection of free expression; it is thanks to this protection that diverse perspectives can be voiced without fear of penalty, thus enabling the expression of values, interpretations, and civic goals. They can only be effective if they are broadly free from not only from censorship and punishment but also from the limitations that self-censorship imposes on an open dialogue and from pressures that silence, "cancel," or limit the free flow of views (I discuss civility, self-censorship, and the expansion of open dialogue in the next chapter). One way to think about the guiding principles that set the boundaries for the two types of inquiry is through the relationship between *intellectual risks* and *dignitary safety*. The search for knowledge depends on the willingness to take intellectual risks, to leave behind existing beliefs and accepted knowledge, to assume that new answers are possible. On the other hand, civic relations and the learning and exploration that they enable depend on dignitary safety: the assurance that all participants in an exchange are valued as equal contributors to the shared endeavor.[65]

While distinct, epistemological and political conversations—the former meant to promote knowledge and the latter which happens in service of social and civic goals—often morph in practice, and the visions they promote serve to mutually strengthen each other. Intellectual risk as well as dignitary safety are necessary for both; the commitment to open expression fostered in a learning community can help students recognize that people who offer dissenting views in the civic context can serve everyone's epistemic goals by challenging all parties to make stronger cases for their stances—such challenges do not exist when all are in agreement. Committing to dignitary safety and mutual civic trust can help a learning community take on difficult questions in a more sensitive and careful way while still avoiding compromise.

To observe the relations—or the spectrum of considerations—between the truth-seeking and the civic missions of higher education, consider an example that begins with truth, facts, and knowledge: In a class focused on meteorology, can a discussion of science accommodate a conversation in which some participants raise doubts about the realities of climate change? Or about the role of human society in accelerating it? From a purely scientific perspective, there is no reason to devote much time to this conversation: climate change is a "closed question"—one on which there is broad agreement and about which continued negotiation is not likely to prove fruitful. At the same time, there might be a pedagogical reason to allow for such conversation to still take place, at least for a few minutes, in a meteorology class: the person raising doubts might be able to learn something new if they are authentically raising the question rather than looking to waste time or needle their classmates. Drawing them in rather than calling them out might be a sound pedagogical and civic approach. Their classmates, too, might learn something—specifically, a respectful and clear discussion can demonstrate to students how to deal with views that, while rejected by the discipline, are still widespread in American society. For these and other reasons, an unfounded claim about climate change might not be the right time to shut down a conversation.[66]

The significant practical overlap between the civic and truth-seeking goals of the university are reflective of the increasingly blurred line between expertise and popular views. In Eyal's words, "in a world where science no longer enjoys automatic credibility, and where competing claims to expertise clash, how far to extend the boundaries of participation in debate about technical matters of public concern?"[67] Absent clear and broadly accepted standards for truth, it becomes more tolerable to simply endorse an approach that mandates exposure to diverse views that are widely held in society even if they lack evidentiary backing. The broader boundaries established by such an approach blur the distinction between the civic goal and the truth-seeking goal of research. There is room for such blurring in certain academic contexts, but this approach should not be allowed to replace the clearer and better-defined disciplinary focus on fact, evidence, and proof. The civic and pedagogic debate is oriented around persuasion, learning, and mutual understanding; the epistemic and scientific debate is oriented around stricter measures of truth and the search for it. Together, the two can guide the shared work that is required for establishing common foundations for public knowledge. The exchanges themselves—the shared work and the disagreements over what might be included, who is an expert, and what the boundaries of acceptable speech should be—are necessary for the building and sustaining of trust, which can help a society overcome the fraying of its civic bonds and the willful ignorance fraying breeds. As trust is both a condition for and an outcome of this work, the work must take place in an ongoing, collaborative fashion, of the type that a student's college years, at their best, can enable.

CIVIC TRUST, DEMOCRATIC HABITS,
AND THE BOUNDARIES OF SPEECH

Engagement with others, including others with diverse experiences and commitments or perspectives, is material to overcoming the mistrust brought on by polarization. Extended and fair engagement, based on respect and an acceptance of shared facts and recognized ways of identifying them, can strengthen the trust that can in turn stabilize the shared epistemology at the foundation of the relationship.

The process of acquiring a belief, subscribing to a certain political or social view, or revising a belief is not solely a rational process. Personal psychology as well as political and group dynamics indicate that we more readily reinforce and expand our existing mental maps than we replace them: we first try to identify views that align with the group to which we already belong rather than consider a fact of perspective independent of who presents it and who believes in it. Our identification with "our team" drives our beliefs more than vice versa.[68] Our social-psychological tendency, as per social identity theory, pushes us to organize our social world into in-groups and out-groups. As Achen and Bartels tell us, "the primary sources of our partisan loyalties and voting behavior . . . are social identities, group attachments, and myopic retrospections, not policy preferences or ideological principles."[69] As Mason demonstrates, even in areas where policy differences are minimal, our political world is organized to pit us against each other in a heated way, leading to in-group/out-group discord.[70] To overcome this discord, colleges can (and do) support the expansion of civic ties across difference.

The shared foundation necessary for participation in civic exchange includes agreements on language, norms of conversation (hence the recurring tussles over civility), and at least a basic epistemic alliance, conditions that can and often are found in the classroom. In some domains, especially in educational contexts, broad protections for open expression rely on an assumption of a shared aim or a shared foundation of values. In higher education, a shared aim might be a commitment to search for a specific truth in an area of interest or a commitment to develop knowledge that can be shared for society's benefit. Clearer boundaries for expression are especially necessary at institutions like colleges and universities, where free inquiry is not only a goal but also a means to achieving other aims, and where free speech does not stand in for a recognition of our equal standing in and of itself as it does in the public square but is also protected in the service of the search for truth.

The closer we get to facts—and to people—the easier it is for us to trust them. Surveys show higher levels of trust in local governments and in local election boards than in national institutions (though sadly those too are in the process of becoming polarized).[71] Local news, which reports on events that can be personally observed or experienced in addition to ones occurring farther away, garners greater confidence than national media, and the downfall of local reporting means significant democratic challenges.[72] In addition to proximity, belief—including belief in true statements—is often anchored in relationships. The development of relational trust over time and the sense of belonging to a community that shares one's values, or that cares about one's well-being, are key tools for countering motivated reasoning, willful ignorance, and Double-Down Dogmatism.

Derek Black, who was raised in the white nationalist movement and has since become an anti-racism activist, emphasizes the centrality of community in his change of heart. He credits trust and new community ties as necessary foundations that preceded his move away from his family and his community of origin to a new one, and he sees these as necessary for individuals to make the epistemological shift from white supremacy to anti-racism. Connecting with diverse friends made him reconsider his bigoted positions; particularly impactful was the insistence of one group of friends on accepting him as a peer despite his expressions of hatred toward their group (they were Jews, and they continued extending their friendship after his antisemitic views became known).[73] His ideological shift—and a new understanding of facts—depended on a prior shift in community and personal relations. These initial changes enabled the epistemic move from one set of facts, interpretations, values, and preferences to another. And while many such moves are less dramatic and require neither changes in one's understanding of the world nor the severing of connections with one's family and friends, this more extreme instance of transitioning from one social, political, and epistemic context to another illuminates the process that such moves entail. Trust in the purveyor of new facts that contradict one's established views, the development of new connections, gradual reconsiderations of one's beliefs, and ongoing discussions can all significantly contribute to an acceptance of facts as such. The relationship between cultivating a new community and cultivating a new set of beliefs is mutually reinforcing. We need a new community to support a new set of beliefs, but we also need to believe in the dignity of our new community members in order to connect to them. As Eric Beerbohm notes, "the moral reasons behind our objections to polarization aren't directed at distribution of beliefs *per se*, but how managing and mismanaging our beliefs impairs our ability to see each other as social equals."[74]

Democratic habits are developed and strengthened when individuals have opportunities to engage in a shared effort based on agreed rules, and in the university context, this shared effort is commonly related to the exploration, acquisition, and dissemination of knowledge. The conducting of such inquiries, at its best, can develop trust through shared effort. But at its worst, it can focus on disagreements around the boundaries of acceptable exchanges or expression, which further entrenches individuals within their opposing ideological camps. Avoiding such entrenchment requires a commitment to truth and a good-faith effort to share norms of research for the common goal of advancing knowledge. Compromise around questions of harm that results from speech might be possible, although any such compromise requires significant scrutiny as to the distribution of harm, and it must be ensured one group does not bring a persistent demand that another group be required to gracefully bear a burden for the common good (much more on this matter in the next chapter). But there is no compromise between truth and lies in a democracy, and there is no room for compromise between a good-faith effort to search for the truth, and a bad-faith insistence on propagating lies in the name of free speech within an institution of higher education.

It is possible to disentangle some aspects of complex conversations and to allow for a substantive exchange about matters such as the construction of social identities, the responsibility of institutions to ensure specific forms of inclusion, and acceptable forms of evidence in various areas of study. To be able to have these conversations, the dignitary safety of all participants needs to be ensured, and their subsequent views and testimonies need to be recognized as contributing to the discussion, even if the truth value and other details of claims can be debated. A connected community with a shared epistemic goal is vital for such explorations. In the final chapter, I discuss processes for holding such conversations in a shared space (such as a classroom), but for now the core of the argument is that the civic and epistemic goals of the academic mission can be, and in practice often are, mutually reinforcing, and they should thus be pursued together through the cultivation of connections on the basis of a shared mission to advance knowledge.

3 · Do I Belong Here? Inclusion and Harm

Among the many executive orders signed by President Biden on his first day in office in 2021 was one that rescinded the previous administration's executive order banning diversity and inclusion training in federal and public institutions.[1] With these competing orders, it became evident once again that the boundaries of inclusion, and maybe the concept itself, are a matter of political struggle. Questions about recognized membership in society generate a host of policy disagreements, many of which go beyond the scope of this book: Who should be included in the census count? What are the goals and details of an acceptable immigration policy? Should public (and other) institutions address group inequity and representation in their ranks? These and many others are subsidiary issues under the sweeping effort to include all members of society in public affairs and to ensure that their voices are heard in public discussions. In this chapter, I focus on how language and speech are entangled in the debate about inclusion and how negotiating the intersection of speech with diversity and inclusion, particularly on campus, affects the democratic public sphere. The struggle over acceptable speech, over what can be said and what must not be said, illustrates the key role speech plays in organizing membership in a democratic society.

Inclusion, broadly understood, means that members of a community see themselves as having equal worth and equal standing and that all members are welcomed into the community as equals. A community (a nation, a profession, a college, etc.) can decide how one is admitted into the ranks and how one becomes a member. Admissions practices determine who can belong, nominally, to a community. After one is formally admitted as a member (via immigration to or birth within a nation, admission to a college, etc.), questions of substantive inclusion arise—namely, what practices and norms will ensure that all members are welcome and are able to participate as equals? For policies on the boundaries of speech, what matters most are acts that ensure the equal treatment of all members. Equal treatment demands, in Anderson's words, a view of democracy as requiring "universal participation on terms of equality of all inquirers."[2] Ensuring the dignitary safety[3] of all members of a learning (or other) community requires that social conditions be treated not as a zero-sum game but rather as conditions that allow all to benefit.[4]

On campus, inclusion is often negotiated today through the lenses of safety and the prevention of harm, especially harm that is caused by speech. This debate is inextricably connected to our current state of polarization. To be inclusive, a community should start by recognizing the forces of exclusion that operate in society and acknowledging the challenges they pose to individuals and to the effort to sustain a democratic public sphere. Exclusionary forces attempt to silence and reject community members based on their immutable traits: people and groups are effectively or formally excluded based on their religion, race, gender identity, immigration status, and sometimes other characteristics such as economic status. When the term *inclusion* is put into common usage, along with the practices it entails, it works against such forms of exclusion and is thus inherently responsive to social conditions. At the same time, the struggle against exclusionary and discriminatory forces sometimes results in demands that the public sphere be scrubbed and purified of a range of views and voices, extending beyond just those that harbor harmful and bigoted perspectives. As is the case with much of what occurs in political and public discourse, these claims propel the ideological camps further away from each other.

In what follows I consider the exclusionary power of some forms of speech and the uses of claims of harm in negotiating the boundaries of speech. I assess "cancel culture," struggles over specific harmful words such as slurs, and demands for civility against efforts to maintain an atmosphere of inclusive and free inquiry. I argue that some forms of speech are wrong in given contexts and can be rejected in such situations; at the same time, harm is often subjective: there is a conceptual spectrum of harm, and responding to claims of harm likewise requires a sort of gradient. Developing a nuanced and contextual view of harm can help maintain an inclusive community.

"I'LL BE CIVIL WHEN YOU STOP LYING": SUBJECTIVE REPORTS OF HARM

The panel was organized in response to complaints about professors' insensitivity to the perspectives of Black and Hispanic students, and others with minority identities. But the discussion devolved quickly: one professor suggested that the students were unreasonably amplifying insignificant, uncommon, or even irrelevant instances of classroom expression. "The survey data shows that conservative students and staff are those who are silenced!" he claimed. "Your reports of hurt feelings are nothing but anecdotes." Some students were incensed. "You are invalidating me!" one exclaimed. "Your survey did not ask about my experience, so of course it is not represented there." The professor was unhappy with the tone of the exchange, and reminded all participants to remain civil. "I'll be civil when you stop lying about who is really marginalized here!" declared the student, eliciting scattered applause from her peers.

•   •   •

Harm, and the effort to avoid it, has animated much of the debate about the boundaries of speech in the public sphere and especially on college campuses in recent years. The ways that harm is perceived evokes a sense of people being vulnerable to malicious others, and these perceptions produce a condemnation of views and actions associated with these others in a vast array of domains.[5] Certain words, statements, and views are excluded or receive strong rebuke because they are understood to be hurtful or harmful to some members of the community, especially those who are marginalized.

But relying on offense and harm as the rationale for limiting speech creates a complication: claims about harm caused by speech are necessarily subjective, and their dependence on personal testimony complicates assessment as well as response. A harmed individual reports the impact hurtful words had on them, and this report is often the only proof we have that a harm occurred, sometimes along with bystanders' perspectives. There is no visible wound, no bleeding—simply a statement from a person who reports they have been hurt. It is a common liberal framing that speech may only be censored to prevent real harm, and identifying such real harm is difficult when all we have is a self-report. Such a report might be sufficient to motivate some response in a trusting relational context, but is harder when polarization and related conditions erode social trust. At higher education institutions, which rely on continued dialogue as a means for learning, a report of felt harm should be taken as the start of a conversation, as a data point—along with other relevant information—that needs to be considered in a conversation about the boundaries of speech. Mutual trust is necessary for such a response.

A lack of trust animates much of the contemporary debate over what sorts of reasons are needed to justify preventing or punishing speech, and it is worth looking briefly at the arguments for both defending and preventing speech. The modern argument for protecting speech, and a large part of the foundations of the legal discussion of speech and its boundaries, is found in John Stuart Mill, as discussed in the previous chapter. Dax D'Orazio notes that Mill "grants government the authority to wield coercive power over the individual to prevent harm done to others, harm is largely understood as material, demonstrable through direct causation and experienced at the individual level."[6] Despite Mill's commitment to a wide range of protected speech, which he defends as necessary for seeking truth, he allows for censorship in cases that cause individual, direct, and significant harm. Preventing (and punishing) harassment, defamation, or libel, for example, are justified based on the demonstrable harm they cause to individuals. In the words of Justice Brandeis,

> Fear of serious injury cannot alone justify suppression of free speech and assembly. Men feared witches and burnt women. It is the function of speech to free men from the bondage of irrational fears. To justify suppression of free speech there must be reasonable ground to fear that serious evil will result if free speech is practiced. There must be reasonable ground to believe that the danger apprehended is *imminent*. There must be reasonable ground to believe that the evil to be prevented is a serious one.[7]

How do we recognize that the "evil" is indeed "a serious one"? Slippage in language sometimes makes this recognition difficult. Harmful actions, often redefined as "violence," might become "indistinguishable from experiences like 'harm,' 'misery,' 'unhappiness,' 'alienation,' 'cultural discrimination' and 'repression.'"[8] The pervasive use of the term "violence" to indicate diverse forms of harm is similarly decried by Sarah Schulman, who notes that the "definition of 'violence' has now expanded to include a new continuum of behaviors and feelings that are also generically used to ascribe a negative value to a person's actions." In her view, which I share, it is misguided to compound all forms of harm into a single broad category.[9] The developments evident in the use of these terms, though, make it difficult to adhere to Brandeis's demand that we focus on what is truly evil if we are to suppress speech.

In addition, Brandeis's reliance on the construct of a "reasonable" ground as a benchmark for speech suppression can create additional difficulties, especially in an educational context, where the development of reason is one of the goals. Calling on students to adhere to the shared norms of reason when they demand that an institution suppress harmful speech is only suitable if these norms are indeed shared, taught, or developed together in that institutional setting, or at the very least communicated clearly and openly. More broadly, the "reasonable person" benchmark can itself miss some of the concerns that reports of harm allude to, particularly when these reports of harm are made by people who are perceived as being "unreasonable" (more on this issue with testimonial injustice below). The subjectivity of some forms of harm is dismissed in the legal context that Justice Brandeis delineates, but even if it does not rise to the level of legal offense, some forms of expression merit a response in educational contexts.

Why is that so? If harm is subjective, how can it be a suitable ground on which to construct rules that bound permissible speech? Speech can cause or perpetuate harm by promoting negative ideas about people, as well as by causing people to feel that they are not valued or not seen as equal. These types of harm are inflicted on those associated with groups that are prejudicially characterized as being unable to contribute to knowledge. As Miranda Fricker demonstrates, women and members of minority groups are often perceived as limited by their "over-emotionality, illogicality, inferior intelligence, evolutionary inferiority,"[10] and are therefore rejected or undermined as producers of knowledge, even when their contributions are based in testimony, or sometimes specifically *because* of the testimonial nature of statements they make. In a learning community, when one is seen as unable to contribute to the shared process of learning and to the creation and dissemination of knowledge, one cannot act and be perceived as an equal member.

Hence, some responses to harms caused by speech might be justified, which makes it necessary to account for the level of harm a person has suffered, especially for the purposes of addressing it and potentially preventing similar harms in the future. The harm done to those who are excluded can extend beyond the epistemic and the dignitary, possibly leading to a reduction in individuals' self-esteem, thus stunting performance in educational and job contexts. Microaggressions can negatively affect the mental health of racial minorities, and hostile work environments can lead to reduced earnings for women, even driving them out of certain professions.[11]

This matter is a pressing one, especially in educational institutions, where inclusion—and the prevention of epistemic injustice—is necessary for accomplishing their mission. The harm that comes from the rejection of women, racial and other minorities, and working class or poor people as participants in knowledge-producing conservations extends beyond these groups; the conversation itself becomes impoverished, and in the context of the learning and research that is typical of a campus community, limits are placed on the reach of inquiry. Some go so far as to suggest that there is also a real loss for hate speakers when hate speech fails to be regulated:

> Hate speech is bad for the autonomy of hate speakers and their targets alike. In evaluating hate speech, we are not just weighing the civil standing and dignity of victims against the supposed self-revealing autonomy of hate speakers. We are weighing an illusory gain in autonomy for hate speakers, against a very real loss in autonomy for their targets. Hate speech is bad for everyone's autonomy: the speakers, and the spoken against.[12]

Therefore, whether the goal is autonomy or inclusion in a community of learning, some forms of harm created by speech need to be addressed. Fricker notes that "prejudice presents an obstacle to truth, either directly by causing the hearer to miss out on a particular truth, or indirectly by creating blockages in the circulation of critical ideas."[13] Indignities inflicted through prejudice and bias thus harm those with minority identities, as well as all others, as they fail to benefit from the truly free inquiry that is possible only when all members of a community are treated with dignity. Jeremy Waldron argues, in agreement with other legal and political theorists, that individuals' inherent dignity is vindicated by the treatment they receive from others.[14] Individuals' equal civic status must be affirmed by their fellow citizens; therefore, when dignity is not afforded to some, the harm they suffer should be recognized. This insight highlights the harms caused to individuals from being associated with a negative prejudice about their group identity; it is significant particularly for higher education institutions who promise equal dignity and rely on it. An open discussion within a given community about what qualifies as harm, and about ways to prevent or mitigate it, is key to addressing issues of inclusion. At the same time, those in power within the community should take proactive steps to express and affirm the values that they seek to uphold, and which they see as reflective of their shared vision for the community.

Some political and legal scholars have made similar cases about the state. For example, Corey Brettschneider delineates a democratic values approach that calls on the democratic state to maintain strong protections for hate speech, including speech by anti-democratic groups, while at the same time expressing its democratic values in an affirmative way.[15] Seana Shiffrin recommends a "thinker-based free speech theory that takes to be central the individual agent's interest in the protection of the free development and operation of her mind," thus again protecting a broad range of views in the public debate, while putting further restrictions on what government officials and elected representatives might say.[16] Along similar lines, but with a focus on the ethics and practice of public exchanges within institutions, I suggest that protections for speech should maintain robust support for diverse views; the recognition that this robust protection creates conditions that might exclude and harm members of certain marginalized subgroups should not be an afterthought but rather part of the foundational understanding of free speech within a given institution. Therefore, both an open discussion about the limits of speech protection and a proactive effort to mitigate the exclusionary effects generated by robust protection for speech should be part of the same framework.

Thus, contrary to the common approach to protecting speech (exemplified by the Chicago Statement, discussed below), an inclusive approach to speech protection cannot merely be a declared commitment to the First Amendment; rather, it should seek to recognize the consequences of commitment to open expression, to acknowledge the ways in which these consequences are not equally distributed, to identify those who carry the burden of supporting open expression, and to mitigate those consequences. To do that, a self-report that harm has occurred must be considered as one important point of information in a discussion about permissible speech and its consequences, along with additional considerations, including the ways in which the broader mission of the school is affected.

Using claims of harm as the sole criterion for preventing or punishing speech can easily undermine the goals of research and teaching—pushing the limits of knowledge and pushing students beyond the limits of their own belief and knowledge. Potential chilling effects should be a concern in a community whose mission relies on an open exchange of ideas. On campus, being narrow in any restrictions put on speech is especially important, because the work of pushing the boundaries of knowledge as well as communicating this knowledge is a core mission. Some of the blunt forms of restriction that campuses have put on speech, including speech codes, civility contracts, and bias reporting systems, produce a variety of negative effects and cause more harm than good with regard to the goal of creating a free and inclusive environment. Beyond their chilling effect on speech, which many—including some courts—have documented and used to counter them, these practices risk being mere band-aids on the real concerns raised by marginalized students.[17] Appointing a bias response team or declaring a list of words unusable on campus is seen by some critics as a progressive overstep that undermines speech. But perhaps even worse, such measures can quickly close down conversations about harm, the boundaries of speech, and ongoing efforts to maintain a welcoming and inclusive atmosphere.

Any decision to limit speech on campus because of its harmful effects should be weighed against not only broad democratic and constitutional requirements but also the practical process of speech limitation and its consequences. It is difficult to delineate regulations in a sufficiently narrow manner, and when the reason for a regulation being considered is a subjective claim of harm, it can be easily questioned and readily abused. Taking a subjective claim of harm seriously as the sole criterion would require treating harm as a threshold (rather than a spectrum) that, once crossed, triggers punishment or censorship. Such an approach might itself be unjust, and it might also be subject to misuse. Once the idea that a claim of harm can be cause for an institutional response takes hold, what would stop bad-faith claims of hurt feelings from being made in retaliation? How ready are those who are harmed by speech to trust any campus official with the decision of what statements should be censored or silenced?

Used as a threshold determination and without a scale that would allow us to weigh or compare incidents, harm becomes a determining factor in demands for protection and prevention. A better response to claims of harm from speech requires two steps. First, harm needs to be distinguished from wrongdoing: the former is a feeling; the latter is a violation of an established right or protection.[18] A subjective report of harm can often be distinguished from a report of wrongdoing. The consequences of each are different, though neither should be dismissed. For example, violating a student's privacy by discussing their shortcomings in a public forum—in class, online, or in an interview—is not merely a matter of harming them or hurting their feelings; it is a violation of a teacher's role, and a breach of the university's legitimate expectations. Cases in which instructors have spoken publicly and pejoratively about their students are not simply an issue of causing pain, although they surely do that too. Such cases have involved both speaking about specific students[19] or speaking about a group of students, most often those who are already marginalized, and questioning their belonging.[20] These instances can rightly elicit a proportional response, such as an assessment of the instructor's teaching or advising duties, or other ways in which they interact with students, hold power over them, or shape their futures.

If a wrong has not been committed, a claim of harm can still be raised and should be taken seriously. The response needs to be weighed in consideration of multiple factors, because a self-report of harm, while meaningful, cannot be the sole trigger for a punitive or even administrative response against the person whose words have caused the harm. Much of this negotiation would ideally happen within the immediate context, in a conversation between the person whose words caused the harm and the students, or others, who feel harmed by them; where this feels impossible, others can get involved—an advisor, a colleague, the department's chair. Thinking about the harm caused by words as a matter that requires repairing trust and maintaining a productive learning environment typically calls for relational rather than regulatory or punitive response. That does not mean that the claim of harm is dismissed but rather that it is taken seriously within its context, instead of giving rise to an administrative response. Speech regulations aimed at preventing harm threaten to create a system of administrative or bureaucratic supports that would not only be censorial but might relieve students and faculty of their relational obligations. Such supports enable them to delegate decisions about what is interesting, appropriate, harmful, or helpful to outside processes, committees, forms, and administrators. A campus affirming its commitment to freedom of speech is not the same thing as it giving up its responsibilities to both consider what the speaker can do and what an audience might do in response. The nuances required for negotiating the academic tensions over free speech and their democratic sources and applications, are better addressed by a discussion about what institutions, including colleges, can do to create inclusive environments where speech in all its variety can be heard.

CANCEL CULTURE

Efforts to scrub public spaces of hurtful and offensive forms of expression have come to be derisively called "cancel culture." Pressuring workplaces, from fast food stands to universities, to fire employees who are caught transgressing; getting publishers to avoid or withdraw book deals with unsavory or offensive authors; shutting down social media accounts that are belligerent or spewing disinformation; pressuring companies about events and sponsorship—all are efforts to advance social causes by declaring certain views unacceptable and demanding strict consequences for publicly expressing them. The depiction of "cancel culture" is commonly negative, portrayed as an exaggerated and even anti-democratic response to any small offense, sweeping up innocent individuals and companies in its wake. Under this view of "cancel culture," a person making an insensitive remark with no harmful intent and an institution or a company failing to abide quickly enough by an ever more intricate public demand for adherence to the ideological orthodoxy of the day are subject to "cancellation": a public outcry calling for firing the offending individual, boycotting the company, or "abolishing" the institution. "Cancel culture" is an elastic term, ever morphing to accommodate specific utterances and shifting ideological lines; Pippa Norris has recently defined it as "collective strategies by activists using social pressures to achieve cultural ostracism of targets (someone or something) accused of offensive words or deeds."[21] The justifications for "canceling" a person—whatever that might mean in practice, encompassing various actions meant to silence or ostracize them—are the offensive action and the harm that this action is presumed to cause.

On campus, "cancel culture" in the form of de-platforming speakers or pressure campaigns to fire instructors is commonly blamed on overly sensitive "woke" students: "expressive freedom is degenerating on campus because of increasingly intolerant, censorious and (sometimes) violent students and the timid administrations that enable them."[22] For their part, many who call for firing, punishing, or de-platforming speakers who have made offensive statements (or worse) are motivated by a desire to prevent harm to individuals and to reflect, as a community, a commitment to inclusion. Demands for accountability for causing harm, particularly to members of vulnerable and marginalized groups, are seen as a step toward a more inclusive public debate in which diverse voices are welcome and heard.

The effort to prevent harm is laudable, especially when considered against the historical backdrop of laws, social practices, and institutional norms that have treated marginalized groups as unequal. Progressive attempts to scrub campuses and beyond of practices and forms of expression that undermine the social and civic equality of marginalized groups—including LGBTQ, Black, immigrant, and religious minorities—reflect a vision of society in which all are treated fairly, equally, and with dignity. However, as Erec Smith has warned, for some activists "the mere performance of change becomes the entirety of the movement"—since current activism, he suggests, focuses too much attention on identity and symbolic acts and too little on actions that can truly empower racial and other minorities.[23] The potential importance of symbolic acts is far from null: Princeton University's president, Christopher Eisgruber, discusses how he learned to recognize the importance of such acts in the process of renaming buildings in an effort to signify the university's increasing commitment to racial equity.[24] But the determination of what the scale of a response should be can still account for the impact of the specific words. Attempts to reduce or prevent the oppression of marginalized groups should be conscious of the difference between words that might be intentionally or neglectfully harmful and words that perform a wrong or enforce abusive power structures.[25] Both types of speech could call for a response, but not the same one.

This vision requires identifying wrongful words, including words that constitute a form of wrongful action, and making the case against them. When a professor at Shawnee State University in Ohio refused to use a transgender student's pronouns and gave a religious objection as his rationale, his choice of words arguably created an unequal or hostile learning environment for the student, and put their gender identity—and their dignity—into question in the classroom.[26] The way the professor chose to use his authority and power in this case does not align with the principles of inclusive freedom. While it might be reasonable to suggest that the power wielded against such words and actions is managed by due process and other mechanisms of accountability, maintaining equal access to a learning environment founded on equal dignity should be the goal. The response to actions that undermine such dignity should recognize the difference between intentional bigoted harm and a flat-footed joke. The boundaries of acceptable expression are hard to pin down and can reasonably shift over time and with changes to cultural practices and expectations. Negotiating these boundaries, and calling for them to reflect a commitment to equity, is a representation of democratic values that are well aligned with higher education's mission and with the broader goals of a democratic public sphere. Democratic debate and the process of learning and free inquiry can become impoverished and even futile when all are not included. But with the inclusion of a broad range of perspectives and people, conditions of trust need to be established. That does not mean that topics or views that seem to stand outside these democratic norms should be silenced, but it does mean that their framing should be based on a commitment to truth-seeking and inclusion.

At the same time, "cancellation"—job loss, public shaming, banishment from "polite society"—does not allow for much gradation in assessment and response. It is easier to make the case for firing a serial harasser of subordinates than it is in other "me too" cases in which the details are murkier or less substantial. It is easier and more justified to call out overt racist speech than to punish someone for a salty joke, an insensitive comment, or an insufficient expression of support for a particular cause. But many of these slopes are slippery, and a demand to cleanse the public sphere of one type of speaker or actor often leads to similar demands about others. That is not to suggest that moral boundaries should not be drawn but merely to point to the unforgiving nature of a model of public action that has no clear due process norms and no sense of gradation. A company can fire an employee because the public response to an employee's actions becomes a burden, whether or not the company's response is grounded in the employee's clear transgression of principles. A college can likewise expel admitted students[27]or fire untenured professors, even though academic freedom guidelines often protect some members of the campus community from easy "cancellation."

But even if "cancellation" is recognized as blunt and inappropriate, at least for a learning community, does that mean we must include all views? Does it make sense to discuss whether the earth is flat, whether there are innate differences among races, or what the relationship between sex (as assigned at birth) and gender is? Are some questions irrelevant, already resolved, or even beyond the pale? Does free inquiry and open-minded exchange require that diverse views on pressing questions always be considered, or are some questions raised in bad faith, to promote bigoted perspectives and thus should not be entertained? These questions illuminate some of the contested boundaries of public debate. Claims of harm that result from discussion of these matters can best be considered by taking into account the distinction between wrongdoing and harm, the gradation of the effect of the speech, and any subsequent actions that have been taken. The goal of considering these would be to find a way to listen to concerns, especially those including self-reports of harm, and to address them in a way that builds on a shared commitment to inclusion and free inquiry.

Doing so has to prioritize institutional structures. In her recent "Can We Talk?" lectures, Anderson focuses on communicating moral concern in ways that might demonstrate a sense of moral superiority and certitude, which can turn off—and turn away—those who hold different values, and whose actions can sometimes be harmful.[28] Anderson suggests that communicating moral concern about behaviors that might cause harm requires humility and openness and should start with testimony rather than statements of blame or principle. Testimony invites individuals to a dialogue and assumes that people with diverse views on a matter can all learn more. This line of inquiry envisions morality as a shared rather than solitary endeavor, but it tends, in Vallier's words, to "overstress the individual, psychological dimensions of divergence, quickly scaling up from bias in the individual brain to large-scale institutional changes."[29] Tools like empathy building and epistemic humility are useful responses to harmful exchanges at the person level, but to address systemic and pervasive injustice they should be supplemented by institutional responses.

When an individual lives in a social-political context that persistently reflects negative perspectives about some of their attributes, the psychological and interpersonal effects need to be addressed. The harm that is incurred by those who live in these contexts, which is to say all of us, is a psychic harm, and the cure has to involve interpersonal and psychic dimensions. However, concerns about translating situational, psychic, and interpersonal interactions into institutional ones still remain. Addressing these concerns is a necessary step because an individual's interactions with institutions engender trust (or mistrust), and this in turn mediates perceptions about those with whom an individual has no direct relationship. In other words, my view of government as an abstract concept is mediated by my experiences as I interact with institutions at the local level;[30] it thus can generate political trust, or a sense that "governmental institutions will follow fair procedures and produce positive results."[31] Institutions— including, for my purpose here, educational institutions—should be the focus of analysis for issues of social relations, inclusion, and harm. Interpersonal relations are often where trust, hatred, forgiveness, and other emotions are negotiated; but institutions are where power relations and cultural interpretations are reproduced, and this is where society can address ills such as mistrust, polarization, systemic biases, and harm.

"I'D MUCH RATHER YOU DIDN'T SAY THAT": PERILOUS AND SAFE SPACES

The mention of racial slurs in class is a flashpoint in the struggle over inclusion, harm, and the boundaries of speech, as the following vignette demonstrates. Geoffrey Stone, a First Amendment scholar and advocate for academic free speech, regularly shared an anecdote in his Chicago Law School class: Years back, a Black student in class argued that the fighting words doctrine was outdated. A white student replied, "That's the dumbest idea I've ever heard, you stupid N-word [which Stone stated uncensored]." The Black student lunged at the white student, which, Stone suggests, illustrates the continued relevance of the doctrine, given that the use of the uncensored word caused the Black student to try to punch the white student. The most recent telling of this anecdote prompted several students to discuss with Stone their discomfort with his use of the word. One student published an op-ed in the university student newspaper critiquing Stone, who is white, for his use of the slur. After the publication of this piece, Stone was approached by several more students, and he subsequently expressed a change of heart on the matter. He expressed that the conversation with the students prompted him to decide to no longer use the epithet in his classes, saying, "As a teacher, my goal is to be effective and I decided that use of the word in that story isn't sufficiently important to justify the hurt and distraction it causes."[32]

•   •   •

Complaints about the use of racial slurs and other offensive language by instructors in class have been multiplying in recent years. As Stone's case illustrates, that does not necessarily mean that the usage is new or that it is expanding; rather, it might be a sign of a new sensitivity to the harm such language causes, or a rising willingness among students to turn to their teachers, to administrators, and to the public in requesting assistance in stemming such harm.

The demand for safety and the call—often mocked—for safe spaces on college campuses require an understanding of the evolving notion of harm. Stone, a preeminent First Amendment scholar who chaired the committee that authored the well-known Chicago Statement (or Chicago Principles), sees free inquiry as the cornerstone of a university education. The statement he crafted declares, "Of course, the ideas of different members of the University community will often and quite naturally conflict. But it is not the proper role of the University to attempt to shield individuals from ideas and opinions they find unwelcome, disagreeable, or even deeply offensive."[33] Many campus controversies around speech in recent years have been framed as issues related to causing and avoiding harm, or searching for safety in the face of potential or actual harm. For opponents of this view, the demand to avoid harm is tantamount to an attack on a core value of the university.

The collective effort to avoid harm is an important step in constructing a free and equal community of inquiry, which is the shared goal in this debate and should thus be taken seriously by those with different positions on the proper boundaries of free speech and open expression. Still, the specifics are complicated, and shifting. It is relatively easy to agree that strong and offensive language is unsuitable for a classroom when directed at a person (or other learning space), especially when used by an instructor. For example, it would be unjustifiable for a frustrated or angry instructor to target a student with an offensive word; it would also likely be incumbent upon an instructor to defuse a situation in which their students target each other offensively. But other uses are sometimes justified as pedagogical devices, which makes the rule harder to maintain. As Randall Kennedy and Eugene Volokh demonstrate, even the mention of the N-word is sometimes justified, particularly in law classes that consider cases pertaining to anti-discrimination, hostile work environments, and other relevant contexts.[34] The case of this racial epithet, and the evolution of demands to ban its use, is seen by Kennedy and Volokh as an overextension of the call to avoid harmful and hateful language in the class. While I differ from their analysis in some ways that I discuss here, I share their sense that the demand to avoid the use of a word—even one with a hateful history—in any and all cases can be exaggerated, and that even if it is justified, a swift and full punishment for those who use the word (in full or abbreviated form, in speaking or in writing) ascribes a magical force to the word itself that cannot be justified in a democratic context. Even if the word were to be banned from all educational contexts—which, even if justified, is hard to achieve—it would be impossible to justify the demand that any user, regardless of context or intent, be terminated from employment and ejected from the community. Colleges (and other places of employment) need to work toward expressing their commitment to inclusion and creating and sustaining a welcoming environment for all without abandoning commitments to other democratic principles like due process and free expression, and while maintaining inclusive freedom.

Offensive language in class is generally inappropriate, as it disrupts the learning environment in a way that places undue and unequal burden on the shoulders of students belonging to targeted groups in the class, including racial minorities, and undermines the trust students and teachers share. Can there be both a clear delineation of what is unacceptable—say, a list of words that should not be spoken—and clarity about reasonable exceptions? And if so, how would a university accomplish this? Jason Kilborn, a law professor at the University of Illinois Chicago (UIC), penned a civil procedure exam question about workplace discrimination, citing an employer who uses "the N-word" and "the b-word" (not spelled out) in a hypothetical lawsuit. The students filed a complaint that resulted in the professor's suspension.[35] Similar fates have befallen many instructors in recent years, including an instructor at Princeton who mentioned the N-word as an example in a class discussion of taboo words.

There are various words that can trigger significant pain and discomfort among students, thus creating an environment that makes it harder for them to learn. As the UIC example above illustrates, both the N-word and the b-word can be painful to hear or read. Creating a list of words that must not be spoken aloud or used in writing and enforcing such a speech code through regulatory or policy measures is not the right step. It is not only an overreach by administration into the classroom that undermines academic freedom and freedom of expression but also possibly illegal (particularly in the United States, where hate speech is protected; the legal conditions are different in most of the rest of the world). It is also most often an ineffective route for a college administration to take because it can hamper discussion where further conversation is warranted, as in some of the examples above, while still leaving open the opportunity for instructors to harm students without accountability when such harm does not include the use of a banned word.

The resolution of the Stone case is a productive path forward, in that it empowers students and invites them to voice their views and educate their instructors about maintaining an inclusive classroom. It is best for colleges to create the conditions for students to speak up, which requires some institutional support. Expecting instructors to listen to students and consider their views seriously often helps too. Some of this work needs to be mediated and supported by the institutions themselves. But students' voices alone cannot provide the full solution, both because students sometimes do not feel comfortable speaking against their instructors for fear of retaliation or out of deference to authority and because students do not have all the correct answers about matters of open expression. The students at UIC responded strongly to what seems, from available details, to be a careful and relevant description of one type of case that students will need to learn to address in their upcoming professional lives, presented in a sensitive manner and without undue intensity. In the fall of 2020, students (and some faculty) at Bryn Mawr College similarly presented strike demands for anti-racist education that seem to trample over academic freedom and pluralism—for example, implementing new required courses that would not be subject to the usual faculty discretion and approval, and changing faculty hiring and promotion practices.[36] Educating students is a collaborative effort, and decisions about proper language use in class, like all other decisions in education, cannot be ceded to students alone.

Given that the university has grown from an institution that once served a small segment of the population to one that serves as an engine for social mobility and equal opportunity, the diversity of identities and views on campus should be reflected in the attention paid to the needs of students.[37] Many colleges are learning to recognize that part of paying attention to the needs of a diverse student body concerns speech and expression. This necessitates rethinking the ways diverse views, perspectives, and expressions are welcomed and responded to.

Even a campus community that is relatively homogenous by certain measures and calm in terms of the relational issues that give rise to free speech concerns still resides within the same diverse, polarized country with more contentious campuses. While the campus may serve as respite or a "safe space" to study and socialize, part of its mission is still to challenge students, to make them think, to expand their intellectual horizons, and to prepare them for their civic roles. To do so, the institution needs to expose students to some of the tensions and disagreements that they might encounter outside of the bubble created by a homogenous social environment. In both theory and practice, there is no reason to assume that maintaining an inclusive environment must clash with the pursuit of knowledge. Quite to the contrary: "The tension between safe spaces and the pursuit of truth is an illusion."[38] An inclusive freedom approach to speech on campus takes seriously the importance of free and open exchange as a necessary condition for the pursuit of knowledge and as a contributing condition to the development of civic and democratic capacities. It lends similar weight to the related demand that all members of a campus community be able to participate in this free and open exchange. This is how campuses can accomplish the goals of free inquiry, open-minded research, and equal access to learning and civic development.

A call for creating an inclusive environment in which all members are respected and where all voices can be heard should be framed and recognized as furthering rather than impeding the realization of a free and open campus. Students sometimes call on campus administrators to support inclusion and diversity by limiting speech,[39] and they cite harms caused to them in cases where open expression allowed for hurtful speech to take center stage. But an inclusive and welcoming campus is one that must recognize the necessity of free speech.

The diversity of views and identities on college campuses, which is essential to the work they aim to do, calls for paying careful attention to these challenges and for finding clear and consistent ways to resolve cases in which free speech and inclusion collide. Looking again at Stone and his use of the N-word in class "for pedagogical reasons," Stone is not alone in this: in recent years, similar cases have come up regularly in the media and in complaints to organizations that work to defend open expression on campus. Laurie Sheck, a renowned poet and novelist and a popular professor of creative writing at the New School, mentioned the N-word in a class discussing the work of James Baldwin. In a discussion about the differences between the title of one of James Baldwin's books and that of its movie adaptation, she brought up the 2016 documentary about Baldwin, *I Am Not Your Negro*. She noted that the title of the film comes from a 1963 interview in which Baldwin mentions the uncensored version of the N-word used also in the title of his book. She, too, used the uncensored word in an attempt to discuss why the directors changed the word in the title of their film. She was temporarily suspended from teaching. In 2018 Lawrence Rosen, a professor emeritus of anthropology at Princeton, used the word in his course Cultural Freedoms: Hate Speech, Blasphemy and Pornography in order to engage his class in a discussion about taboos. He asked if it would be worse for a white man to punch a Black man or to call him the N-word, using the uncensored version of the word. Following student complaints, Rosen decided to cancel the class. In law, there has been a common distinction between the use of a slur, which is deemed illegitimate, and mention of a slur or curse word when quoting, analyzing, or otherwise discussing it in a pedagogical context. But this distinction seems not to hold as a useful delineation between acceptable and unacceptable use in class. The students in Stone's class felt hurt by his use of the uncensored word in class, even as it was mentioned as a quote within an illustrative (and, as he notes, accurate) example of the meaning of the legal doctrine of "fighting words."

How, then, can the harm caused by speech be assessed when students report biased, hate-based, discriminatory, or other hurtful language in class? One possibility is to never allow hate-based utterances; the examples above suggest that this type of speech code can be too sweeping and is thus unjustified. It is not possible to always categorize offensive language as an instance of expressed hatred (for example, to understand the mention of a racial slur as an instance of expressed racism). Rather, it might be useful to take three variables into consideration for the purpose of delineating the boundaries of acceptable speech in class—namely, *who is speaking*, including their racial identity, their intentions, and their position in the classroom; *who the audience is* and what the audience's expected reception of the language used by the speaker is; and *what the justification is* for mentioning slurs, epithets, and other hurtful terms within the relevant context of social structures, relations, and pedagogical aims. These are the considerations that can help place a specific instance of such speech on the gradient of harm and, therefore, help determine the way in which a resolution might be crafted. This is not to suggest the implementation of a systematized, bureaucratic categorization of offenses and a rubric of responses, but rather to suggest which aspects matter when assessing and addressing an event that generates reports of harm.

The first question we should ask when looking to assess offending speech is "Who is speaking?" In this context, the position of the speaker and their identity often matter. The cases mentioned above all involve white professors, although that is not uniformly the case with contestations over mentions of racial slurs. An instructor bears responsibility for creating and maintaining a positive learning environment, and thus their use of language should be deliberate. Identity-related power dynamics can matter, and those can account for the speaker's identity, as well as the audience's, as I will discuss next. Asymmetries of power, both those historically between racial groups and those between instructor and students in the classroom, should be taken into account when assessing the permissibility of this type of speech. Similar considerations can apply in the context of negative terms related to women or other groups, in which both the social power dynamics and the gender identity of the speaker can be relevant. While Kennedy and Volokh reject this consideration in favor of an equal measure of speech protection to speakers of all racial (and presumably other) identities,[40] it seems that a more nuanced view of the matter, beyond speech protections, is warranted. The argument is not that universities or workplaces, or the law, need to carve out separate requirements and protections according to race or other identity attributes. Rather, I recommend that speakers take these matters into account as a matter of social norms and that responses from students and especially from college administrators allow for more nuanced reactions—currently, the main responses institutions employ are either inaction ("we support the speaker's freedom of expression") or termination.

In addition, the intentions of the speaker should matter, to the extent that those can be discerned from the situation and from relevant contexts. While intentions can be opaque or complex, and while they are usually not decisive in assessing racist expression—and hate-based expression in general—there is often a reason to distinguish different reasons or intentions for using epithets and similar language. For example, an instructor or a student might quote or read offensive language out loud in a way that is relevant to research, literary practice, or discussion with no incendiary intention. This would be an instance in which the distinction commonly made between use and mention,[41] which sees the use of offensive language as inappropriate and the mention of its usage as more permissible, is relevant. This is possibly useful when incorporated as a consideration of the entire context of an incident—again, it is obviously impermissible for an instructor to swear at a student, while there might be some contexts in which a mention of a curse word is relevant and appropriate—but the distinction does not by itself help us discern an appropriate from an inappropriate mention. It does, however, highlight the importance of paying attention to a speaker's intent—namely, discerning what the speaker aimed to do when uttering an offensive term or word—as well as the impact of the utterance—namely, how the words are taken, and what kind of exchange has ensued.

More controversially, a speaker can use humor that is off-color, and potentially offensive, for various reasons, such as illustrating a point or attempting to defuse a situation. As is the case with other uses of offensive language, humor can be used in different ways and to further different causes, and as Luvell Anderson carefully demonstrates with regard to racial slurs, the mere exclamation "it was a joke!" in and of itself does not resolve the issue.[42] Humor complicates the distinction between use and mention—or it at least blurs the two—as a joke can mention offensive terms but can also be a form of using them. Intention is thus harder to discern.

This does not render intention useless, but it does demand additional considerations when evaluating whether the utterance of an offensive word is justified. Because of the disparate impact of words on different audiences, and because the reasoning behind usage relates to the audience, the identity of the audience matters too. A racially diverse group of students may reject the mention of a slur in class as we have seen, but there might be a stronger explanation for the instructor's decision to make such a mention if, say, the audience is law students and the mention is relevant to their education, as in many of the cases mentioned here, which is also the view unequivocally voiced by Kennedy and Volokh. They suggest that at least in the case of teaching law students, epithets need to be spelled out because of law's professional expectation for accuracy in reporting: "Practice like you play, because you will play like you practice,"[43] they note. If you cannot hear a word quoted in class, you will not be able to act professionally when hearing it quoted in court. However, this might be an argument unique to law schools and not necessarily generalizable to other contexts. Further, Kennedy and Volokh's argument that judges and juries prefer to hear uncensored versions of the events they adjudicate is itself contextual and subject to change. The generational effort to expunge the public discourse of slurs and epithets may reach these levels of the judicial system as well, and while some will lament such a development, others might celebrate it. Preparing students for the "real world" must take into account the possibility that these same students might reject some facets of this world and set out to change them.

The second variable that is relevant to discussing appropriate responses to controversial classroom speech is the audience—the students, or whatever other people the speaker has in mind when uttering controversial speech. The demographic makeup of an audience is not a conclusive factor in deciding which words one might use, but it can and should be a consideration. For example, a male instructor making off-color jokes about women in a coed class can cause one form of harm among his female listeners, but he can also generate concerns among his other listeners. A male instructor using offensive language about women when speaking to an all-male audience can still be hurtful to members of his audience who are committed to gender equity; he would surely also be doing harm to the important democratic and social value of gender equity, regardless of his audience's feelings about his language. In the racial slurs cases mentioned above, at least some of the concerned students were white. They did not see themselves as harmed by the use of the slur, but they did observe that it might undermine the inclusive learning environment for their Black peers. In the Stone case, it was a group of Black students who finally changed his mind. They were correct that Stone should not use the word in class: while a college or university cannot and should not engage in creating speech codes or censoring professors, Stone's students had the power to show him that his use of the slur was painful in a way that distracted them from equally engaging in this class.

Finally, pedagogical context matters. A slur can be used to offend someone, or it can be used to, say, quote Baldwin or Randall Kennedy in a manner that is respectful and relevant. Scheck had a reasonable pedagogical purpose for using the N-word when discussing Baldwin's work and the related shift in terminology (there are a few similar cases involving teaching Baldwin). However, I contend that nothing would be lost in the Rosen and Stone cases had they censored the word. Or, possibly, something would be lost—a clear feeling about what is taboo or what constitutes fighting words, respectively—but something more significant would be gained: a classroom where all can equally learn and feel valued and welcome.

The harm caused by mentioning epithets, slurs, and other utterances depends on the speaker, the audience, and the justification—in short, context matters for understanding claims of harm and properly responding to them. Stone was open to hearing his students and recognizing their pain, and his response was to avoid mentioning slurs again. In other contexts, a more elaborate engagement, sometimes with others in the institution, is called for. Some ambiguity remains for the application of this framework, and here I do not offer strict and conclusive rules that either permit or ban any specific words. This ambiguity is inherent to determinations of harm, which, as noted, are subjective and have many hues beyond black and white. Not all contexts can be covered by a concise rule, and the work of education is to create norms of conversation and to negotiate tolerance. As such, the process for deciding what is permissible must include the views of the students and instructors' pedagogical justifications while also recognizing that the classroom does not operate in a normative vacuum and its decisions should be based on a sound normative framework that relates to the overall mission of the institution.

With that said, the question of how we might respond to breaches remains. What to do when a professor decides to use hurtful words in class, in contexts that are questionable or even impermissible by the framework I offer or the norms of their institution? This type of speech is protected; it is free, but it is not without a price. And the price is being paid disproportionately by minority students who are at best distracted and at worst demeaned and silenced.

Efforts to strictly and formally regulate classroom speech are therefore futile; they also undermine the epistemic work of knowledge construction and shared development of norms, both key aspects of learning. An established list of words that should not be used in class might also turn into a lightning rod, inviting people who are either strongly committed to free expression or acting in bad faith to use these words (or versions of them) as a challenge or as a matter of principle.

The response to an unjustified use of a slur should thus be educational rather than legal. State and federal governments, along with the justice system, should see their roles in regard to speech protection in higher education as limited to providing the legal context in which these institutions operate, such as defining the boundaries of protected speech in democratic society. Campus administrators can communicate their expectations for the kind of atmosphere they seek to promote and clarify the mission of the shared work done on campus and the values they seek to uphold. They can create avenues for recourse open to those who see their rights or needs as being undermined by the actions of their peers, colleagues, or professors. But the main work in these domains remains in the hands of instructors and students, and negotiation itself is part of the solution. Will they get it wrong sometimes? Surely. Some professors will use offensive language that excludes and silences rather than opens minds. At other times, some students will push too hard, looking to silence ideas that challenge them. This is part of the process of developing shared norms and developing trust, foundational to an inclusive and productive learning environment.

A misplaced complaint or the misguided use of a word in class is the price that must be paid to maintain classrooms that are open to inquiry and to learning. Universities should implement structures and norms that ensure that this price is not only paid by certain members of their communities, and that the norms created are not only built on respect for all but also are locally created in classrooms and in other groups through a participatory process that includes diverse voices. Shared agreements go beyond imposed norms to encourage participation by all members of a community who are affected by the community's norms and who have a stake in their enactment.

CIVILITY: IS IT EVER A VIRTUE?[44]

The Chicago Statement asserts: "Although the University greatly values civility, and although all members of the University community share in the responsibility for maintaining a climate of mutual respect, concerns about civility and mutual respect can never be used as a justification for closing off discussion of ideas, however offensive or disagreeable those ideas may be to some members of our community."[45]

Civility, as both a stylistic and substantive constraint on conversation, is often depicted as a precondition for a fair conversation, or even a just one.[46] Avoiding insults, aggression, and statements that undercut or humiliate one's interlocutor (or ideological opponent) is portrayed as a necessary imposition that allows for conversation to take place, to proceed, to be productive. Even in cases in which unjust laws, policies, or power are protested or opposed, civility is a common demand, as is evident in notions such as "civil disobedience," a sanitized and idealized form of engagement. Civil disobedience is broadly understood as acts of resistance that are transparent, nonviolent, and non-evasive, in which actors behave with decorum, showing themselves to be dignified and, therefore, trustworthy.[47] Civility in low-stakes forms of engagement, like conversations across divides, is expected and sometimes demanded as a norm that makes the exchange possible.

Civility is productive in that it draws our attention to the need for shared conversational norms, so that all participants and potential participants in an exchange know how they can engage and can do so without threat of harm. However, as civility is commonly depicted, it sets a high and exclusionary bar for participation, and at the same time, it sets too low a bar for the views that are permitted into the discussion.

The bar is set too high in that civility excludes emotional appeals, expressions of anger, tears, and raised voices; it pegs forms of speech that are typical of some cultures as inappropriate in the norms that it sets for civil conversation. Significantly, civility overlooks power differentials for speech: if one person holds the microphone and has the power not to share it, those who find this person's words objectionable have few options to make their voices heard. And if they raise their voice in anger, cry, or try to get a word into the microphone, they are deemed uncivil, and their words are therefore shut out from the conversation. This outcome is a form of epistemic injustice.

At the same time, the bar of civility is set too low in that it allows noxious ideas free rein as long as they are voiced in proper and decorous ways. Ensuring that all people can participate in a discussion and be listened to as equal members of a learning community in a college classroom or similar setting requires different criteria, ones not rooted in current visions of civility.

Like other general concepts discussed here—inclusion, diversity, harm—civility has been co-opted into our polarized political debate. Ideologues regularly charge their opponents with incivility or demand more civil discourse when faced with strong disagreement. Civility turns out to mean different things in different contexts: for some, a speaker's bigoted views are uncivil; for others, their opponents are the ones breaching civility norms by strongly rebuking the speaker. This is not to suggest that both are similarly correct, or that their views should be seen as equivalent from a democratic perspective. Rather, it is to suggest that the concept itself needs to either be pared down to some foundational core that can be shared across political ideologies—for example, by focusing on specific discursive norms—or otherwise that civility should be disposed of as a guiding principle in public discussion.

Beyond a basic, technical agreement on discursive practices within a given context—for example, avoiding ad hominem and aggressive attacks in congressional debates—or ensuring a fair distribution of airtime in class, the notion of civility itself is no longer useful guidance for democratic public debate, and its usefulness in educational institutions is very limited. Instead of focusing on a robust notion of civility or descending into fights over who acted in an uncivil manner (Those who kneel during the national anthem? Those who mention slurs? Those who engage in "locker room talk"?), the focus should shift to norms of exchange that suit a given context and that can be negotiated by participants within the boundaries of an institution's values.

THE COMMON GOOD, TRUST, AND DEPOLARIZATION

Determinations about the boundaries of speech delineate who gets included and who gets excluded from a conversation and community, particularly in learning communities. Negotiating the boundaries of speech is crucial for regenerating a shared epistemic foundation, a sense of civic trust, and a renewed commitment to democratic civic culture. But I argue that the policing of the boundaries and the ongoing discussions regarding permissible and impermissible speech do not suffice for the task at hand. To push back against processes of polarization and social distrust, inclusive communities need to at least make a sense of shared interests into a possibility: they need to justify their role as communities (rather than mere bureaucratic entities) by making possible a common good that is more than the aggregate of their members' private goods. The notion of the common good, as Waheed Hussain notes, defines an important dimension of a political community in which members are expected to relate to each other in ways that go beyond their private interests:

> Members of a political community stand in a social relationship, and this relationship also requires them to think and act in ways that embody a certain form of mutual concern. The common good defines this form of concern. The common good incorporates certain basic requirements of social justice, as citizens must provide one another with basic rights and freedoms and they must not exploit each other. But the common good goes beyond the basic requirements of justice because it requires citizens to maintain certain patterns of conduct on the grounds that these patterns serve certain common interests.[48]

The common good can be thought of as the facilities (or institutions and goods), interests, and practices that define the shared dimensions of a political community. Without a recognition of its importance, it is hard to envision a sense of trust, solidarity, or even coordination among members of a society, and it is hard to expect that its institutions will function effectively. When power struggles, mistrust, polarization, and a fractured understanding of reality typify a society to the extent that they do in the contemporary United States, the common good is diminished as an aspirational dimension of society. Shared institutions of governance exist, but trust in them is limited. Assumptions of good faith and the possibility of connections across differences erode. A sense of shared fate is undermined by stark economic inequities. It becomes harder to communicate the ways in which members of the same society are bound by the same rules, institutions, norms, and basic values.

Given the documented growth in negative attitudes toward those who hold opposing partisan and policy views, the first steps toward a solution must recognize the viability of diverse views and rehumanize ideological opponents. Reducing the centrality of a partisan in-group and animosity toward an out-group (or the opposing party) is possible when shared national identity is prioritized[49] and the shared fate of diverse groups is made the center of attention.[50] In addition, animosity is reduced and respect can be increased when speakers are willing to share personal narratives in a nonjudgmental way and focus on relationships rather than on persuasion.[51] In Danielle Allen's words in *Our Declaration*: "Only when others tell us about themselves, and about what they see, have we any chance of setting their happiness and ours in relation to one another. Hold fast to this idea, and one has the root of democracy."[52]

Recreating opportunities for engendering trust and pursuing shared projects or goals can be more productive for revitalizing democracy than trying to persuade each other about matters of ideology or political vision. Working together on practical shared interests that have tangible benefits for diverse groups—focusing on the shared aspects of our fate—is a key (though not sole) aspect for the strengthening of democracy. Higher education institutions are well positioned to do so, but they have to be careful in this work because they tend to establish and expand a single network of individuals and institutions that they depict as trustworthy, and this leads to some students endorsing this network while rejecting a different network of trust into which they were connected earlier in life.[53] This pattern is often seen with first-generation students, as well as students with less common ideological affiliations.

In recent years, campuses and organizations have been busy developing programs aimed at negotiating differences of ideology and identity, crossing divides, and developing a shared civic context where discussion is possible.[54] Preliminary studies show that these efforts are worthwhile and that even a one-time workshop can generate real effects on participants' attitudes.[55] Other studies indicate that even political campaign volunteers, who tend to be more partisan and to have a strong affective affiliation with their cause or group, depolarize when they are asked to engage in deep interviews during canvassing with members of the public who disagree with them. The process of asking questions, listening carefully to answers, and looking to understand the reasons someone espouses an ideology contrary to one's own tends to generate empathy and reduce affective polarization.[56] Campuses are ideal contexts for putting the lessons from these studies into practice, not only through structured forms of engagement but also through the informal, ongoing exchange that is part of campus life in the classroom, in the dorms, and on the quad.

The story of Derek Black (told at the end of chapter 2), who was raised as a white nationalist and now works as an anti-racist activist, demonstrates the power that relationships can have on reducing mistrust and on rethinking extremist views.[57] What was concerning about Black was not so much that he held different views from his more progressive friends but that he held hate-based and discriminatory views and attitudes toward religious and racial minorities. His story would not have been as inspirational to many if the relationships he developed in college had led to persuasion in the opposite direction, were his college friends to have joined his white supremacist cause and signed on as contributors to Stormfront. The desired impact of relationships on beliefs and attitudes is not direction-neutral: the aim is to cultivate better connection and trust, greater commitment to truth-seeking, and stronger civic ties.

To generate trust built on a shared epistemological foundation, a personal exchange can make a significant difference. Some studies show that a personal and nonjudgmental exchange of narratives on a politically contentious topic—for example, discrimination against transgender people—can foster more tolerant attitudes.[58] Other studies indicate that the effect of an interpersonal structured exchange across ideological differences can generate positive feelings toward the ideological out-group, and thus increased trust and reduced animosity—and this effect may be sustained beyond the exchange.[59] Social reasoning, defined not by the content of reasons but by our responsiveness to those with whom we reason, allows individuals to learn to consider the reasons others offer for their views even if they remain unpersuaded. We learn to see them as *their* reasons and therefore as understandable to us as moral choices that another person can make.[60]

Therefore, beyond interpersonal exchange, the common good must evolve in the context of a community, or in an institution that serves it. For a concept or goal to be considered as contributing to the common good, it needs to take into account the interests of all rather than some members, and it needs to be nonpartisan. The main thing to keep in mind is that "the common good consists in the fact that there are reasons to act together to bring it about."[61] The common good is not in and of itself a sufficient reason for action. The substantive reasons to act in the service of the common good are in what brings it about, as well as what it brings about.[62] On campus, the common good sustains dialogue into the future, and it allows for learning, connection, and growth to flourish.

Focusing on local contexts, on people in our proximity with whom we share some familiar routines and habits, and especially on those who can be part of an extended connection are all key to creating a revitalized civic context. This statement is supported by evidence from many studies—including those sparked by Putnam's *Bowling Alone*, which documented the decline of American civic life and the centrality of local ties to health, well-being, and other positive outcomes—but it should not be read as a nostalgic call for a return to bowling leagues and PTA meetings. There is little room for nostalgia for the days of yore: the familiarity and connection of local neighborhoods or towns in the imagined olden days—the 1950s are the most common frame of reference here—were frequently the result of racial redlining and the exclusion of women from the workforce. Moreover, the call to (re)create local institutions that serve as engines for renewed civic life comes in the context of increased disconnection from the fabric of society[63] and feelings of loneliness and isolation, which were common even before the pandemic and its social burdens.[64] At the same time, technology makes new connections possible. As discussed in the first chapter, the combination of personal disconnection and the availability of global networks only a keystroke away creates the conditions for radicalization across distances. The spread of conspiracy theories and violent extremist ideas indicates that the potential inherent in the ability to cross borders and connect with like-minded others through new media does not always lead to the realization of a humanistic vision. Hatred and lies, protected by rules of privacy and open expression, spread quickly and create senses of connection and affiliation. Civic and local ties, particularly those that encourage exchanges and connections across different views and identities, can provide at least a partial antidote to these trends. Virtual echo chambers and information bubbles are hard to break online, though introducing some serendipity and diversity into search engines and news algorithms can do some of this work. But given the self-directed nature of these processes, and the fact that they are most commonly conducted by a person sitting alone in front of a screen, it is harder to counteract isolation and immersion in a limited pool of sources by changes to platforms and algorithms alone. Various civic groups have sprung up in recent years as the damaging effects polarization and mistrust have on the political sphere have become evident. Their focus is on in-person, directed, and intentional exchanges of views, aimed at creating trust and shared understanding.[65] These are significant and productive endeavors. One of their possible limitations is that participation is voluntary, meaning that many of the individuals participating in these conversations are already inclined toward civic renewal and understanding, and the conversation might not reach others who are less so inclined. While that does not invalidate the importance of these exchanges and the significance of such groups, it points to the need to have civic conversations and similar exchanges in contexts that would include individuals with other inclinations too; supporting such exchanges in educational contexts—where people would join for other reasons but also where they have the time and connections to be able to pursue ongoing conversations across differences—can also be useful.

Focusing on the boundaries of permissible speech within an institution—and in the democratic public sphere more broadly—should help create an inclusive middle ground. Instead of calling for the inclusion of all ideological voices, including hate-based and bigoted ones, or calling out all who do not adhere to one particular comprehensive political vision, a more nuanced approach would recognize the institution's mission, values, and history, the population it serves, and the democratic necessity of sustaining a public space that is both inclusive and diverse in terms of the people and views it welcomes.

The demand for safety and protection from harm recognizes that the clamor of diverse views and competing arguments that takes up so much space in classrooms, dorms, labs, civic groups, and other diverse and public spaces on campus can be not only exhausting but also diminishing for some members of campus. The demand for safety is partially addressed but is not fulfilled by being able to escape into an

affinity group. Freedom of association and the centrality of certain features of identity to one's sense of belonging together justify the continued role of identity-based connections on campus, despite legislative
challenges. Republican-controlled state legislatures are proposing and
passing laws that prohibit such contexts in public universities. A variety of bills were proposed in 2020[66] that target both safe spaces and
freedom of expression: they seek to bar public colleges from allowing
classes, activities, or events that promote "division between, resentment of, or social justice for" any "race, gender, political affiliation, or
social class," thus limiting the academic freedom of instructors and
students to discuss issues of concern.[67] A student looking for an accepting and familiar space within a community that might feel alien
or alienating to an eighteen-year-old can reasonably turn to those who
share a salient aspect of their identity for social connection or mento-
ring, as well as for intellectual exploration. Banning these connections
does not serve the purpose of well-being, academic freedom, or free
expression.

Thus safety can align with both free speech and inclusivity, and together they can serve as grounding aspects of the common good. The
work of reconciling these aspects is itself the work of building trust,
reducing tension, and depolarizing the ideological realm. This work is
incentivized by the fact that both open expression advocates and those
who seek to promote and expand inclusion can readily find their work
self-defeating. When social justice advocates call for the curtailment
of free speech through censoring speakers and canceling events, they
neglect to recognize what politics and history can teach us: that curtail-
ing speech out of concern for harm to marginalized groups can readily
lead to censorship and punishment directed at the very groups such
measures intend to protect. Once censorship based on content is ad-
ministratively possible and socially accepted, what is to stop people in
power—administrators, religious majority groups, others—from limiting speech by dissenters, opponents, or anyone who threatens the
status quo?

On the other hand, advocates who insist that unfettered free speech
is a necessary condition for the open-minded free inquiry that makes a
university worth its name sidestep the fact that when many on campus
are already effectively silenced, inquiry is in fact neither free nor open-
minded. It remains the prerogative of those who have the tools and
support to join the conversation and participate in the main activities

on campus, including research, active learning, and established social roles. Many gender, racial, and sexual minorities, first-generation students, and other individuals who may not see themselves (or be seen by others) as belonging or possessing the tools required to hit the ground running remain outside the conversation, which impoverishes the conversation and hinders the search for truth and knowledge. Inclusion should be used not to limit speech but to support students on campus, citizens both in the public sphere and online, by expanding both opportunities to exchange views and a capacity to productively respond to speech so inoffensive.

In the revitalization of democracy, inclusive practices can help alleviate mistrust through an open exchange of testimonies, ideas, and perspectives. As Allen writes, "distrust can be overcome only when citizens manage to find methods of generating mutual benefit despite differences of position, experience, and perspective. The discovery of such methods is the central project of democracy."[68] Democracy in polarized times requires a commitment to negotiating and protecting expressive and political speech with broad legal requirements and a thin, flexible commitment to an inclusive atmosphere. The final two chapters explore ways to enact this commitment: first in K–12 schools, where most of the nation's children learn to become citizens and to practice free expression in a diverse setting; and then in higher education.

4 · Freedom of Speech and Habits of Democracy in K–12 Schools

"Democracy has to be born anew every generation, and education is its midwife."
JOHN DEWEY

If college campuses are to advance the common good, reduce polarization, and help rebuild democracy, the institutions and the sector need to commit to this goal.[1] Many higher education institutions are indeed making this commitment.[2] But to achieve this goal, the students the institutions serve need to know their own rights, they need to learn about democracy, and they must be experienced in using their voices. Familiarity with free speech, not just as an idea or a legal concept but also as a lived practice, is uncommon for young people. Most have little experience with institutions that foster open expression, particularly the open expression of youths; and most also have limited exposure to open debate. This chapter assesses the ways in which schools are framing student free speech and what they might do to strengthen it so that young people are able to use their voices and develop their democratic attitudes—in school, on campus, and beyond.

As with other events that induced national reckonings, the January 6 insurrection had many commentators turn their gaze toward the nation's schools. Some have lamented a lack of civic education, and some have suggested that better schooling could have prevented the attack, and some have argued that schools should now work to reduce both extremism and polarization. As is often the case in the wake of instances of civil discord, interest in civic education rises and then ebbs when the focus of education debate inevitably returns to standardized test performance.[3] Civic education is important, but it cannot be expected to solve such significant social problems until schools are able to commit to giving students opportunities to develop democratic habits. And, as Daniels rightly laments, "it is hard at this moment to imagine civics being restored fully to the K–12 curriculum in a coherent and consistent way, given the hyper-partisanship that has called even the most settled civic norms into question."[4] While there is limited agreement on whether civic education courses alone boost formal measures of participation, such as voting,[5] a broader investment in and attention to civic issues in school strengthens civic competence and efficacy. I do not focus here on the broader issues related to teaching civics—though such a focus would be warranted, particularly with an eye to how partisan divides can be overcome.[6] Rather, I focus on speech: the erosion of speech protections for students[7] and teachers;[8] the need for more political content, speech, and debate;[9] and the need for learning to discern the quality of arguments—particularly their truthfulness.

Schools, and particularly high schools, are faced with two key challenges to creating an atmosphere of open inquiry. The first challenge is cuts to civic education programs and corresponding demands placed on teachers to focus classroom time on attaining measurable achievements in other areas.[10] The cuts—though they have been reversed in some states in recent years—make it hard for teachers to find classroom contexts in which open discussion can be cultivated and sustained. The second challenge is the legal view of student free speech: recent decades have seen courts permitting increased limitations on students' expression in class. The landmark *Tinker* decision, which permitted the use of black armbands to express opposition to the Vietnam War, also established the requirement that student expression not disrupt the learning environment.[11] In the decades since, and until the 2007 "Bong Hits 4 Jesus" case (approving the suspension of a student who unfurled a nonsensical banner at a school event), courts have expanded the demands on maintaining a productive learning environment and have declined to protect a broad variety of student speech, including lewd speech and student newspapers reporting on uncomfortable topics.[12] Therefore, it is common for high school graduates to come to college with very limited basic knowledge about politics and governance, and with very limited experience in institutions that foster an open exchange of ideas. Students who come to college after (or while) spending some time in the workplace are often in no better shape, as workplaces regularly forbid or punish the expression or discussion of controversial views.[13]

Legal scholars have described a continued decline in the courts' willingness to protect student speech. Even in earlier decisions, such as *Barnette*, in which the courts sided with appealing students, the courts "did not establish that students possessed an affirmative right to advance their own opinions, on topics of their own selection, much less in the face of school officials' objections. The right to sit out, in other words, did not necessarily confer the right to speak out."[14] The *Tinker* decision allowed student war protesters a stronger voice, but since then the courts have continuously restricted students' speech rights under the banners of preserving a suitable learning environment, out of deference to administrators and teachers, and for other similar reasons. The courts have generally not taken minors to be citizens, deserving of full constitutional protections, and have instead portrayed them as citizens in training, whose views are therefore not material to the democratic or institutional discussion.[15] And while the "Tinker Test," established in 1969, noted that student speech is protected so long as it is does not "materially and substantially interfere with the requirements of appropriate discipline in the operation of the school" and does not conflict "with the rights of others to be secure and let alone,"[16] subsequent decisions have expanded the scope of what is required for a suitable learning environment, and developed a set of caveats and exceptions to the Tinker Test.

In addition to declining support for student speech in the courts, state legislatures have also passed numerous laws in recent years that restrict "disruptive" student speech. The definition of "disruption" in these state laws is often broad and murky, leaving practitioners significant discretion to decide when a student deserves to be not only reprimanded or suspended for classroom behaviors but also arrested, charged, and jailed.[17]

Concerns about speech rights thus animate legal and jurisprudential efforts. But not when it comes to school children: Justice Roberts, despite describing himself in 2019 as the "most aggressive defender of the First Amendment on the Court," does not see students as deserving of the same protections it provides to adults.[18] Lower courts agree: courts in both Michigan and Rhode Island have dismissed cases that sought to demand equity in access to quality education on the grounds that literacy, or civic education, is necessary for equal citizenship. In his opinion, Judge William Smith sounds a supportive note: "This is what it all comes down to: we may choose to survive as a country by . . . educating our children on civics, the rule of law, and what it really means to be an American, and what America means. Or, we may ignore these things at our and their peril."[19]

As courts restrict speech rights and treat young people as being too young to have their own views, schools also take up this vision and apply it to their testing-focused curricula and to a mute-button-ready remote learning environment. The increasing focus on behavior and school discipline further limits attention to students' speech rights.[20] Students are regularly treated by judges, policy-makers, and school administrators as vessels for the advancement of one agenda or another, or as mere future workers and taxpayers, committed to uplifting our shared economic future. Future prosperity is a fine goal, but it cannot suffice alone. A society is more than an economy, and American democracy is broader than the sum of its businesses and employees. Students need to learn how to become effective members of this complex, and arguably eroding, democratic society. They need to learn to speak up, to speak their minds, to connect across divides, and to be allowed to make their own mistakes.

Unlike other democracies, the United States puts very few limits on hate speech, and citizens are encouraged to use "more and better speech" in response to hateful, bigoted, and other harmful speech. Many young people today are skeptical of this approach[21] and express a preference for more limitations on speech, especially when it harms members of marginalized social groups. Whether or not one agrees with this view—I give this view further consideration in the next chapter and argue that dismissing it is not practically reasonable and may also be unjustifiable—it is no surprise that young people are ready to endorse a more restrictive view of speech after spending twelve years in public institutions that stifled their voices. Schools are increasingly regulating bullying and cyberbullying—an important responsibility, which is sometimes defined in overly broad ways; they expect civility—which is, again, a good habit, but sometimes results in a chilled environment for speech. Schools are permitted by the courts to censor school newspapers to preserve the school's "brand."[22] The courts allow schools to limit lewd and improper speech. Teachers and administrators reasonably shy away from discussing topics that create public rifts and, increasingly, draw scrutiny and rebuke from school boards and legislators. Where would students learn to appreciate the promise of open expression?

No one is born with the skills and knowledge to be an engaged citizen, and we need more engaged citizens to sustain this unique form of government. The First Amendment is phrased to limit government regulation of speech ("Congress shall make no law . . . abridging the freedom of speech"). A politically engaged, well-educated new generation is seen as the solution to many social ills, and it can indeed be this solution. But schools should be recognized as operating not outside the social and political realms but within them. Political will and the social commitment to recognize and resolve social issues are necessary if the school system is to effectively take on and attempt to alleviate issues ranging from racism to economic inequality to insufficient patriotism. Whatever the civic traits that we value, or whatever the issues we seek to resolve through the schools, it is not enough to assign schools these tasks and hope for the best. "If we want active citizens who care about democracy and are willing to work for it, then the requisite traits need to be cultivated,"[23] teachers and schools need to be guided, supported, and funded properly so they can accomplish these weighty tasks.

To help schools prepare students to revitalize American democracy, students' civil rights are a good place to start, and this involves protecting student speech as well as teaching students to use their voices. While the courts might help determine when it is appropriate to punish a student for hurtful, bigoted, or otherwise inappropriate speech, the work that must be done in schools goes way beyond sketching the boundaries of permissible speech. A key step in revitalizing democracy is investing in schools and supporting them as they prepare the next generation of citizens.

A healthy democracy requires deep civic learning, which has been suggested to incorporate the mastery of civic knowledge, along with creativity, the development of civic identity, and civic attitudes and values.[24] A strong civic education, of the type that is rarely available these days to American K–12 students, teaches young people how to be authentic, informed, and engaged democratic citizens who know what they value and what kind of society they want to live in, who understand social institutions, and who know how to raise their voices.

Civic education is key to an active and stable democracy. In *Our Common Purpose*, the authors assert that education must go beyond "names and dates" and that "the American citizen today must be prepared to acknowledge our nation's mistakes, to recognize that we have grappled over time to improve our imperfect union, to find pride in those struggles, and to recognize that, at our best, everyone is in-cluded . . . citizens today must be able to deal with ongoing debate and argument, be able to engage in debate, find compromise."[25] The centrality of open expression, as a broad commitment on the part of schools rather than as merely a topic for a lesson, is key to this type of civic education. Students could be taught about open expression di-rectly, particularly through learning the history of students' open ex-pression. They can be exposed to the evolving boundaries of their own speech so that they might begin to consider that it matters.

This sort of teaching might be a productive first step in address-ing young people's views of open expression, but it does not address the other issues that weaken American democracy. The problems of polarization, the erosion of truth, lack of trust in one another and in public institutions, and the resultant struggles over the boundaries of expression are reflected in Americans' views of the public education system. Nearly 90 percent of American children attend public schools, and while most parents tend to approve of their children's schools and trust them, this support is uneven. Some elites and others, particularly on the right, express significant suspicion toward teachers' unions, re-quired curricula, and the notion of public goods available to all that are provided by the government. Some minority groups, especially African Americans, maintain an attitude of distrust toward a system that has failed to serve them well for generations.[26] This same system can also be called upon to resolve these concerns, but only insofar as its doing so is supported by the public and by its multiple regulatory and supervisory structures. Civics education and related educational interventions that aim to prepare youth for their roles as citizens are seen as necessary for overcoming the challenges that democracy faces today in the United States (and in some other countries where popu-lism is a significant force). Schools can produce citizens who would be better trained to recognize fallacies and to prefer truth over them, and to be prepared to hear views beyond their own. To accomplish this goal, support for schools' work at the federal and community level will be necessary, so that teachers are trained and supported in this work.

If they receive such support, as a recent bipartisan recommitment to civic education indicates might be possible,[27] what might they do to accomplish the task of educating future citizens? The focus here on education for free speech is key to understanding democracy and to developing the habits and attitudes that sustain it. Schools can start with some of their curricular offerings, especially those that involve media literacy; they can also focus on developing a greater variety of classroom opportunities to develop democratic skills and habits. K–12 schools can help support the revitalization of democracy through a clear focus on truth and freedom of expression. Tweaks to school policy and practices can revamp the protection of free expression for teachers as well as students, which would strengthen the civic and democratic preparation students receive in schools.

The protection and expansion of freedom of expression is partly a matter of political ideology, which follows the positions staked out in the campus speech battles. The concern long held by liberals that schools might be used to shape children's minds in ways that would stifle diversity of thought[28] has been taken up by some segments of the political right. Select conservative and right-wing perspectives portray public schools as oppressive factories meant to churn out citizens who align with progressive ideologies. Using the term "government schools" to describe public schools, some advocates for religious and private schools have been promoting school choice as a way to juxtapose the conservative ideological bent they favor against a progressive ideology that they presume is propagated in schools. The struggle over the 1619 Project, and the related discussion of enslavement being key to the American origin story, demonstrates this tension. To sum up the controversy, some conservative speakers see the teaching of the 1619 Project, along with the general depiction of slavery in various curricular materials, as promoting a rejection of patriotism (or of a specific, color-blind version of racial equity) or as indoctrinating children to think about the United States in critical ways. They would prefer an educational focus on their favored version of patriotism. These positions illustrate the perspective of some conservative speakers who depict public schools as left-leaning institutions of indoctrination—much like how colleges are depicted in parallel debates.

These ongoing public clashes animate much of the discussion about public schools and the appropriate modes of expression within them, including discussions of effective pedagogical practice, ideological orientation, and legal and jurisprudential principles. As the debates ebb and flow, teachers continue to prepare students to be civic actors who learn to share the public sphere with diverse others with whom they need to reach shared decisions about collective action. The climate they maintain in class and the practices they model and promote around truth-seeking and open discussion can support the development of democratic habits as well as any curriculum.

Efforts to protect open expression in schools do not focus on concerns about compelling or silencing certain ideologies. Contrary to the current debate about college campuses, the struggles over open expression in K-12 schools—including the standout legal cases discussed below—center on a mix of political and nonpolitical topics, and many of these relate to concerns about learning generally rather than voicing a particular perspective. Hence, the protection of open expression in schools can readily fit into the discussion of education for citizenship.

Civic education is increasingly recognized as a key aspirational goal of public schools, even as both policy and practice remain uneven in its implementation. Scholarship about education has long recognized preparing students to become citizens as a central justification for schools being a public endeavor—why would one resident agree to the use of their tax dollars in funding the education of their neighbors' children if not for the stake they have in having an educated citizenry?[29] Advocacy groups and policy organizations increasingly join the chorus calling on districts, states, and the Department of Education to invest in the effective preparation of democratic citizens.[30] While the scholarly and advocacy work promoting civic education is growing stronger, supporters of civic education are still swimming against the strong tide of standardization and a staunch focus on "the basics"—math and reading, mostly—which take up most of schools' time, attention, and funding.

Some of the fragilities of American democracy are becoming apparent—particularly those that stem from the inability to discern truth from lies in news reports, online exchanges, and political statements, as well as those that result from bitter partisanship and eroding trust. With the growing recognition of these fragilities, it is clear that teachers could be better supported than they currently are in attending to the civic development of their students. Curricular offerings, from one-time programs, workshops, and visits to full courses, are being developed by academic and advocacy organizations and are being made available to districts and teachers, who can implement these in addition to the curriculum they develop themselves. Such offerings tend to go beyond the transmission of factual information—how a bill becomes a law or the structure of the three branches of government—and venture into domains that support the development of civic skills and democratic habits. They do so by engaging in issues that affect local communities, by raising and considering controversial issues in class, and by supporting students in developing their views and voices. However, teachers often report that they do not feel confident—and do not see themselves as being properly trained or supported—in raising difficult and controversial topics of discussion in class. Nor do they always feel prepared to deal with such issues when they spill into the classroom, either when highly visible news events occur—elections, impeachment trial, war—or when students bring a disagreement from the hallway or home into class.

Recent studies on the unsteady state of American democracy focus on the need to teach children rational skills of argumentation and of discerning truth from lies, politically motivated statements, and conspiratorial thinking. Philosopher Quassim Cassam suggests that to overcome the current epistemic predicament we face, we must use arguments and evidence to rebut conspiracy theories and educate our children, equipping them with critical thinking skills and intellectual virtues so that they are inoculated against conspiracism. He further suggests that we unmask the propagandistic nature of conspiracy theories, as doing so might lead to embarrassment among those who hold unfounded beliefs.[31]

But the focus on critical thinking skills, while important, will not by itself suffice as a solution to concerns about the democratic erosion that results from the decaying state of truth and heightened concerns about harm in contemporary democracies. Arguments alone, and the strengthening of children's epistemic capacities, will not improve the social and political conditions that have led to the current fraying of democratic ties. The habits of democracy, which are shared, civic, and social, need to be mended before children can use any newly developed critical thinking skills to argue their way into a stronger political union. If these habits are developed through a shared process of truth-seeking and open discussion, they can overcome the single-minded nature of conspiracy thinking and the polarizing effects of sorting and mistrust. Sharing the process of information production, assessment, and distribution—sharing the judgment of what is reliable and what should be shared—can produce trust, if it is done within broad, clear norms of speech and exchange.

To enable the development of democratic civic skills, schools need to maintain a robust context in which students can voice and share their views. Strict and punitive boundaries that focus on strict hierarchical structures of authority do not allow students to develop the connections and the capacity and inclination to engage across differences that are necessary for democratic revitalization. Next, I consider how two of the most important practices meant to enable the development of democratic habits—namely, media literacy programs and discussions of hard topics—contribute to this goal.

TRUST, TRUTH, AND MEDIA LITERACY IN K–12 SCHOOLS

After the 2020 elections, misinformation about voter fraud was rampant. Tracy Freeman, a high school teacher in Illinois, sought to support the development of her students' media literacy and ability to discern true facts. In the days after the election, one student said they'd heard that Pennsylvania had bused in ballots bearing the names of dead people. "The student wanted to say it was factual," Freeman said. "So then the class automatically said, 'What are our sources?'" Freeman usually requires that students cite two, and the student did name two outlets: Fox News and The Gateway Pundit, a far-right outlet. Freeman proposed in class discussion that they expand their search this time. They checked their local news station, which wasn't reporting anything about the supposed Pennsylvania incident. She showed them an interview with a law professor, who explained that there wasn't widespread evidence of fraudulent voting.

Finally, Freeman suggested that they wait a week. They could keep listening to on-the-ground reporting from national news outlets like NPR ("They're in the middle of rallies with microphones—they'll have people who will find out for us," Freeman said), and the student could look for other evidence, as well.

When they checked in again, the student was reconsidering his initial claim. "He said, 'I think I'm making a sweeping generalization,'" said Freeman.[32]

•   •   •

It is easy to blame exposure to unreliable media sources as the root of misinformation and unfounded beliefs. There is some truth to this claim: networks of like-minded ideologues can easily connect across

distances to create sealed information bubbles in a spiraling and rad-
icalizing process (as discussed in chapter 1). Social media platforms
are not just a new medium for communication—they create new exchanges, relationships, and content that did not and could not exist
without them. The struggle over how to regulate this type of speech
will continue in legislative attention to Section 230, which protects
social media companies from liability for the content that is posted
on their platforms, and in the courts. But regulation is not going to
resolve the issues that these new exchanges bring about. Platforms
can add a label to posts warning readers that claims are misleading or
"disputed," but to address disinformation, users will have to develop
media and (dis)information literacy. Many schools already take on this
role, which is seen as part of their language arts learning or social studies and civics.[33]

Media literacy is essential to creating a shared epistemology, which
can counter many of the ills afflicting current media platforms—in particular, the tendency of users to participate in creating a spectacle by
believing and sharing misinformation. A shared foundation of facts
must start early, and as a part of this process, the youngest members
of a political community need to be ushered into the practice of evaluating their sources of information and assessing the trustworthiness
of claims. It is being done in some places already, most notably in
Finland, where a curriculum that advises students about identifying
lies, mistakes, and hoaxes, and encourages them to engage in news
consumption and also civic action has recently become mandatory
with clear and positive results.[34] Similar curricula are available in the
United States, and implemented in some districts, although they are
not universally used.[35] If there ever was a time in which students could
be expected to rely on encyclopedias and newspapers for reliable information, that time is long gone, with answers to many questions at
the students' fingertips, for better and worse. The broad availability
of information of varying quality is affecting older generations, who
were not trained in learning to discern reliability with these types of
sources.[36] While younger people may be more adept at understanding
the online environment, it is still misguided to portray them as "digital natives" who need no guidance as they peruse information, news,
and data; in fact, studies continue to show that many young people are
having a hard time assessing digital sources.[37]

But traditional media literacy programs cannot address the issues raised by insulated information bubbles, where ideologically motivated misinformation spirals and echoes without check. To be relevant in the current media landscape and in today's polarized debate, media literacy programs need to address intentionally manipulative media[38] by extending their reach further into new sources in a collaborative, rather than merely analytic, fashion.

Programs that teach children (and adults) to assess a source of information itself remain within the bounds of the information bubble, rather than looking to connect and compare the source to other sources. This is to some extent the case with SIFT, a program that teaches children to assess the sites they are using.[39] The focus on a single source and its reliability is less effective in the context of disparate and insulated media streams marked by ideological affiliation. The process illustrated by Freeman, the teacher described in the opening of this section, is reflective of current approaches that aim to compare different sources and look to triangulate the data they provide. Another benefit of this approach is that while such a comparison can be done by a single person, it is more effectively done in teams. Team efforts to assess sources—and to learn more about the information the team seeks—allow team members to connect, compare notes, and help each other in the processes of debiasing, building trust in each other and in their sources, and assessing their outcomes together.

Preparing students to manage reality in an era of misinformation and truth decay[40] is key to helping them navigate this age of increasing polarization. As news, information, and truth itself become politicized, and given the decentralized and participatory nature of many platforms, the role of media literacy is not limited to identifying and assessing reliable sources of information, though this remains a critical step. Politicization exacerbates the difficulty of using facts to debunk entrenched views, including unscientific and unproven ones.[41] As discussed in earlier chapters, polarization and insularity contribute to the circulation of mis- and disinformation in that individuals and communities are confined, commonly as a result of personal choices that are fed and escalated by algorithms, to echo chambers and information silos where competing views are rarely heard. Being exposed to a single set of perspectives and facts—accurate or otherwise—leads to a diminished habit of questioning or critically assessing one's perspective.

Key guides for educators recognize that the vitality of American democracy depends on citizens' ability to discern reliable and truthful information, which they mostly access through digital sources.[42] Most young people are unable to do so consistently and effectively.[43] Awareness is rising among teachers and, especially, policy-makers about the risks created by this lack of media and digital literacy. Subsequently, more states are requiring the inclusion of this subject in their curricula, and teachers and administrators are choosing to include it in language arts, civics, or other classes.[44] More scholarly attention is being paid to documenting youth media literacy and to addressing it through the use of innovative programs.[45]

The responsibility for teaching and assessing media literacy can fall to English teachers. Teachers are recognizing the urgency of this need. For instance, in 2019, the National Council of Teachers of English passed a resolution calling for a renewed emphasis on teaching "civic and critical literacy," including efforts to "support classroom practices that examine . . . dishonest discourse and arguments."[46] The importance of assessing sources of information, dishonesty, and the reliability of arguments students encounter is relevant in the English (or language arts) classroom, but it can also take place in the history classroom or in social studies, as well as in the sciences, where climate, evolution, and other subjects rife with misinformation and controversy are discussed.[47] But assessing sources of information for reliability is not all that is needed: tackling motivated reasoning, and the willful ignorance that sometimes accompanies it, is an essential part of becoming "media literate" as well. To do this effectively, clear goals and responsibilities need to be assigned at the school.

Young people, like their elders, are influenced by their political affiliations in assessing the truth of claims presented to them. Political knowledge does not mitigate the tendency to positively assess the truth of a statement according to prior political preferences, but exposure to media literacy programs does influence the extent to which young people trust inaccurate information.[48] Attending a media literacy program is also associated with the motivation to seek information and the development of news analysis skills, which together contribute to young people's inclination to be civically engaged.[49] Therefore, effective media literacy programs, ones which include a focus on cultivating the abilities to discern reliable sources, to assess information independently, to analyze arguments, and, especially, to do all of these together, are key to developing effective civic engagement skills.[50]

Today these essential programs make up an occasional part of various required curricula and subjects, but they are not any specific educator's responsibility in most schools. Assigning this responsibility to a specific person—for example to a specific subject teacher, or to the school librarians who can train and support teachers as well as provide their own programming—would help. The Common Core and other standardized approaches to curriculum have pushed media literacy skills aside, and these skills need to be brought back to the center of learning.[51]

In addition to helping young people discern accurate from inaccurate information, media literacy programs have the benefit of increasing youth participation in political discussions and information-seeking online.[52] Media literacy can "situate the engaged citizen in environments where they recognize the capacity they have to form connections and extend their communications to a large group of interested peers."[53] I turn now to the importance of training students in how to do this effectively across political and other divides.

OPEN DISCUSSION OF HARD TOPICS

In a diverse seventh-grade history class, the end of a lesson about the New Deal is devoted to a whole-class discussion about primary documents from the era. Jenny, an African American student, notes: "I kind of disagree with Sarah only because of the African American [document] and then, the songs. Because if you can't help, like everyone, how can that be a success? If African Americans are kind of left out of the whole New Deal then it can't really be a success for the Americans because African Americans are Americans as well." Eric, the teacher, who is white, responds with approval. A white girl speaks next: "Okay, uh, what a lot of people are saying with the African Americans, you have got to remember that not the entire country and everyone—like a lot of, yes, it was mainly white people being bailed out from the Depression, however, not all white people are the same and that's what everyone is kind of lumping them together. And you've got to remember that there is a certain number of people that think about the African Americans and they stand up for them, so once they get out of that they can make the movement to get the African Americans out of that . . ." Devon, an African American student, interjects: "Wait—what!?! She said that white people get out then Black people get out!?" Lea (to Devon): "Essentially. Okay, so the Depression is like a big jail cell. The cops are like—okay, so basically the Depression is like the cops. And, well, whoever got them into the Depression is the cops, the Depression is like the jail cell. White people get out first, and then, everyone is kind of lumping all white people together." Eric [interrupting]: "So you're agreeing with Jenny here that this is not a success for similar reasons Jenny stated, the fact that not all people are getting helped: either they're not getting helped or they're not getting helped at the same time." Lea: "Well I'm saying yes it wasn't a success but then eventually it was a success..." Other students chime in to clarify: "She's saying it takes a while." Eric: "How reliable is that document? Let's talk about that. Is it a trustworthy source?"[54]

•   •   •

Even students who benefit from media literacy education, those who agree on ways to validate and cross-reference sources and avoid lies and mistakes, must have the opportunity to practice sharing their views and considering them through open exchange. Views, opinions, beliefs, and even interpretations of facts do not spring up wholly formed in one's mind. They evolve in a social context, and conversation—discussion—is therefore a necessary context for learning to appreciate and benefit from free speech. The structured environment of the classroom is the main place where this can happen for most students.

Facts are often best discussed within their broader contexts, so their status as true or false can be understood within their own significance and in relation to the ways in which they are created and shared, or the impact they have. Therefore, in this context as well, truth and inclusion go hand in hand, as assessing facts and people's views and understanding, as well as their motivations for sharing their views and understanding, lead toward the same democratic goal. The guardrails against anti-democratic pressures, such as disinformation about issues of interest and about fellow citizens, include careful attention to the boundaries of speech. Within the school community, in addition to such guardrails, educators need to be supported in threading civic connections focused on meaningful conversations about hard topics, as in the classroom conversation about the Depression era. To do so, students should be able to trust their teachers and peers, at least in the basic dignitary sense that ensures they will not pose social identity threats to them, as well as in the epistemic sense that allows them to assume that difference of views will be used to advance everyone's knowledge rather than be framed as a zero-sum competition.[55]

The aim of discussing hard topics should not be to sharpen political divides but should rather be to reduce the affective polarization among students—or in other words, to help them see people with opposing opinions as acting for reasons that are acceptable (even when one continues to not accept them).[56] The goal is thus not to change minds or reduce polarization or differences in views, but rather to create a sense of shared fate among students, both as members of the classroom community and as members of the same nation. As Paula McAvoy notes, this approach is particularly relevant in times of significant polarization and civil strife: "The appeal of shared fate is that it attempts to shift how one identifies with politics."[57] Thinking about what binds a nation together—and in particular, thinking about the institutions, histories, languages, and geographies that make up a nation—is a way to create a shared foundation of both reality and identity—a shared understanding of facts, a shared vision of the issues the country faces, and a shared sense of the unique capacities that can propel a nation into a shared future. Clearly this description is aspirational, and chapter 1 has already delved into polarization and the many divides that pull citizens apart. But the educational endeavor, rooted in boundless optimism about what investment in young people can produce, can commit to establishing a shared sense of knowledge and fate. To do so, students and teachers should not shy away from hard conversations or paper over differences with abstract visions. Rather, they should engage in an open exchange across the real differences that divide the nation—ideological, racial, and otherwise—to find ways to share both knowledge and values across these divides.

Educational practices both inside and outside the classroom can facilitate the development of a sense of shared fate, which is at the core of democratic culture and at the heart of the educational process. It is not only curricular decisions and pedagogical practices that can be used to reflect a commitment to democratic values, but also disciplinary decisions. Thus, for example, as Campbell Scribner and Bryan Warnick note: "A central goal of restorative justice is the restoration of dignity."[58] Maintaining, or restoring, dignity for all students (and teachers) is a key condition for the learning and moral community that schools need to sustain if they are to promote their democratic goals. Censorship and silencing, much like other forms of exclusion, cannot serve this goal.

It is not enough to recognize the importance of hard discussions in the classroom. Teachers need backing and support, which also includes training from their superiors for when a discussion goes into territories that cause offense or anger—an eventuality that should be avoided when possible, but is bound to occasionally arise. Pedagogical and instructional practices[59] and curricular guidance[60] can help teachers facilitate effective discussions.

To remake the civic fabric—the democratic culture that is required to sustain a democratic public—the electorate and the broader population must be empowered to act and to be able to respond to the current challenges concerning the boundaries of the public sphere. The key issues that are threatening democratic stability at this time are polarization, including politically motivated reasoning and the erosion of trust in institutions and in the 'other side,' and truth decay, including the widespread issue of mis- and disinformation, which is exacerbated by the wide availability and quick evolution of virtual connectivity.

Classroom discussion is key to generating the first threads of civic trust, through the protection and expansion of open expression in the classroom, and to sharing diverse views that can be considered, argued, amended, endorsed, or rejected. In addition, as McAvoy asserts, "when students deliberate in politically diverse groups, the group's views pre-post do move people toward consensus and away from ideological poles."[61] Such an open exchange is vital to the development of democratic values and habits. As Will Kymlicka powerfully puts it, "the ability and willingness to engage in public discourse about matters of public policy, and to question authority . . . are perhaps the most distinctive aspects of citizenship in a liberal democracy, since they are precisely what distinguish 'citizens' within a democracy from the 'subjects' of an authoritarian regime."[62] Substantively, it is central to democratic speech within institutions not only that institutions focus on legal and constitutional protections from government intervention, regulation, or limitation of speech as the First Amendment requires, but also that citizens are able to develop their voices— that they can learn to have a discussion. As Diana Hess defines it, "discussion is a particular approach to constructing knowledge that is predicated on the belief that the most powerful ideas can be produced when people are expressing their ideas on a topic and listening to others express theirs."[63]

Despite the courts' retreat from the protection of student speech rights, educators can recognize that an open classroom climate where diverse views are aired and debated is productive for the development of democratic skills. Students in classes with "rich and frequent" discussions have been shown to be more engaged, learn more, have a higher level of political knowledge, and, importantly, be more interested in listening to diverse views.[64] Classroom discussions led by teachers who are well trained and supported by their communities and leaders, which enable students to develop early skills and habits of democratic debate, are material to the revitalization of the democratic public sphere. There is a long road for American (and other) schools to go before teachers are properly trained and have their speech protected.[65] Students can be prepared to meet, tackle, and overcome extreme polarization if they already have the basic habits of listening, speaking, and discussing; these habits can be developed at home and in other contexts as well, but most crucially, they can also be developed in schools, where students are most likely to hear diverse opinions in a structured and sustained way.

Schools are also public institutions, and as such they are best suited to train students to prepare for engagement not only with diverse others but also with authority and institutional hierarchies. It is necessary to the development of such democratic habits to debate key policies and controversial issues in class: as Hess notes, "we need to teach young people that what they think about such issues deserves airtime—both in and out of school. Their views matter, not because there's something special about young people, but precisely because there is not. Their views matter because all views should matter in a democracy."[66]

To some extent, expecting schools to facilitate the development of civic trust by encouraging open discussion of hard topics is akin to asking schools to lift themselves out of the current conditions of democracy by their bootstraps, and to lift society along with them. To learn to be both willing and able to communicate across divides, classrooms need to be based on trust and good faith—a tall order in this polarized time. As in society at large, as Hess and McAvoy state, "political polarization can cause distrust within classrooms, between teachers and

students and among fellow students."[67] Recent years have seen a proliferation of civic efforts to support schools in this work, with groups
like CivXNow and iCivics establishing organizational efforts to build
capacity and work to equalize access to quality civic training for teachers and their students.[68] This rise in interest and investment, where
welcomed by schools and their communities, can invigorate the civic
opportunities teachers can provide.

Having hard and open conversations in class is a central tool for
generating civic trust and for protecting freedom of expression in
school—it is a key democratic habit. Teachers can only have these
conversations if they are trained to do so and are supported by their
supervisors as well as by community members, including parents. Like
all learning processes, these conversations will, as a matter of course,
include mistakes, missteps, and possibly some hurt feelings. But they
will also be a part of a process that will help students learn to try on
different ideas; to acknowledge the lived experiences, diverse backgrounds, and social contexts of others; and to start building a shared
network of learning. Even in relatively homogenous schools, some diversity of experience, ideology, and identity is present. Exploring and
building on diversity through open discussion of controversial topics
can help students learn the skills and develop the attitudes necessary
for crossing our increasingly overlapping social fractures.

5 · Campus Speech and Democratic Renewal

Contestations about safety and about truth have increasingly animated polarized and extreme public debates in recent years. Safety, and the effort to reduce or prevent harm, is foundational to the effort to create an inclusive and open atmosphere that allows all members of a community to participate equally without intimidation. While safety as a concern is sometimes depicted pejoratively (with terms such as "safetyism" and "coddling"), it is an essential aspect of the core democratic value of non-oppression. Truth, and in particular the path leading to knowledge and reliable information, is another cornerstone of a democratic public sphere. A shared epistemology is necessary for shared governance: to negotiate policy, a society (or its representatives) must agree on facts. A number of issues define democratic practice, such as the role of expertise, the knowledge held by the populace, and this knowledge's standing in relation to expert knowledge; available ways to consider, understand, question, or debunk existing knowledge; and the assessment of political lies. These issues play out in legislative offices, on social media, and on the streets, and in recent years they are also centrally present on college campuses.

The current struggles over the meaning of truth and over the conditions of inclusion and safety present an expansion of earlier "deplatforming" attempts on college campuses and provide an opportunity to consider key matters of civility, resistance, and the possibility of a common ground. These struggles provide an opportunity to create new pathways for building social trust, more inclusively than in the past—an effort that requires commitment by institutions and sectors rather than solely engaging individuals. Given that open-mindedness and receptiveness to considering views different from one's own are not so much a personal trait as an outcome of interactional and interpersonal contexts,[1] building environments where such receptiveness is possible is key to overcoming the current democratic predicament. As Annette Baier suggests, "where there is little or no mutual trust . . . it is hard to see how trust could get started except with the help of a third party, trusted by both the others."[2]

This struggle is typical of American universities, although similar tensions have been evident in recent years in Australia,[3] Canada,[4] the United Kingdom,[5] and other democracies. Colleges and universities provide a context in which social and civic trust can be cultivated. Social and civic trust, which is distinct from individual trust, operates not within the context of personal connection but rather as part of an institutional context. Even if individuals can establish, sustain, or rebuild personal trust—and even if extended families can manage to have an honest conversation in which members can either persuade one another or at least reestablish a sense of mutual trust—it would likely not be enough to generate a sense of public, political, civic, or social trust. The rethreading of civic and political trust has to occur within the context of an institutional or civic context, and it needs to address social identities and civic commitments instead of primarily relating to personal connections.

I focus on the establishment and sustaining of civic trust because it is in short supply in the current democratic civic culture,[6] and it is necessary for the strengthening of democracy. Among the influential institutions, such as newsrooms and schools, that help establish civic trust through defining membership and belonging and advancing knowledge for the benefit of society, higher education has a special role, placing it at the forefront of current discourse.

It should not be inferred that those who attend college, or those who work there as teachers and researchers, have special standing as members of a democratic society. It is true that education levels tend to correlate with civic and political efficacy and that higher educational attainment predicts higher rates of participation in electoral and other formal processes.[7] At the same time, civic standing should clearly not depend on education level: as a matter of principle, all members of a democratic society have inherent equal standing, regardless of their education or other accomplishments (or traits). The special status that colleges and universities have as institutions in a democratic society is derived from their contributions to the knowledge society has about itself and about the world. The role of research in posing salient questions, in expanding the knowledge society has at its disposal, and in establishing the shared epistemic foundations on which a democratic society must stand gives institutions a special role in the discussion about the path to a stronger, more equal, and more sustainable democracy.

Institutions are central to the way in which people experience the diversity of the nation and the functioning of the public sphere, and it is therefore important to consider local and interpersonal relations along with structural and institutional aspects. Interactions that occur with and through institutions are key to revitalizing the public sphere. Establishing trust in institutions and establishing trust in others through sharing institutional affiliations are two separate processes, but they can work together toward the same desirable goal. So, if citizens interact positively with a public health insurer, they can rather significantly amend negative attitudes toward the Affordable Care Act;[8] when parents interact with public schools, they can at least develop positive attitudes toward their local institution, even if this does not always translate to an appreciation of public education more broadly;[9] and if consumers of news read or watch a report on local events about which they had first- or second-hand knowledge, they extend greater trust toward the news media.[10] Interacting with diverse others through schools or learning about them through positive or neutral news reports, sharing a parent-teacher association or other civic organizations with them, and attending school or higher education institution with them—all of these can contribute to the rethreading of the civic fabric, through personal interactions and especially through the mediation of public institutions. The trust built can extend to both individuals and the institution itself.

Campuses fulfill their civic role when they support free speech that is anchored in their democratic and truth-seeking projects. The processes of truth-seeking and knowledge expansion on campus rely on an assumption of fallibility, and thus on the recognition that all members of the campus community (and others) can potentially contribute to this shared mission, as long as they work within its broad norms. As Mill clarifies, "complete liberty of contradicting and disproving our opinion, is the very condition which justifies us in assuming its truth for the purposes of action; and on no other terms can a being with human faculties have any rational assurance of being right."[11]

While free speech operates in various institutions in ways that reflect its democratic significance, it has a unique role on campus. In
a democracy, free speech responds to each person's fallibility, and
therefore to the equal dignity that society affords to each member as a
potential knower, as someone who can contribute.[12] The same is true
on campus, but in this context, there is an additional aspect in regard
to the protection of open expression: with the focus of its mission on
seeking true knowledge, a college or university must be open to trying out a variety of ideas and perspectives, including heterodox ones.
While in a democratic public sphere the protection of open expression
demonstrates the dignity afforded to all, the boundaries on campus
also reflect the shared commitment to correct mistakes and advance
knowledge in service to society. As such, disciplinary boundaries and
norms regarding the content and style of exchange reflect not only
the equality of all members but also a commitment to their shared
research and learning goals. Therefore, "the mission or end of an institution may both ground requirements for freedom of speech and
constraints on misrepresentations,"[13] producing unique boundaries
to acceptable forms of speech within the institution, including unique
rules regarding misrepresentations and lies,[14] hurtful and harmful expression,[15] and speech that violates professional norms.[16]

A close look at the struggle over free speech on campus illuminates the actual and potential contribution of college campuses to
democratic culture. The struggle over the boundaries of permissible
speech—or expanding the types of speech that should be prevented
on the basis of the harm they cause—has affected campuses in significant ways. In many states, new regulations and legislation continue
to emerge, banning specific speech—for example, forbidding employees and contractors from supporting the BDS movement, which advocates the boycott, divestment and sanctioning of Israel, or restricting
diversity and inclusion training workshops for staff.[17] On many campuses, faculty, administration, and students have a hard time reconciling conflicting views about the boundaries of acceptable speech in
the classroom and beyond it. These struggles represent broader social tensions, and decisions in this domain are consequential to the
way speech is perceived and addressed in society.[18] The boundaries
of speech are not just about the jurisdiction of the First Amendment
or about colleges' commitment to academic freedom and free expres-

sion. Higher education institutions train people for positions that give them social, political, and economic power in society, and that should influence the way that they internally organize their work, and create access pipelines into academe and other professions that require academic training.[19] Recognizing that higher education holds this instrumental value for society clarifies the centrality of free speech on college campuses: the protection of an open, inclusive, and productive dialogue is at the heart of colleges' service to society. Attending to the boundaries of free speech at colleges and universities allows society at large to consider the standards of truth, the boundaries of tolerance, and the possibility of an inclusive democracy in an era characterized by polarization and extremism. A discussion about free speech on campus serves these instrumental values of higher education by leading us to consider the ways in which these pressing questions shape campus practices and policies.

The institutional changes I discuss and recommend here can support a revitalized civic culture that can serve to mitigate the corrosive effects of polarization, mistrust, and democratic erosion by focusing on the ways in which citizens relate to one another, think of and with one another, and treat one another. Revitalizing democracy will require broader structural reforms.[20] Such reforms can result in improved levels of political trust, "trust which each member of a society has that government institutions will follow fair procedures and produce positive results."[21] The discussion this book presents is not structural or legal but rather relational and institutional—it attends to the social aspects of the democratic civic infrastructure, and suggests ways to bolster it. Conversations about the boundaries of speech and the ways in which they affect policies and practices on college campuses are a part of this discussion. They should be read as one important area of focus for the revitalization of the civic infrastructure of American democracy. Speech, and especially campus speech, is a central area of focus because it can help build the shared epistemic foundations necessary for a functioning democracy. At the same time, the issue of speech can also clarify some of the questions of inclusion and voice in democratic contexts, answering questions such as: What views are welcome and what views are anathema to a civic dialogue? What are the evidentiary criteria, or the boundaries of truth and reliability, in a discussion of fact? Who might speak, and how should others listen to them? And what are appropriate responses, both by the audience and by the institutions in which the speech takes place, to speech that is harmful, objectionable, hurtful, or hateful?

Many look to the application of First Amendment principles, or the expanding jurisprudence around them, to resolve tensions regarding open expression. Among legal scholars, the reigning view adheres to that of Justice Brandeis, as encapsulated by Erwin Chemerinsky: "I think that Justice Brandeis got it exactly right when he said, the best remedy for the speech we don't like is 'more speech not enforced silence.' When I say this I know that more speech cannot cure the pain of hateful speech. But more speech in the context of a college or university can proclaim the principles of the community that we aspire to live by."[22]

The main concern that remains with this formulation is the weight it affords to the word "we" in the final sentence. The notion that "we," either as a university or as a nation, have a sense of the principles of the community that we aspire to live by—or can even agree on enough facts and procedures that would allow us to deliberate about such principles—seems fantastical at this polarized time.

Even though this vision of embracing more speech to counter hateful expression is insufficient for contemporary universities, the core point made here by Chemerinsky (and Brandeis) holds true: it is generally unjust to use the law to censor, prevent, or punish hateful speech. As Nadine Strossen emphasizes, "even if constitutionally protected 'hate speech' did notably contribute to the feared harms, and even if 'hate speech' laws would meaningfully help to reduce them, we still should reject such laws because non-censorial measures can effectively counter the feared harm."[23] Hence giving authority to anyone on campus to determine the boundaries of acceptable speech is a dubious idea, particularly in a polarized time; and allowing that authority to decide what to censor, or what punishments to dole out for objectionable or hateful speech, can easily backfire. At the same time, it is especially necessary on campus to ensure that the "non-censorial measures" Strossen mentions, some of which I describe in detail below, are in fact developed and utilized.

The use of softer measures alleviates some concerns. It is perhaps significant to note that many of these tensions lie well beyond the reach of the law. The same is broadly true about deceitful or hurtful statements shared by individuals or private entities in person. Significantly, there is typically legal guidance for speech on college campuses, whether private or public (though the rules differ between them), and therefore the focus in most cases of disagreement should be not on litigation but rather on institutional efforts to preserve open expression and inclusion at the local level.

Moreover, the jurisprudential approach to the First Amendment has long relied on a capacious, expansive view of expression that includes emotional appeals, spectacles, lies, donations, and boycotts. A deep organizing principle of First Amendment jurisprudence is to distinguish between political speech, which is broadly protected, and economic or transactional speech and expression, which are more directly seen as reasonably regulated. A pressing concern in today's academic and legal debate is the virtual sphere, where, as Suzanne Nossel reminds us, the First Amendment offers no guidance as to when "content is too vitriolic, bigoted, deceitful, or misleading to be shared online."[24] These debates focus on a broader set of actions encompassing diverse forms of expression and are distinct from a more restricted or deliberative account, one that would mostly protect arguments and is generally more suitable for addressing campus concerns.

It seems to casual observers that the current campus speech battles are recent and unique to this polarized era. That is not so. Suzanne Goldberg notes that "a quick look back to the early 1990s, among other times, shows commentators squaring off much as they do today about the tensions between protecting free expression and ensuring meaningful equality."[25] In the introduction to their widely read 2009 book on academic freedom, Matthew Finkin and Robert Post explain the need for their contribution: "In the past decade, frequent and fierce debates about the nature of academic freedom have resulted from a systematic and sustained effort to discipline what some regard as an out of control liberal professoriate."[26] They illustrate the concern with a case from the University of North Carolina at Chapel Hill (UNC): "The current climate of controversy is exemplified by the outrage that erupted in 2003 when the University of North Carolina assigned Barbara Ehrenreich's *Nickel and Dimed: On (Not) Getting By in America* as required reading for incoming freshmen."[27] Nearly two decades after the events that follow, that story sounds tired and familiar: the outraged board denouncing the alleged "Marxism" promoted by the selection of the book; the angry professors and students; and the tussle over independence of thought versus representation of minority (that

is, conservative) views. Questions of academic freedom and the protection of institutional autonomy remain salient today as well, but this
story from 2003 at UNC seems almost quaint in its details: there was
no physical violence, as there was at Middlebury College in 2017, and
the school didn't spend millions of dollars on security, as Berkeley
did in 2017. There was no disparagement or outright bigotry against
identity groups, in contrast to contemporary cases that invoke racist,
antisemitic, or white supremacist views, including the struggle at UNC
over the appointment of Nikole Hannah-Jones to the Knight Chair.[28]
And no disinformation was propagated. The misapplied and dispar-
aging accusations that the committee assigning Ehrenreich's book
was promoting "socialism" or "Marxism" and the suggestion that the
university was aiming to indoctrinate the students into a progressive
agenda remain central refrains in contemporary attacks on campus
open expression and on academic freedom, but the issues at hand have
become more extreme and more pressing.

A survey of UNC students conducted nearly two decades after
the Ehrenreich controversy reports that the state of speech on campus remains relatively stable.[29] Most students support protections
for speech, aspire to greater ideological diversity, and observe that
their professors do not attempt to influence their views. At the same
time, some 13 percent of students support "de-platforming" speakers
(though there is no evidence they actually engage in such efforts, as
controversial speakers continue to visit), and a similar number report
that they self-censor their views in class.

How, then, can campuses embroiled in their own controversies help
ameliorate these tensions? I turn to this question next, before offering
practical steps that members in different roles on campus can take.

BETWEEN CAMPUS AND DEMOCRACY

Campuses today are arenas where the contemporary struggles over
the boundaries of expression, the role of expertise, and the meaning of
inclusion are fought. In the past few years, the campus speech conversation can crudely be described as offering the choice between being
a censor who cares about equality and being a bigot who cares about
free speech. But campuses can serve as both anchors and models for
revitalizing democracy by creating spaces where common ground can
be found.

Higher education engagement with speech is distinct, and the debates over free speech on campus do not apply to democratic concerns about speech in all its diversity. At the same time, I suggest that these institutions are positioned to be central in the tackling of core issues in today's democratic backsliding. A main driver of democratic decline is the loss of a shared epistemology, or the fact that we no longer share the same factual world. The main mission of higher education is to search for and disseminate knowledge and truth. Therefore, universities and colleges can help mitigate some of the struggles over facts and reality by introducing ways to identify truth from fiction, as well as by direct introduction of scientific and other truths.

Further, higher education institutions are serving a greater and more diverse share of the population than ever before, and their reach can thus extend to a greater number of segments in society. They serve their members for extended and significant periods of time, providing them with opportunities to develop new skills and attitudes and to forge ties across various divides. Finally, institutions of higher learning are located in many different communities across the country and they serve these communities in various ways beyond their central educational mission. They connect to local communities by providing jobs to local residents, supporting local businesses, working with schools and other institutions, and so on—some of these ways of connecting create friction or raise concerns about inequities, but together they generate opportunities for civic exchanges.

The common good is made accessible by diversity, extended interaction, and commitment to truth-seeking in a complex community. As Michael Sandel notes,

> if the common good can be arrived at only by deliberating with our fellow citizens about the purposes and ends worthy of our political community, then democracy cannot be indifferent to the character of the common life . . . it does require that citizens from different walks of life encounter one another in common spaces and public places. For this is how we learn to negotiate and abide our differences. And this is how we come to care for the common good.[30]

If social and civic trust is required to strengthen democratic civic life, then creating significant opportunities to develop trust in young adulthood is key to this process. Generationally, young Americans today report starkly lower levels of trust than older Americans—in a 2018 Pew poll, 60 percent of Americans between the ages 18 to 29 agree that most people cannot be trusted (as compared to 29 percent of Americans 65 and older).[31] Moreover, there is growing evidence that one's level of trust is itself a democratic habit rather than an emotion that fluctuates in response to outside stimuli or political circumstance.[32] Mark Warren has argued that one of the ways in which democracies can support social trust is by enabling institutions that cut across particularistic ties—institutions like schools and universities—to spread interpersonal and socially mediated evidence of trustworthiness; in other words, in contexts such as educational institutions, where the positive outcomes of trusting another person or a local institution can be evident, young people can learn that trusting others and trusting institutions can be warranted.[33]

Exchanges on campus can be related directly to the free exchange of ideas—free inquiry that is aimed at advancing scientific and social knowledge. This is the case in publications, research exchanges, and sometimes teaching and presentations that aim to push the boundaries of knowledge. But a lot of campus talk could also be understood as a part of "everyday talk," the free-flowing conversation that makes up public and civic life.[34] While this type of exchange is regularly thought of as less significant than talk related to research and inquiry, and as less central to public life than strictly political talk (such as campaigning or voting), it is often central to civic development.

Why focus on campuses? Campus leaders can serve an important role in strengthening democracy and creating a new era of solidarity and connectedness, social cohesion and shared goals. Daniels notes,

> to be sustainable, a democracy must find ways not only to channel the thrumming plurality of viewpoints, experiences, and dogmas in society, but also to fuse these perspectives into some approximation of a shared purpose, a public agenda.[35]

This ideal is advanced through the moral commitments voiced by many young leaders on college campuses. In some small ways, colleges could be seen as a form of "experiments in living" that is aimed at getting students ready for their lives as free people (the "liberal" in "liberal education" comes from the Latin *liberalis*, which means "befitting a free person"). In this view, college is not just about job preparation or other skills, but about soul-craft. Through their education, students get the opportunity to think critically about the values that guide them and to test out their ideas and ideals within a campus community. The experiment in this construct takes place at the individual level—much as Mill saw his own early life as such an experiment[36]—an experiment in trying to conduct one's life in ways that comply with certain moral principles.

Still, there are some limitations in treating college campuses as spaces where open expression and dialogue across difference can be established and as spaces that can serve the broader democratic goals of truth and inclusion. While it is easy to look at American historical experience—as well as that of other countries—and envision the role of colleges in revitalizing democracy, various factors restrict their ability to carry out this role. Most critically, not all young people attend college, and given the overlapping fissures that encompass ideology, geographical regions, and levels of education, it is crucial not to compound ideological differences, instead of alleviating them, through a focus on the role of colleges. This concern can partially be eased by sustaining robust and mutual connections between colleges and their surrounding communities, and especially by focusing not only on charitable contributions from a college and its students to a community but rather through mutually beneficial and sustained connections. Civic capacity, efficacy, and participation track education levels in significant ways, and therefore the local ties cultivated by colleges should consistently include communities around the college that are not represented in its membership.

Attending a four-year college and completing a degree creates a significantly different opportunity structure from not attending college or attending only some college. These overlapping class and ideological differences create diverging social and economic trajectories for individuals as well as communities and families. Colleges, seen as arbiters of opportunity based on perceived merit, contribute to the erosion of the common good in public life.[37] Given the sense that those who are admitted into college and succeed in and through academic work deserve the fruits of their work, colleges contribute to the view that inequalities in society are justified—they merely represent natural differences in personal endowment and help sort people to where they belong on the socioeconomic ladder. In this sense, colleges contribute not only to growing inequalities in opportunity for stable and well-paying jobs but also to the sense that those who win the race to such stable and rewarding employment and the benefits that come with it should feel that their accomplishments belong only to them. Those who do not "make it," who do not manage to get into or through college in a way that provides financial and related stability, have—by inference—only themselves to blame. Of course, as Sandel accurately notes, this is not a fair description of the process, as many unmerited factors—many attributes and circumstances that one is not responsible for and cannot be blamed or praised for—go into educational attainment and success. The role of luck in these processes should not be minimized, and subsequently, we should reject the attribution of college success to one's moral worth.[38]

Students themselves might constitute a hurdle to fulfilling the role of colleges as labs for democracy. As noted in chapter 4, students come to campus with little experience operating in an institution that values and protects their freedom of expression. Most public schools serve areas that are increasingly ideologically aligned, so students encounter limited ideological diversity; and schools can censor, prevent, and punish student expression in a variety of ways, based on court precedents that permit such actions, premised on the vague standard of preventing disruption to the learning environment. Most colleges do not introduce freedom of speech, expression, or inquiry in their new student orientations or like contexts.[39]

Faculty are expected, in the ideal formulation of college, to provide the foundation of true knowledge and the disciplinary skills to discern truth from mistakes and lies. They are also expected to facilitate and resolve hard conversations across differences about both open and closed questions that come up in class. But a faculty member is not always ideally positioned to take on the role of a facilitator of a hard conversation. Many higher education instructors are overburdened, underpaid, and do not have the kind of job security that allows them to take on hard conversations with confidence. One recent survey of faculty pointed to these concerns, as well as faculty's lack of training in defusing difficult moments in public settings like a classroom and the number of students in their classes, as complicating their ability to serve as effective facilitators of civic conversations about hard topics.[40] Colleges and universities serve only a segment of the population, which means they are not fully suitable to serve as training grounds for democracy: it is not democratic to systematically allow for select citizens to attain greater skills as civic actors. On the other hand, this is already the case today, given the correlation between education level and civic participation (the third factor here is economic).

In spite of these limitations, institutions of higher learning are still well situated to serve as training grounds for democracy and as locations and contexts for cultivating a revitalized democracy, with innovative ideas and young people committed to developing and applying them. In their variety—including two- and four-year, commuter and residential, public and private—colleges need to recognize some of the ways in which the sector replicates overlapping fissures in society, as well as their capacity to intentionally work to bridge them.

POLICY AND PRACTICE

Creating and maintaining a sphere of open expression, one that not only protects free speech but also invites dialogue and connection across difference, has long been a focus on many college campuses. These efforts can make a key contribution to the revitalization of democracy, but they must be practiced throughout campus and taken as the shared responsibility of leaders, faculty, students, and staff (in other words, this role cannot be the sole responsibility of the staff in the student life office, despite their ample talents). The work of strengthening democratic habits and practices in colleges starts in the admissions office, continues in the classroom and at the leadership level—including the university's board—and extends to students.

Colleges and universities operate within the bounds of constitutional and legal expectations, and like all institutions they are limited in their expressive and other practices. Still, there are specific rules that apply to them, in some cases expanding and in other cases contracting the limits of what students, faculty, and leadership might say or do.

Public universities are bound by the First Amendment to ensure their policies are neutral regarding the content of speech. This commitment to neutrality means that they cannot promote religious, ideological, or other particular views, nor can they prevent or punish speakers for expressing such views. In this way they differ from private institutions, which can be affiliated with organized religion, as many are, from Yeshiva University (which has refused to allow an LGBTQ group to organize) to the College of the Holy Cross and Notre Dame, from Jesuit colleges to Liberty University. Private colleges can subscribe to factional ideologies, as in the case of Hillsdale College. Legislatures, especially in GOP-led state chambers, have increased their efforts in recent years to place further limitations on public colleges (and schools) through legislation that threatens with expulsion students who participate in protests, that requires the submission of syllabi to state legislatures so they can be investigated for perceived ideological bias, and that prohibits the teaching of "divisive concepts," especially those related to the history of race in the United States as well as to gender and sexuality.

What follows is a set of policy suggestions and practical strategies for colleges to help them to live up to their roles as labs for democracy, particularly in the context of a polarized democracy. In our contemporary context, open expression remains a point of cultural contention, catalyzing the struggle over the boundaries of tolerance and illuminating the lack of a shared factual foundation. When trust and other civic habits are in decline, and when the value and boundaries of speech are a matter of ongoing struggle, colleges can be not only arenas where these battles are waged but also anchors for change.

I collected or developed the practical tools offered here at colleges and universities I visited around the United States as well as a few other countries experiencing similar tensions (especially Canada, the United Kingdom, and the Netherlands). In most cases, I was invited to visit the campuses to either discuss the scholarly aspects of my earlier work on open expression on campus or to help develop policy or resolve challenges and crises. I engaged with leadership, staff, faculty, and students across these many campuses, and many of the suggestions below were developed in exchanges with them. Many of the issues that arise in different countries are similar, though there are of course local differences. For example, colleges in the UK tend to have a significant focus on religious concerns, especially with regard to the inclusion of Muslim students. The gender identity debate on college campuses has also been louder there, though recent legislation in the US seems to be heading in a similar direction. And, of course, each country's legal landscape is unique.[41]

In *Free Speech on Campus*, I argued that the population served by a college should be taken into account when crafting open expression policies and practices.[42] I noted then that campus demographics affect a campus's speech struggles because speech reflects the relationships on campus, and those relationships change with the makeup of the student body. If colleges are to serve as labs for democracy—if they are to develop policies that are not merely reactive but also proactive in their effort to revitalize democracy through the opportunities they offer their students for engaging with each other as civic equals across diverse perspectives—they should not only take into account the population that they serve but also address inequities in accessibility.

While affirmative action programs directed at underrepresented minorities have been in place—and in legal contention—for decades,[43] many colleges have in recent years started paying more attention to the economic backgrounds of their applicants. As understandings of diversity and inclusion become more nuanced, the need to respond to the concerns of diverse groups that are newly visible on campus—while maintaining an atmosphere of free inquiry—also becomes more urgent. The remainder of the chapter advises higher education leaders, faculty, and students on how they might work to succeed in establishing an environment where all people and all ideas can be heard.

EXPANSIVE SPEECH AND FREE INQUIRY

Bard College's Hannah Arendt Center found itself at the center of a controversy in 2017 when organizers of the conference Crises of Democracy: Thinking in Hard Times invited a leader of the far-right German populist party Alternative for Germany as a speaker. Dozens of academics signed a letter criticizing the decision and the legitimacy it afforded the politician. The center's leadership and the college's president pushed back and defended the decision. The politician was interviewed on stage by a thoughtful, and critical, interlocutor.[44]

•   •   •

Daily and ongoing decisions by many constituents on campus manifest and sustain the commitment to search for knowledge. For the boundaries of speech on college campuses to remain broad and to enable free inquiry, the way we spend our time on campus matters. Bard and the Arendt Center were right to continue with their event, not simply because the expression in question is protected by law (which it is) but especially because of the details of the event: it was optional for students rather than mandatory, so those who might find it hurtful could avoid it; the politician was interviewed critically rather than simply provided with a podium and a microphone; and the broader context was clearly focused on a commitment to democracy. Beyond all these important details, the speaker was already holding a position of power. Disinviting him would do nothing to the power he holds, and the invitation confers no further power on him; it rather allows the audience to engage with ideas that—while hurtful not only in hearing them but also in their real-world consequences—are not generated within academe and cannot be addressed through speech restrictions.

Below are some illustrations of how leaders, faculty, and students can spend their time in ways that help maintain broad boundaries of speech through application of the ideals discussed thus far.

Leadership

An institution's leaders should make conscious and careful determinations through ongoing conversations with others on campus about the boundaries of what is permissible. The general guideline should be a commitment to maintaining broad boundaries of speech that are consistent with legal requirements and with the institutional mission. Universities can legitimately prohibit or punish some expression that is legally permissible—for example, misrepresenting research or credentials, acting in an unprofessional manner, or otherwise working against the institution's mission. Like other workplaces, universities can establish boundaries of behavior, including speech. The boundaries of acceptable expression should be set by the mission of the institution, and by the call to search for truth through shared work and through the inclusion of diverse perspectives and voices in the process of inquiry.[45]

If a statement, perspective, or other sort of expression has an exclusionary consequence—if it silences some voices—it can legitimately be seen as incongruent with the institutional mission. But what should the outcome of this determination be? Ideally, it would generate not a backlash resulting in censorship or exclusion (firing an instructor, suspending a student), but rather counteraction from within the institution—its members and leadership would express their values and their commitment to the inclusion of the threatened voices and perspectives. In this way, speech remains robust while the commitment to and practice of inclusion are preserved.

Strategy: Take Your Time

The pressure to respond quickly to events, always a factor for leaders, is amplified by pressure campaigns organized on social media—and sometimes by traditional media. Waking up to find your institution in the eye of the storm, an experience shared by many college leaders, generates a sense that swift action is required. Most often, a deep breath and communication with as many stakeholders as possible to find out the details of the event and the proper course of action is a better call. For example, Smith College responded swiftly by firing white staff members who were accused by a Black student, in a social media post, of inappropriate treatment. The ensuing struggle made the issue much worse for the college and went on for more than two years.[46] Taking more time to study the claims, to talk to the student and the employees, and to hear the concern about both the specific incident and the broader atmosphere would have generated more goodwill and a better outcome, both on campus and in the media. To have this extra time, to be afforded the grace to conduct an investigation or develop an appropriate response, leaders and community members cannot wait for a crisis to occur. Trust builds over time, and when trust is prevalent, it is possible to count on the generosity of community members who believe their institution will act in a fair way. Some voices may remain insistent and loud in demanding immediate action, but they should not determine which steps are taken to address any given issue.

Strategy: Making Public Statements

Colleges and universities are regularly called upon to speak about contemporary issues. This is evidenced by the outpouring of statements in the summer of 2020, following the George Floyd protests. This wave of statements once again raised the question—should colleges speak on these issues? And, more importantly, how do they move toward taking action after speaking? Colleges invite and cherish a diversity of views, but at the same time, they represent certain values. The statements universities make (in response to events on or off the campus) are one of the ways universities are able to represent these values.[47]

When the democratic state protects free speech (including hateful speech), it still has a duty to express its values: as Brettschneider writes, "while the state should protect the rights of these groups, it also has the duty to make clear that it is not complicit in their opposition to the ideal of free and equal citizenship. The state should criticize discriminatory groups, and in the case of the most extreme hate groups, condemn them . . . [that is] the simultaneous role of the state in protecting rights and criticizing discriminatory messages."[48] The university, of course, is distinct from the state in important ways, including its roles vis-à-vis expressive rights. Even public universities have a unique autonomy with regard to the regulation of speech, as discussed earlier—and private institutions even more so. Moreover, the university speaks in many voices: while its leaders can state their vision, department heads, chairs, deans, board members, faculty, and students can also all make statements that circulate and sometimes define the institution. But there are still parallels in higher education with the vision of the state that Brettschneider offers, especially in the dual commitments that higher education institutions should express by taking a clear stand in support of open expression—especially extramural speech but also most classroom speech—while at the same time stating the values that the institution stands for and taking steps to uphold these values.[49]

Especially for students, the message of the leadership is significant. Admitting a student to a college is akin to telling them that they are welcome at the institution, that they belong there, and that their voice and ideas are welcome. If someone's views within the institution, or a speaker involved in some incident, communicate a contradicting message—namely, that people like you do not belong here or that you are not a valuable member of the community (because of your religion, citizenship status, ethnicity, gender, or other identity)—it is incumbent upon the institution to clarify where it stands and to reinstate the message of welcome and inclusion.

Campus leadership has many ways to express support, dismay, approval, or rejection beyond simply deciding whether to censor or punish speech or let it occur. In particular, administrative leaders are often called on to respond to events within and beyond the campus and to thus communicate their values to campus members. How should they respond to these calls?

When Should a Statement Be Made? National and global events sometimes generate an expectation that leaders of educational institutions will make a statement (as well as business leaders and other public figures). Some matters are easy: if you send good wishes for a holiday that many of your students celebrate—say, Christmas—then also send some good wishes for Lunar New Year if some of your students celebrate it. Other matters are harder, as was evident in some of the delayed and tortured responses from higher education leaders in the wake of the protests following George Floyd's murder at the hands of a policeman in Minnesota, in that they capture the tension between expressing institutional values and refraining from choosing a side in a political debate. This difficulty increases when the institutional values themselves are implicated in the political debate. Leaders should keep in mind that no matter how carefully they try to traipse among the raindrops, they are bound to get wet, given that not only specific institutional missions but the value of college itself—and its core mission—has been politicized. The goal of public statements about significant events should thus be to express these values in an inclusive manner rather than to try and avoid controversial implications. A simple restatement of relevant values in light of a recent event is sometimes sufficient when presented alongside the sharing of relevant resources on campus. Sometimes a statement alone is not sufficient, though, and a leader has to commit to further action that will reflect these values. For example, in light of the racial reckoning following the George Floyd protests, many institutions have taken a closer look at the ways in which they reflect a commitment to racial equity in their practices, and some have committed to actions such as hiring in relevant research areas or holding public events on related topics. Princeton University went further by committing to uproot the remnants of its historical institutional racism.[50]

Truth-seeking does not require neutrality about speech or the abandonment of judgment regarding the value of specific statements. To the contrary, judgment is at the core of truth-seeking, and rejecting false and offensive statements does not undermine the truth-seeking mission but rather protects it. Such a rejection does not have to take the form of censorship, and it rarely does. A college or university can state its values clearly and reject some perspectives without censoring words or punishing speakers.

Given the ubiquity of instances in which there is an expectation by some community members that a statement should be made, top leadership should reserve its statements for the most significant issues. Most statements are best made by the leaders closest to the issue at hand, which could be a dean, a department chair, or another person in a relevant leadership position. If a member of the campus is implicated in a controversial action, the leader closest to that person's position is the best person to make a statement, so that it will be the best-informed, most relevant reflection on the issue. Keeping the creation of the statement at a level directly relevant to the matter at hand also communicates, beyond its content, the institution's respect for its own division of responsibility. If it is revealed that a football chat has been rife with misogynistic remarks, the coach or the athletic director would be smart to put out a statement about their value commitments and expectations in addition to any consequences that must be discussed. If an admitted student's acceptance is rescinded following revelations of inappropriate conduct, the admissions director can speak to the decision even if higher level administrators were involved. If a faculty member is embroiled in a public scuffle over their views, their chair or dean can make a statement. The reality that many institutions face today is that a multitude of issues are amplified by internal or outside groups who initiate petitions and mass letter campaigns, making demands for statements or action. These conditions are stressful, but they should not guide swift action.

When KKK flyers were posted around Saratoga Springs, New York, Skidmore College students demanded that the college make a statement. The administration demurred. They coordinated a response with the town (whose leaders made a statement and offered security) and decided that amplifying the hateful message by denouncing it would not help in this situation; as one college leader noted, "if the students don't know by now where we stand about the KKK, we have a bigger problem." Ensuring that the institution represents its values day by day is often more important than making a statement.

What Should the Statement Say? Knowing how to craft a public statement is the expertise of communications professionals, and here I simply intend to consider practical ways to express the argument at the heart of the current discussion: that the institutional goals of truth-seeking and inclusion can be pursued together while maintaining a strong commitment to free inquiry and expression. The goal of a public statement in response to an incident involving a campus community member is to situate the offending party, their views, and their actions within the context of the institution, its people, and its values. It is important to acknowledge that the event in question—hurtful tweets, toxic language in class, a talk by a controversial speaker—has caused disruption and hard feelings. A stated commitment to the legal and institutional protections of open expression can clarify the boundaries of a response. For example, such a statement might clarify the reason behind a decision to continue employing an instructor who voiced controversial, untrue, or bigoted views. But if the community member's views in question are presented as inherently contradictory to the institution's values—for instance, if a faculty member expresses racist views, rejects the reality of historical events, or subscribes to anti-scientific theories—simply noting that the view is protected by the First Amendment is often insufficient. If a leadership statement presents the tension between the commitment to protected speech and the commitment to inclusion and belonging of all members, or if it highlights the tension between protected speech and the institutional commitment to knowledge and truth-seeking, then it must also chart a path to the resolution of that tension. In order to do that, it needs to firmly position itself on the side of protecting speech by declining to censor and censure speakers while defending inclusion and truth by taking active steps to sustain and promote these values.

Recent years have given leaders a steady stream of opportunities to hone this craft. Faculty members are at the center of many of these instances—facing the ire of online mobs for marginally unpleasant speech or failed jokes; using epithets in class; refusing to support students applying for study abroad in Israel; questioning vaccines and public health measures; or publicly supporting or opposing Black Lives Matter, affirmative action, DACA, Zionism, torture, or the impeachment of the president. There is no shortage of examples. Once it is decided, as is appropriate in most of these cases, that the speech in question is protected, leadership needs to decide whether the issue merits making a statement to the campus community. Such a statement would note that while the speech is protected and that leadership is committed to free speech, leadership also recognizes that some members of the community pay a price for this protection, and then the statement would offer a way to redress or account for this price. Sometimes the way to rectify the wrong that some members face by being exposed to offensive ideas—and by the fact that such ideas are protected—can be as simple as articulating the institution's values in the statement, but in other cases, making a commitment to participating in a conversation with the community or holding a special event is helpful. In other cases, institutional support for activities sponsored by student groups that see themselves as undermined by the protected speech is appropriate. For example, when a professor or a speaker questions the support that a "sanctuary campus" offers to DREAMers, the institution can subsequently sponsor or support cultural events organized by undocumented students and their supporters to reiterate its commitment to their well-being and inclusion. The expressive value of such actions can be more meaningful than mere words, and they are sometimes warranted.

What about Neutrality? While the First Amendment requires the government to remain neutral in regard to specific matters, institutions—including public ones—can still have a mission and hold a set of values that supports their mission. Expressing that mission does not mean that each and every member of the campus (or the department, or the school whose head is making the statement) supports the institution's mission and values. Protecting a broad array of views does not always mean institutional neutrality; sometimes it means representing its values, including the expansion of the boundaries of knowledge and a commitment to inclusion. It is important to keep in mind that some forms of neutrality are necessary, as they help cultivate the exchange of views across ideological, religious, and other lines. The university has a lot of power over its students and employees, and it also holds some power in other domains. If it favors one ideological view, it might in effect be silencing some of its employees or demanding that members of the campus avoid voicing perspectives that fail to toe a particular line. One common issue raised on college campuses has to do with staff who feel that their views, which do not align with the views of the majority on campus, are not accepted or may get them in trouble. Such a diversity of views among staff should in fact be embraced by colleges, as it can provide some counterweight to an orthodoxy of views on certain campuses.

How do you know when a line that demands the institution step in and prevent or sanction speech has been crossed? Because a lot of hateful content is either protected or also mainstream in today's polarized politics, the lines are shifting to accommodate more speech that used to be marginal, but the pain that these changes cause needs to be recognized as well. An institution legitimately responds to hateful speech not by aligning itself with one political or ideological camp, which is not a good idea for most institutions (and is unacceptable for public ones), but by affirming broader values and acting on them.

Faculty: Planning Your Time

Strategy: Lesson Planning for Controversy

Instructors need to think about how to address controversial issues in the same way they think about lesson planning. It is important to think about the objectives that are sought in discussing controversial topics: allowing exploration of personal views, exposure to alternative views, or development of counterarguments.

It is also important to think about content, and especially to consider what topics and perspectives should be recognized as controversial and what should be talked about as plainly true or accepted. Decisions about "open" and "closed" topics are specific to a discipline and a point in time. In the health sciences, the complexities of views about vaccines and the internal scientific debates about vaccines have exposed the need to discuss vaccine hesitancy as a legitimate topic, even as the organized anti-vaccine movements may not have any valid arguments to offer. Another example is marriage equality, which even a few decades ago might have been presented as a controversial topic, but is now the law of the land in the United States and can be legitimately presented as a "closed" topic.[51]

Pedagogically, instructors should think about when to teach in directive and nondirective ways. Directive teaching means that the instructor aims for students to reach a certain conclusion or obtain particular knowledge by the end of class, and nondirective pedagogy means the instructor invites diverse views to be argued for and maintained. For example, if a student makes a case for climate denialism, the goal of a directive approach would be for the student holding that belief to recognize that their view is not only controversial but also misguided and in opposition to the consensus of the scientific community. At the intersection of hatred and misinformation, those who question or deny the Holocaust present a similar challenge that calls for directive teaching.[52]

Classes are meant to teach content, but they are also part of the overall process of preparing students for their professional and civic lives. As such, one of the goals of any class is to prepare students for critical thinking, media literacy, and citizenship. To facilitate this, the classroom has to make space for students to make mistakes and try out different views, including controversial ones. This calls for some courage on the part of both students and instructors, who should bring in relevant topics and make room for diverse views about them. Sometimes this is planned as part of the course syllabus, and the instructor should be prepared for the ensuing debate. At other times, the world outside the classroom will slip in and claim some space. Instructors would often do best to allow at least some room for such occurrences, rather than merely sticking to the lesson plan. Avoiding hard topics, or maintaining neutrality in the face of difficult events happening on campus or in the world, will chill speech and prevent valuable conversations from happening. Speaking across political and other divides and navigating differences are useful skills for many fields and topics and can make real contributions to many courses.

Strategy: The Five-Minute Rule

An open conversation in the classroom works best when diverse views, experiences, and perspectives are voiced. But sometimes group dynamics make that difficult to accomplish, particularly when there is broad agreement among many—or certain outspoken—students in class. To make space for perspectives that are less commonly held in a class, are not fairly represented, or are marginalized, the five-minute rule can help. With this rule, anyone who feels that a particular point of view is not fairly represented, has not been considered, or has not been taken seriously can point this out and call for this exercise: The group takes five minutes to consider the perspective on its merits, looking to understand and make the case for it before offering any criticism. Some common and useful prompts are: What is new or interesting about this view? Why would someone believe it? And what would it take for you to believe it?[53]

Transgressions in class can take the form of bigoted or hateful expression that exclude members of some groups—women; gender or sexual minorities; religious, ethnic, or racial minorities, etc. Transgressions can also take the form of denying scientific consensus about vaccines or climate change. Ideally, these can be investigated or discussed using the strategies suggested here, or the best pedagogical practices the instructor can muster. But there are also cases in which the instructor can reasonably say, "You are pushing against our shared norms for this class. If you have questions about this matter, we can discuss them after class, but this is not how we speak here."

Students: Your Time and Attention

Engaging Controversial Speakers: Your Attention, a Precious Resource

One of the most significant resources we have as citizens is our attention, and the decisions we make daily on how to allocate it are at the core of civic learning in a polarized time. As Lorreta Ross, a Black feminist activist, reminds us, we can call people out for transgressions; we can call them in and engage in an effort to find common ground; or we can call off the engagement with them and decide to spend our time in more productive ways, thus avoiding the distraction and heartache that can be caused by listening to some views.[54]

As citizens, students have a choice to make, especially when a speaker is propagating hatred or is looking to benefit—to earn notoriety, money, further invitations—by eliciting rage: they can decide to engage or to not pay attention and, by withdrawing their presence and response, take away the speaker's incentive. Whether an event deserves a rebuke or a shrug is a matter of context, and it is reasonable to suggest that some events should not pass without response while others can simply be ignored. The latter response also preserves the energy, attention, and labor of students, especially those who feel affected by an event. In some cases, direct engagement is a productive response—attending an event that represents a point of view with which one disagrees, or asking hard questions. This is useful if the speaker offers a perspective that can be of interest, even to those who disagree, and if they are there to engage and organizers provide real opportunities for engagement. In events where this is not the case, a good response might be a protest, or providing alternative programming either simultaneously or at another appropriate time. In other cases, walking away is the most effective to communicate disapproval. In all of these, students can take the lead, but they should be able to expect the institution to support them.

When colleges begin to open their doors to outsiders, the invitation to speak on a college campus should be presented as an invitation into an intellectual community that comes with responsibilities to the members of that community. This commitment to the exchange of ideas takes advantage of a feature special to campus talks—they bring many different people from a community together in one place.

A growing menu of practices can help speakers fulfill their responsibilities. For example, after the well-publicized clashes over Charles Murray's visit, Middlebury College has been experimenting with a format in which speakers have time to present their ideas and then audience members discuss them together in small groups.[55] Given that the goal of a visit should be engagement with ideas, new formats that go beyond speaking to the audience—whether in person or virtually—are a good place to start. Students in many colleges are taking the lead in developing or calling for new opportunities to engage, and these changes make a vital contribution to a free and inclusive climate.

University Boards

Understanding the Democratic Role of Learning Institutions

University boards have an important role to play in protecting broad boundaries of expression on campus. While they do not often seek guidance on these matters, I have had some exchanges with full boards or individual board members, and here I offer a quick note on how they might see their role in this regard. University boards (sometimes called trustees, regents, boards of governors, or similar titles) are charged with selecting the top leadership of the institutions they lead and with steering the institution in its significant financial and policy commitments, approving hiring for certain roles, and similar executive decisions. Board members are often selected for their political ties, financial contributions, and service in similar roles for units within the organization; they are often political and business leaders and tend to skew conservative. This note on ideology would not be of significance if not for the politicization of higher education institutions generally, and specifically of speech within them. In recent years, members of some boards have expressed their commitment to advancing an atmosphere of free expression as a main goal.[56] The Board of Regents of the University System of Georgia declares that its institutions "must promote open ideas and academic freedom on their campuses ... policies should not unduly burden the free expression rights of students, faculty, and staff. Any parameters placed on the time, place, and manner of expression must not be based on the content of the expression."[57] The Board of Regents of the University of Wisconsin System amended its open expression policies in 2015 and again in 2017 to include rules

restricting student protests (more on that below), based on the perception that such protests undermine the free expression rights of speakers and audiences against whom protests are carried out. In Arizona
and Iowa, public universities are now charged with submitting reports
about compliance with free speech policies and are required to amend
their policies in accordance with approaches that demand viewpoint
diversity, often raised as a way to create greater representation for conservative ideologies.[58]

These mandates demonstrate the slippage between a commitment
to free inquiry, which is a laudable aspect of a board's role, and impos-
ing a politicized vision of the same. The decision of the UNC board to
upend the process of hiring journalist Nikole Hannah-Jones with tenure to the Knight Chair at UNC's journalism school, following the rau-
cous public debate over her 1619 Project, demonstrates how a board
can fail to respect institutional autonomy and faculty governance. In
many such cases, including an earlier case at UIUC involving Steven
Salaita (whose tenured appointment was similarly denied at the last
moment, in his case because of his harsh political expression on social
media), boards are acting as ideological partisans rather than as institutional partners and leaders, joining the current culture wars instead
of rising above the fray to play a leadership role in their institutions
and society.

A board is at its best when it strives to support the institution it
leads, its independence and autonomy, and the fulfillment of its broad
mission. While some of the recent speech policies mentioned above
are framed as being in service of the core mission of the university—
namely, the protection of free inquiry—the details point to an effort to
limit the autonomy of university leaders, promote conservative voices,
and limit student (and in some cases faculty) expression.[59]

THE BLESSING OF A CONTRARIAN VIEW

The small college's administrator was on the phone and clearly concerned. "Can you join us for a discussion on free speech? Our community is under a lot of stress. How soon can you come?" Our conversation revealed that a young faculty member had started a "free
speech" speaker series, with assistance from an outside organization.
The invited guests included some scholars, as well as some popular
culture characters, including a YouTube celebrity known for their

harsh attacks on liberals and "snowflakes." The atmosphere on campus was tense and angry; when students protested the bigotry some of the speakers expressed, they were filmed and ridiculed on social media. At the dinner after my talk, the young man organizing these talks declared his commitment to the principles of free speech and suggested that none of the events he organized were meant to offend.

A few years later, I received a similar call from the administrator of a large private university. "Can you join us this month for a talk and a discussion with students?" A center at the university had hired as a fellow a former Trump administration official who had enacted immigration policies that many students were opposed to and that some students had experienced as direct threats to themselves or their family members' prospects as residents of the United States. Known for his brash social media presence, the former federal official continued to clash with students on social media, and his followers enacted coordinated virtual attacks on students who were critical of his views.

•   •   •

In each case, the campus community engaged in a fierce discussion over the boundaries of speech. And in each case, as in other instances of controversy cited earlier in this book, many in the community felt that the events prepared them to take on diverse—even unacceptable— views. Many have learned how to make the case for their beliefs and, in some cases, were ready to take on new challenges to the boundaries of acceptable expression when they occurred—as they invariably do.

Some students and faculty find the introduction of certain views to be not only inappropriate but also hurtful, harmful, or even violent. Attempts to "de-platform" or silence some speakers is justified as a way of preventing harm that would come from their views being expressed. In some cases, including the ones described above, the harm seems to be more than metaphoric, as in the case in which certain students' images and words were dragged into the social media public sphere as objects of ridicule. I want to use these difficult illustrations to make the counterintuitive claim that in many cases, and for most institutions, the introduction of views that go beyond the realm of acceptable to most campus members is a blessing, even when it comes in disguise.

Contrarian—and even extreme—views can offer a few contributions to campus discussions. First, many of the contrarian views espoused by faculty or visiting speakers, while marginal on some campuses, are in fact rather common in the broader community and the nation. The former Trump administration official was probably a minority voice on the campus where he served as a fellow, but he had just stepped down from a position of power and authority, and a significant part of the population supported his, and the administration's, work. It is useful for students (and others) to have the opportunity to hear these views from a person who subscribes to them and hopefully to listen to their perspective as part of a dialogue or other forum in which open and mutual exchange is welcomed. The goal of such an exchange is not to change any participant's mind—though that is surely a possible outcome—but to learn to understand what brings another person to think in such a different way, to consider their arguments and their vision. And, as Daniels rightly notes, "conservative students need to feel that their campus is one that invites their views in the endless refinement of ideas through reason."[60] The outcomes of such an exchange for a participant or audience member can include at minimum some clarity about how to argue *against* the position they disagree with more effectively—and, hopefully, the ability to make a clearer case for their own position, even when that position remains unchanged. Significantly, the outcome of a well-structured dialogue or forum, especially if it is not a one-off opportunity for engagement, would allow all sides to find some shared values, views, or commitments that would make the polarized distance between camps seem less uncrossable. If the goal is not persuasion but rather learning about one another's positions and developing a clearer understanding of the variety of views on a topic, a contrarian speaker can help do that.

A second benefit of representing uncommon views on campus is that engagement across polarized divides—whether through membership in a small student club, through organizing a speaker series, or simply by the voicing of an unpopular view that one has kept to oneself—minimizes the tendency of like-minded groups to push their members further toward the end points of the political continuum. Progressive students, when discussing progressive ideas, tend to push each other further to the left and make greater demands of "purity of thought" or ever stronger adherence to value commitments from their peers. Without the presence of outsiders in a student group, the group will often single out and sometimes even demonize some of its own members. This phenomenon is of course not unique to one ideological group but rather is typical of all groups that share an ideological commitment.[61] Engaging with "outsiders," or those who hold significantly different ideological views, helps students recognize that calling out their peers for small transgressions from an orthodoxy of thought is both futile and unjustified, shines a brighter light on the diversity of views on matters of common interest, and allows students to find shared language and opportunities to look beyond minute differences and work together in shared projects, at least within their own ideological camp if not—hopefully—beyond it.

In addition, a contrarian view, even one that causes some turmoil or hurt feelings, can help demonstrate the prevalence of an issue and thus mobilize an effective response. For example, a bigoted speaker can help clarify for well-intentioned but passive allies that bigotry is still a living issue in society and at an institution, not a problem belonging to the past. While expressions of bigotry of course are unfortunate and require timely responses, they can also help highlight the necessity of addressing bigotry even in an otherwise "nice" department. In prompting this focus and clarity, they can help students and leadership develop support for investing in resolving persistent structural issues.

I do not claim that any speaker who expresses uncommon views on campus should be seen as bringing such a blessing. Some speakers may just look to incite violence or spew hatred; some are looking to enrich themselves by touring campuses and enraging students without bringing the benefits of ideas or dialogue. The line is hard to draw, as most such lines are, and depend on the speaker, the institution, the topic, and other considerations. But overall, if a visiting fellow, speaker, faculty member, or student (alone or as part of a club) is bringing to campus views that are not commonly heard within the campus community, it should be seen as an opportunity.

Leadership

What Is a Disruption, and When Does It Cross the Line?

Acts that visibly establish distance from hateful views are vital to the goal of maintaining a shared public sphere, particularly in the context of a learning community in which all are welcome.[62] Rae Langton convincingly makes the case for "blocking" in response to hate speech: "blocking interferes with the evolving information taken for granted among participants in a conversation" by exposing presuppositions or highlighting "smuggled" information through statements, questions, jokes, and even physical gestures.[63] Conducting such public and visible distancing acts goes beyond the recommendation to respond to hate speech with "more and better speech." Efforts to persuade haters, bigots, and bad-faith actors ("trolls") with more speech is often futile, insufficient, or even counterproductive, as it can expand the reach of their message without creating a real opportunity for discussion or persuasion. It is critical that these visible acts remain within the boundary of justified public action, meaning they should not themselves become acts of violence, silencing, or hatred. Sustaining a dialogue into the future is only possible to the extent that the rift created by both hate speech and the responses to it can potentially be patched in later discussions, a responsibility that is borne by all but often rests, in effect, on the offended party.

However, colleges should still develop and enact practices that seek to ensure all can express their views. The Chicago Statement aims to do that by calling for "consistency across cases" and developing "procedures for event management to reduce the chances that those engaged in disruptive conduct can prevent others from speaking or being heard."[64] The University of California, Irvine, has developed a set of policies that aim to delineate appropriate forms of protest and to clarify the consequences of crossing them. Such policies can be helpful in some cases.[65] However, in other cases, a lot depends on the responses in the room. When Penn students protested during a talk by a former ICE official, the event was called off by the organizers.[66] But some believed that had the students been allowed to protest for a few minutes, then a dialogue could have ensued, which may have led to a different outcome—for example, the students might have been permitted to raise their signs from the back of the audience, or the students might have been allowed to ask the first questions (generally a good practice).

Some student protests today are restricted by state laws and policies, an unfortunate development that limits civic practices on campus. In 2017, the Board of Regents of the University of Wisconsin System implemented a policy that, with some qualifications, requires "any student who has thrice been found responsible for misconduct that materially and substantially disrupted the free expression of others at any time during the student's enrollment shall be expelled."[67] A recent law in Illinois requires that public educational institutions adopt a pol-

icy prohibiting and subjecting to sanction any "protests and demon-
strations that infringe upon the rights of others to engage in or listen
to expressive activity." Additionally, the law requires administrators
to suspend for at least one year any student who is twice found to be
responsible "for infringing on the expressive rights of others."[68] This
seems to be an effort to protect outside speakers from the progressive
students who have fiercely demonstrated against such speakers in
prior years. Republican lawmakers in Tennessee demanded that public
universities forbid student athletes from kneeling in protest of police
racial violence while the national anthem plays before their games.[69]
These, again, are restrictions on protest that themselves silence speech
rather than invite engagement.

Rather than focusing on disciplinary measures, and framing the
tension as one between oversensitive students and the realities of the
harsh "real world," guidance on campus should seek to foster conditions conducive to developing shared norms, agreements, and practices. This does not mean that every side of every dispute has to be
included in an agreement or reconciled with; rather, this means that
efforts should be made to sustain a dialogue with as diverse a group of
ideas and people as possible, and to be clear about the reasons why any
rifts remain, and about the form they take.

These efforts should be developed while keeping in mind that students may come to campus with a distorted or vague understanding
of what constitutes "disruptive" behavior with regard to methods of
appropriate dissent in response to a speaker's (or instructor's) view.
In many states, broad and possibly unconstitutional laws are being
passed that provide significant power to schools and local police over
students' speech and mundane disruptive behaviors.[70] Similar stat-
utes have targeted public college students in recent years, threatening
expulsion in cases of repeated disruption of university events.[71] These
legal limitations on disruption are based on the expanding jurisprudence against the "heckler's veto"—that is, if there is a concern that
"a speaker's opprobrious remarks might incite others to misbehave,
the constitutionally sounder response is to enforce rules against the
audience's nonspeech misbehavior."[72] In other words, disruptions can
and should be regulated and limited, so as to prevent the silencing of
a controversial speaker. Still, the rules must be properly tailored, especially given that the proverbial "hecklers," too, have constitutionally

protected speech rights, and they may be trying to express their own perspective through their disruption as well.[73]

Flyers, Posters, Flags, Banners

A confederate flag flown outside a student's window. A banner suggesting a faculty member should be fired. Antisemitic imagery posted on bulletin boards. Expression on campus is not limited to words, and struggles over art displays, posters, and ideas presented through images are as complicated as struggles over ideas spoken or published.

Posted materials, from banners to flags to art displays, sometimes create a stir on college campuses. As these materials have legal protections similar to those of spoken statements,[74] colleges need to develop clear policies about what might be posted, where, and by whom.[75] When racist and antisemitic posters flooded various colleges campuses in 2017, it was easier for those colleges who had clear policies to remove the incendiary content. In some cases, the individuals who created and displayed these materials were outsiders who were looking to film workers removing their posters so they could claim a violation of their First Amendment rights. Regardless of the legal merits of such a claim, if campus policy does not allow outside groups to post notices, the issue is more easily resolved with no injury to campus debate. Similarly, when an outside Greek organization posted party invitations on one university's bulletin boards that included derogatory depictions of women, that campus's clear sense of who is allowed to post event notices and clear guidelines for the content of posted materials helped mitigate some of the fallout. Such clear guidance can be difficult to achieve on campuses that have a tradition of creative, spontaneous graffiti in some locations (as was the case the University of Minnesota, where messages graffitied on a bridge have long been common, but pro-Trump messages created a stir).[76] But it is important to develop this guidance in order to protect free expression and openly discuss and communicate its boundaries.

The reasons for having clear policies about posted materials go beyond avoiding legal trouble, and they are not intended to merely create bureaucratic hurdles. The atmosphere on campus is affected by such materials—from inspirational signs to circulated petitions—and it is therefore necessary for the institution to create guidelines around them. Is it legitimate to post the name or photo of a student or a professor as means of accusing them of sexual harassment? This issue became pertinent at a few colleges, where it generated strong feelings and discussions, as well as at least one lawsuit blaming a college for failing to protect someone accused. Where might student groups display political messages? At Emory University, the chalking of sidewalks and staircases with messages supporting the Trump administration, especially those that promoted its anti-immigration stances, elicited a strong reaction from immigrant and Muslim students. At both Mount Holyoke College and later at Bryn Mawr College, a student flying a confederate flag outside their window prompted demands for rules that forbid such displays, which ended up turning into a conversation about impact (in one case, the student agreed to either remove the flag or move it inside, while the other chose to keep flying it).

There can be no general policy about posted materials that would fit all colleges. Public and private, large and small, technical and liberal arts, urban and rural, residential and commuter—different institutions will have different needs depending on the populations they serve and what sorts of outsiders have access to their campuses. Residential areas—dormitories or other types of housing—require different rules too: what can be chuckled at or ignored in a public space can feel intrusive and hurtful if posted by one's door. Art galleries merit different considerations—and more openness—than bulletin boards. Religious institutions may have stricter guidance than nonaffiliated universities.

Overall, these are issues that colleges should take into consideration before posted materials cause strong responses on campus. Key questions for guiding the policy development process should be: How can the institution protect the broadest possible boundaries to speech and expression, inviting all to share their views, ideas, and creative perspectives, while maintaining a welcoming environment for all? And are there boundaries that cannot be crossed without consequence? Conversations about these questions should include leadership, faculty, staff, and students, and the answers should include clear guidance and responsibilities.

For some who favor boundless expression and worry about censorship, these guiding questions might sound worrisome, as they do point to the possibility of limiting speech through institutional design. That is indeed so, and this concern should be on the minds of administrators who delineate and enact these policies. But it should be widely agreed that some forms of expression, such as displaying threatening and targeted materials, are both unacceptable and incompatible with maintaining a suitable learning environment. While it is important not to micromanage expression—so as not to chill students' creativity or the true open exchange that can be observed on walkways and greens across campus—it is inadvisable to have no rules about posted expression.

Staff

On many university campuses, the people expected to directly address the daily matters of speech controversies are the staff responsible for university life, student well-being, and civic organizations. The work these professional staff take up related to speech and its boundaries mostly involves mediating disagreements, helping to plan events that would allow for all to participate, and supporting students and faculty in taking on this work. Here, I offer a strategy that I have recommended in the past—namely, using free speech observers as a way to ensure inclusion—and I offer an additional strategy that might help to increase the capacity of staff in doing this work—namely, working with organizations that share the same goals.

Strategy: Free Speech Observers

Free speech observers have been trained and dispatched at the University of Pennsylvania for many years. I have written about them in the past[77] and here will briefly reiterate the service that these campus members provide to the preservation of open expression on a diverse and inclusive campus. Volunteers come from the ranks of campus members: staff, faculty, and graduate students (though upperclassmen may volunteer as well, especially in undergraduate-only colleges). They undergo a short training that familiarizes them with campus guidelines and policies and with basic tools of mediation and de-escalation. They are dispatched in pairs to events and other contexts where disagreements around acceptable speech are anticipated. Organizers of campus events request their presence (they do not show up uninvited). They are also present where there are protests, sit-ins, and visits from uninvited outsiders that can cause a stir, as is the case on many campuses with the presence of "street preachers" who profess hatred toward women, LGBTQ people, and religious minorities. Free speech observers wear name tags that identify them as such and have no disciplinary authority—they merely observe to ensure that everyone's speech rights are protected and that campus policies are followed. If someone stands in violation of such policies—for example, if they are disrupting a scheduled event, if they are protesting loudly near a classroom, or if they attempt to silence protected speech—free speech observers inform them of their violation and request that they cease the inappropriate action and express their views in a more acceptable way. For example, if a student is interrupting an invited speaker, the observer will ensure that the speaker can continue their talk, but they will also ensure that the student's protest, or counter-speech, can take place and be heard and that the protester is not thrown out of the event. In the vast majority of events in which they are present, their low-key, matter of fact guidance is sufficient to resolve these matters.

Strategy: Organizations That Bridge Divides

In recent years, numerous local and national organizations that aim to advance depolarization and to bridge political and social divides have been established (or expanded): Braver Angels, Red and Blue Exchange, Intercollegiate Civil Disagreement Partnership, BridgeUSA, Healthy Democracy, Civic Health, and American Public Square are some of the many groups that work to engage students in structured opportunities to connect across social and political divides. Campus staff can invite such groups to assist in their ongoing work to bridge divides among students. Similarly, groups such as the Political Union organize events in which policy issues are discussed in an openly political yet collegial way. The opportunity to think about politics or policy through an ongoing engagement with ideologically and socially diverse groups should be available to all and can surely be made available at many college campuses. The goal of such opportunities is not to persuade participants to change their policy stances or ideological persuasion, though this is a possible outcome in some cases. Rather, their aim is to help reduce affective polarization: to demonstrate through engagement that people on the other side of political and ideological divides are often motivated by similar values and concerns, or at least to help participants recognize and empathize with diverse others. This work is taken up by student groups with support from faculty advisors and from campus staff, and the opportunities to engage in it can be expanded through working with outside organizations.

Faculty

Open expression of diverse views on campus happens first and foremost in classrooms. One of the pressing issues facing college instructors is how to deal with controversial issues and hard conversations in the classroom. This concern arises as significant both when faculty choose to teach topics that they know will cause some difficult conversations in the classroom and when they assign materials that can cause distress or disagreement. Likewise, it is an ongoing concern among faculty who assume their topics or materials to not be controversial but still observe that tense classroom exchanges can erupt and disrupt their lesson plans.

One of the key reasons that administrators, instructors, and other people in positions of power reject subjective self-reports of harm is that they seem insufficient as an evidentiary basis for punishing offenders. If a student reports that their instructor spoke in class in ways that cause harm and pain, the administrator receiving this report can (mistakenly) feel that they need respond immediately. They often respond either by accepting the report at face value and taking action against the instructor or by questioning the report's validity ("Were these the actual words used?") or its significance ("Is that really so hurtful?"). However, these are not the only two options. Taking reports of harm at face value, in the dignitary context, does not require punitive responses, though other responses may be required. In other words, a report of a subjective sense of dignitary harm should at least initially be accepted at face value. A person should know how they feel and should be trusted when they disclose their feelings. But this report of harm is not the same as a report of wrongdoing, which has a higher bar. It should lead to some response, which could be further investigation, an effort to facilitate reconciliation, or an investment of resources in efforts to rebalance power or voice. But this sort of subjective report does not necessarily mean, and often will not mean, that there was an incident of wrongdoing that requires punishment or a similar form of intervention. Take for example the increasingly common case of instructors using racial slurs in class "for pedagogical reasons" (a practice that, as noted in chapter 3, I find to be gratuitous more often than not). In many cases, this practice reasonably creates a sense of subjective harm. However, that does not mean that the instructor in all or even most cases should be censored, censured, or fired. But it does mean that we need to find appropriate recourse for students and offer both guidance and support to instructors.

It is important to reserve space for controversial topics in classroom conversations. Some instructors increasingly shy away from controversial discussions. This happens, among other reasons, because a growing share of instructors do not enjoy the protections of tenure or other forms of job security. They worry about strong disagreements in the classroom resulting from the broader polarized environment, and they worry that they are not trained to manage such disagreement in a productive and contained manner. These instructors' concerns are valid. Still, bringing these topics in is an important part of the role of higher education instructors, and their colleges should find ways to support them in doing so. It is impossible to challenge students' beliefs if instructors attempt to always assuage them or refrain from bringing in controversial topics and views. If controversy or marginalized opinions are not brought in through readings and conversation, then we are not allowing our students to challenge themselves, to learn to make the case for their own views, and to try out new beliefs and positions. Bringing in controversial topics is important not only because it can change or expand students' minds but also because it gives students a chance to really understand their own positions and why they hold them. Doing so is common in humanities and to some extent social science classrooms, but it is also relevant in the natural sciences. Addressing disagreements about the validity of climate change in an environmental science class or taking on disputes about the efficacy of vaccines—in a public health class, of course, but also in a virology class—can help students learn what these positions are and, ideally, how to argue against them, or how to consider the evidence in support of accepted science.

Strategy: Free Writing

One way to deal with unexpected events, especially those happening outside the class, is the free write. Especially in the case of outside events that create a difficult atmosphere in class—a mass shooting, a spate of hate crimes, the enacting of a policy that hurts some members of the community (for example, the Trump administration's Muslim ban)—the instructor can take a few minutes at the beginning of class to acknowledge the event and its impact. They can allow a few minutes for students to write down what they think and feel and what questions they might have. The instructor can then spend a few more minutes of class time inviting students to share some of these and to continue the conversation later. This approach is productive both for exchanging diverse views in a thoughtful and careful manner and for allowing students to co-process their views and emotions before they move into the planned material.

With today's polarized environment and the context of social media and related pressures, it is even more pressing for institutions to prepare for these hard conversations and to ensure support for instructors who might misstep while making an honest attempt to accommodate diverse views and help students process differences and hard events.

This strategy is one of many that can allow instructors to find a balance between creating a steady place where students can express themselves and one where they are challenged to consider new and sometimes disruptive ideas and views. Learning is oftentimes an unsteadying experience. The experience of learning is one in which you lose your balance intellectually—and sometimes in how you understand yourself. Feeling at sea can prove to be the best time for learning, as it provides an opportunity to reassess what you think and why you think what you do. When an instructor creates a place that is itself steady, it gives students a sense that they are welcome and they therefore feel they have the ability to try new ideas. This is the thin meaning of the much-maligned "safe spaces"—the classroom as a context in which students can try out ideas, including outrageous ideas, or ones they are considering rather than simply expressing or endorsing. Contrary to the Chicago "letter to freshmen," such a safe space does not preclude but rather enables a robust intellectual exchange.[78]

Strategy: Establishing Norms of Classroom Conversation

Different courses, classrooms, and institutions, and—of course—different instructors call for unique classroom norms. It does not make sense to offer a template here, because there is no template that can cover both Intro to Biology and a doctoral proseminar on politics. What is critical to all courses, though, is the importance of establishing clear and shared classroom norms, of defining them at the start of the course, and, ideally, including the students in the process when possible, either up front or as the semester unfolds. There are two key points to keep in mind across diverse classroom contexts: First, everyone in class belongs, and all students' questions and comments are welcome. Second, learning is an ongoing process, which is everyone's shared goal. The instructor can openly acknowledge that they may make mistakes, take a wrong step, and not say the right thing, and the same can happen to any of the students. But the group can agree up front to be generous and to have a strategy for talking together. Expecting and offering generosity and the space to correct mistakes can create an ongoing classroom conversation in which amends can be made when needed. One way to express such generosity is to ask: What do I see or feel? And what might others see or feel? Asking these questions gives students an opportunity to explore what it might mean when someone else might think or feel very differently from them. Another expression of generosity is giving others, including the instructor, time and space to correct mistakes they may have made, in a response they gave or failed to give. Such generosity requires established trust, and establishing shared norms early in a course creates a solid foundation for such trust.

Strategy: Mutual Observations

While teaching is a core responsibility for many professors and all other types of instructors, it is rare that teachers in higher education receive any training, professional development, or instructional support. Developing a syllabus, conducting a lecture, and facilitating a class are skills that professors are often expected to come by naturally as they devote their time to research or even when they are hired solely or mostly for their teaching work.[79] Many disagreements and clashes between students and their instructors come down to basic pedagogical practices, classroom norms, and relationships that allow for a conversation to take place. I cannot take on the whole breadth of this matter here, but I can recommend a simple practice that does not require a broad reevaluation of training for higher education instructors (useful as that might be for other purposes): Instructors in higher education are rarely observed in their work, but being observed can yield significant benefits for an instructor's teaching, especially—

though not exclusively—in the improvement of pedagogical practices related to the boundaries of speech. Am I failing to notice, misinterpreting, or ignoring some of my students' voices inadvertently? Am I speaking in insensitive ways that I am unaware of? Could I have brought additional perspectives into the discussion? An observation by a well-meaning peer, or by a professional (from a center for teaching and learning or its equivalent on any campus) can help identify areas for improvement in a supportive way and prevent frictions where they could be unproductive.

Students

Campuses provide spaces and contexts for action, and many institutions recognize the centrality of civic skills to the learning that college is meant to provide. Given the limited experiences that most students have had in civic engagement and open dialogue across divides prior to coming to campus, campuses need to be intentional in their support of student activists and leaders.

Strategy: Student Collaboration across Identity Groups

Students are often drawn to participation in affinity groups with others who share their identities or views. That makes sense: those at residential colleges are often away from home for the first time, and in any case, students find themselves in a new environment, so it makes sense for them to look for "their people." These associations, which often offer a safe haven, an anchor, and a home, can also open up to engagement with others. Students can ask for support from their institutions for events that draw in more than one student organization. This is one small way that colleges can support shared contexts for collaboration.[80] Supporting a pizza dinner, a field trip, a speaker, or another student event that would involve groups that do not typically engage with each other, or groups that are often at odds, is one way colleges can weave a more robust civic fabric on campus.

Many universities—and departments, and student groups within them—aim to ensure that a diversity of opinions are heard, even when these views are not well represented within the community. Sometimes institutions seek to serve this goal by securing outside speakers who come to share their less common or even controversial views. In recent years, as the progressive ideological leanings of college campuses have drawn greater attention, the industry of campus invitations has become more lively and sometimes more lucrative. On many campuses, it is becoming evident that student organizers have developed alternatives to de-platforming, including protests, alternative events, boycotts, and interruptions to the event within acceptable limits. To the extent that a broad and diverse set of voices is heard, and to the extent that dialogue across differences can continue, these are all welcome developments.

A Final Word

The lesson plan called for engaging with the raging "school board wars," with a focus on arguments about the teaching of a broadly construed "critical race theory" in schools. Analyzing a statement from a group opposing such teaching took longer than expected and extended until the class period ended. The instructor felt that the message her students were left with as they shuffled out was imbalanced and even painful: that they should prioritize arguments against teaching in K-12 schools about race, about racism, about the history of slavery. She started the next class by saying, "I thought, and still think, it was important to consider the range of perspectives our fellow citizens voice about these matters. Some of these may be the views of people in this class. It is important to understand anti-CRT views—like any views— within their historical, social, and political context." She invited her students to continue the conversation from last week for a few more minutes: What did you think of the arguments? What counterarguments can you offer? How does it relate to this week's reading? The conversation was lively, animated, sometimes fierce. No one ended up being canceled. I, the instructor in this story, left the class grateful for the relationship with my students and the environment of open expression that allows me to continue the conversation.

· · ·

Universities' role in responding to the political challenges of our time continues to evolve. Hiding behind a cloak of objectivity, trying to stay above the fray of politics, is unfeasible as higher education is already politicized, has already been drawn into the struggle over knowledge and truth, diversity, and inclusion. Students are debating the value and price of free speech; professors are losing their jobs for speaking out in class or on social media; federal funding for scientific research is subject to political wrangling over what may be prioritized, studied, and publicly communicated. Trying to maintain a distance from political debate, to remain a "referee," would also be a missed opportunity because institutions of higher education are among the best positioned to respond to the pressing needs of democratic societies today. They "should be at the forefront of modeling a healthy, multiethnic democracy."[1] As the struggles intensify over defining the boundaries of truth against a rising tide of mis- and disinformation and over defining the meaning and practices of full inclusion in a pluralistic society, universities should intentionally join the conversation.

Democratic institutions have been weakening in the United States and other democracies, resulting in changes to civic culture and an erosion of democratic commitments. The processes that have led to this decline are fiercely debated. Democratic erosion may be the result of changes in news media and the rise of social media or of actions taken by populist leaders, or a number of other causes. Within the resulting shifts in political allegiances, freedom of speech has become a lightning rod for partisans. The freedom to express controversial, marginal, oppositional, and contrarian views is well protected in democracy at large and especially in the context of learning and research. Like all other freedoms and rights, the freedom of expression has never been boundless, and its boundaries have always been contested. But the politicization of the very concept of free speech is newer, as is the politicization of—and direct attacks against—major social institutions whose main role is to assess, communicate, and expand what we know.

The struggle over free speech requires a direct response, one that recognizes its political context and addresses the boundaries of speech directly as a political and civic matter. In this book, I aimed to provide the justification and shape of this direct response: I argued that institutions of higher education should implement inclusive freedom practices, that they should prioritize truth and the evidentiary processes that lead to reliable knowledge, and that equal participation in educational and academic conversations calls for attention to be paid to the unequal burden that unalloyed speech can create. I offered some practical ways to lift this unequal burden while maintaining a strong and clear commitment to free speech and free inquiry, and to educate the next generation, from a young age, about the democratic and scholarly importance of these values. While I strongly believe, based both on my experience working with many institutions of higher education and on my academic work, that this is the most justified and effective approach to take in response to current speech struggles, I recognize that its details can be debated. Some would prefer to permit expression that in my view is too exclusionary to tolerate; some may have a strong case for being more restrictive, or more punitive, in specific instances of intentionally harmful expression. This is a healthy debate to have, within and beyond academe. Whatever exact boundaries are drawn, either as a sector, or by specific institutions and even departments or schools within a given university, it is key to take up this challenge directly.

To do so, it is important not only to cool down the rhetoric around speech and its boundaries but also to reach some agreement over the nature of the struggle. It is evident in the public debate that many across diverse political and ideological affiliations are concerned about the state of open expression on college campuses. Legislators are trying to intervene, university administrators are struggling to respond to outcries, and new organizations that aim to address faculty or student concerns continue to emerge. But the nature and severity of the "crisis" remains elusive. The Foundation for Individual Rights in Education documents over five hundred cases of instructors being punished, terminated, or threatened with consequences for expressing protected views between 2015 and 2022.[2] Is this a large or small number of cases? The trend is unclear, and the cases seem sparse for a sector that encompasses thousands of diverse institutions in which classes and events take place every day. With what seems like a limited number of difficult cases, it is evident that many more events are taking place without raising concerns, hence underscoring the contribution of the higher education sector as a space where speech is robust, supported, and welcome.

There might be other uncounted, missed opportunities to share diverse opinions and views. Some are concerned about self-censorship and the social silencing of divergent views, especially instructors and students who may choose not to voice their views out of fear of social ostracization or punitive actions. The decision to self-censor or to remain silent is very hard to capture and quantify. It is also hard to know what was lost: sometimes the decision to hold one's tongue is noth-

ing more than simple politeness, or a reasonable choice to avoid unhelpful friction. At other times, something valuable is missed and the
conversation is stifled. While it is hard to collect data on this matter, a
commitment to open expression requires creating and protecting opportunities for those with views outside of the campus (or classroom)
mainstream to speak their minds. Making this commitment is key to
the intentional work that must be done to expand the civic space for
exchanging views and perspectives on campus.

An argument commonly heard today is that efforts to expand the
conversation on campus must work against students' opposing tendencies. Indeed, various surveys suggest changes in students' commitment (or that of young people in general) to open expression. These
have proliferated in recent years and have been suggested to show that
"kids these days" fail to recognize the importance of First Amendment
speech protections. Many assume that the source of young people's
growing unease with speech protections is that the youth of today
are coddled, or that they are "snowflakes," softer than the true men
(people?) of yore. But the picture that these surveys paint may not be
simply attributable to their parents' failures or some societal shortcom-
ing. When some students say that they oppose hosting a racist speaker,
are they rejecting the principles of the First Amendment, or are they
looking for ways to ensure that a diverse student body feels welcome
and able to speak on campus? Even if the tactics that students employ
or support are sometimes unhelpful, or even inappropriate, students'
views should not be dismissed out of hand. Their views are interpreted
by some as authoritarian or anti-democratic, but I suggest that they
can be interpreted in many cases as an effort to expand the scope of
democracy. The generational change around open expression might
best be described not as intolerance to diverse views but rather as embracing diverse people and an effort to reconcile that embrace with
protections of intolerant speech. Young people are looking to broaden
the benefits of speech so that more can enjoy them, including those
with minority identities. This process is accelerated when the struggle
over the boundaries of speech becomes a subject of contention.

Using the construct of "cancel culture" to explain or condemn these
phenomena is bound to exacerbate the problem, not alleviate it. The
attempt to silence a view you abhor is as old as politics, and the label
"cancel culture" can fit actions across the political divide, going back
generations. I attempted to offer here a more productive approach to

protective speech and maintaining an inclusive community, one that could help heal democratic divides and shore up shared epistemic foundations. It requires sustained attention and a genuine commitment to a shared society, an assumption of general goodwill on all parts, and an ongoing dialogue—all of which are in short supply in the public sphere today, and all of which can be found more abundantly on campus.

Whether my approach to speech and democracy is accurate, the goal of strengthening support for free expression is one that can be shared across political divides. Making sure K–12 students are familiar with democratic structures and rights is necessary but not sufficient. It is essential that young students to learn to voice their views and share their ideas, that they develop the habit of carefully listening to others' diverse experiences and views about complex issues affecting society, and that they are able to actively consider the sources of information they gather. All these are key steps for protecting and strengthening democracy, and moreover, they are steps on which many agree across political divides.

Finding common ground within the generational and ideological struggles over free speech is possible; like other scholars and organizations, I have been helping colleges and universities do just that, and I have seen both the challenges and the possibilities of creating an honest context in which ongoing dialogue takes place. When young people experience the power of their connections, the flexibility and resilience of their ideas, their voices and actions can help bridge some of the fissures that divide us. Their schools and colleges have a role to play in helping them harness this power, and doing so will help elevate the thinking and the voices of younger generations, the institutions that serve them, and ultimately, democracy itself.

Acknowledgments

The person on the other side of the line is often distraught: A controversial speaker has been invited—how do we respond? Someone plastered invitations to a hateful event—must we keep them up? In the last few years, I have visited many colleges and universities, in various countries, as they have struggled to address speech challenges and develop policies that align with their mission. I am grateful to the many higher education leaders with whom I have shared difficult moments as they genuinely and open-mindedly sought ways to protect open expression and inclusion on their campuses. I anonymize them in this book, but their stories and their views inform this work.

Conversations with the 2020–21 fellows in (virtual) residence at the Edmond J. Safra Center for Ethics at Harvard University helped me think through this work, as did the center's faculty under Danielle Allen's leadership. I am especially grateful to Meira Levinson, Adrienne Stang, Jacob Fay, Adam Hosein, Steven Campbell, Catherine Elgin, Eric Beerbohm, and Gina Schouten. I am grateful to the center, and to Penn GSE, for the sabbatical funding that allowed me to write this book. I am lucky to have more wonderful colleagues than I can list here. Peter Agree, Suzi Dovi, Joan Goodman, Abby Reisman, Pam Grossman, Ted Ruger, and Annette Lareau always push me to clarify and improve my ideas and to check if they work in practice. My engagement with the Andrea Mitchell Center for the Study of Democracy at Penn, first under Rogers Smith and then under Jeff Green, helped crystalize my ideas and provided a platform for sharing them, as did my work with Penn's SNF Paideia program under Michael X. Deli Carpini's leadership. Jennifer Morton and Sophia Rosenfeld offered friendship, comments on this work, and an invitation to speak to their insightful students. I benefitted from conversations with Cerri Banks, Michelle Deutchman, Amalia Daché, Howard Gillman, Sarah Ropp, Catherine Ross, Geoffrey Stone, and Nadine Strossen. Many Penn and Harvard doctoral students enlightened me during many enjoyable conversations about free speech, inclusion, and campus life, including Megan Bogia, Monika Greco, Abigail Dym, Penelope Lusk, Nora Reikosky, and Dustin Webster, who have all read and helped improve earlier drafts. John Tilson co-convened the PESGB virtual summer school of 2021 with me, along with Ben Kotzee, where a version of most of this book's chapters was read and discussed. I am grateful to all participants for their feedback. I am lucky to work with my wonderful editor Elizabeth Branch Dyson and the team at the University of Chicago Press.

This book is dedicated to the memory of my sister, Maya Raday. She would have written a different book: hers would be funny. I miss her every day.

My family is always game to discuss hard cases, and to think with me, even when the world shuts down around us. Eran Noah, Itamar, Amalia: the best parts of this book, from first to last word, echo with your voices.

Notes

INTRODUCTION

1. Private institutions have greater autonomy in this domain than public ones, as the latter are limited by the First Amendment's demand for neutrality by governmental actors (among which public universities are counted). See Erwin Chemerinsky and Howard Gillman, *Free Speech on Campus* (New Haven, CT: Yale University Press, 2017).

2. In *Whitney v. California*, 274 U.S. 357 (1927), Justice Brandeis wrote, "If there be time to expose through discussion the falsehood and fallacies, to avert the evil by the processes of education, the remedy to be applied is more speech, not enforced silence."

CHAPTER 1

1. Hannah J. Martinez, "Harvard Undergraduate Council Endorses Removal of Gov 50 Instructor," *Harvard Crimson*, updated September 30, 2020, https://www.thecrimson .com/article/2020/9/28/UC-endorses-gov-preceptor-removal.

2. Robert Talisse, *Sustaining Democracy: What We Owe to Each Other* (Oxford: Oxford University Press, 2021).

3. Alexander Meiklejohn, *Free Speech and Its Relation to Self-Government* (New York: Harper & Brothers, 1948); see also Robert Post, "Participatory Democracy as a Theory of Free Speech," *Virginia Law Review* 477 (2011): 617–32.

4. Geoffrey R. Stone, "Free Expression in Peril," *Chronicle of Higher Education* 63, no. 3 (August 2016): B9.

5. Knight Foundation, *The First Amendment on Campus 2020 Report: College Students' Views of Free Expression* (Washington, DC: Gallup, 2020), https://knightfoundation.org /wp-content/uploads/2020/05/First-Amendment-on-Campus-2020.pdf.

6. "FixUS-Ipsos: America's Values, Goals, and Aspirations," Committee for a Responsible Federal Budget, 2021, https://fixusnow.org/americas-values-poll.

7. Ronald J. Daniels, *What Universities Owe Democracy* (Baltimore: Johns Hopkins University Press, 2021), 19.

8. Daniels, *What Universities Owe Democracy*, 233.

9. I develop this approach in Sigal R. Ben-Porath, *Free Speech on Campus* (Philadelphia: University of Pennsylvania Press, 2017).

10. For a tracker of current legislative efforts against protests and similar speech activities, including (as a separate category) on campus, see International Center for Not-for-Profit Law, "US Protest Law Tracker," last updated January 26, 2022, https://www.icnl.org/usprotestlawtracker.

11. For a summary of current legislative efforts to restrict protests, see Eric Halliday and Rachael Hanna, "State Anti-Protest Laws and Their Constitutional Implications," *Lawfare*, October 25, 2021, https://www.lawfareblog.com/state-anti-protest-laws-and-their-constitutional-implications.

12. For a report on a host of 2021 laws limiting specific curricular content, especially about race, racism, and slavery but also about gender and sexual identity, and other matters, see "Educational Gag Orders," PEN America, accessed January 30, 2022, https://pen.org/report/educational-gag-orders.

13. H.B. 1218, 93rd Gen. Assemb., Reg. Sess. (Ark. 2021).

14. *Masterpiece Cakeshop v. Colorado Civil Rights Commission*, 584 U.S. (2018).

15. *Meriwether v. Hartop*, 992 F.3d 492 (6th Cir. 2021).

16. For a libertarian defense of similar values, see Jacob T. Levy, "Black Liberty Matters," *Niskanen Center*, September 20, 2017, https://www.niskanencenter.org/black-liberty-matters.

17. Shanto Iyengar and Sean J. Westwood, "Fear and Loathing across Party Lines: New Evidence on Group Polarization," *American Journal of Political Science* 59, no. 3 (July 2015): 690–707.

18. Emily Badger, "Americans Are Afraid. Not for Themselves, but for the Country," *The Upshot* (blog), *New York Times*, updated November 3, 2020, https://www.nytimes.com/2020/11/01/upshot/election-democracy-fear-americans.html.

19. Recent literature about the difference between views on the right and left sides of the political map focuses on the growing distance between these median views; the question of whether the elite, party leaders, or the general population initiate moves from the center toward ever more extreme sides of the political map; whether both sides are equally responsible for such moves or one side contributes more to the distancing; and whether concerns about these movements should mostly focus on changes in policy views or on reduced exposure to views typical of the other side due to social sorting based on residence, institutional affiliations, and media consumption.

20. Danielle S. Allen, *Talking to Strangers: Anxieties of Citizenship since Brown v. Board of Education* (Chicago: University of Chicago Press, 2004), 46.

21. Lilliana Mason, *Uncivil Agreement: How Politics Became Our Identity* (Chicago: University of Chicago Press, 2020).

22. Roberto Stefan Foa and Yascha Mounk, "The Signs of Deconsolidation," *Journal of Democracy* 28, no. 1 (January 2017): 5–16.

23. Kai Ruggeri, Bojana Većkalov, Lana Bojanić, Thomas L. Andersen, Sarah Ashcroft-Jones, Nélida Ayacaxli, Paula Barea-Arroyo, et al. "The General Fault in Our Fault Lines," *Nature Human Behavior* 5, no. 10 (October 2021): 1369–80, https://doi.org/10.1038/s41562-021-01092-x. Ruggeri et al. illustrate how it is the perception of polar-

ization rather than polarization itself that causes negative attitudes about the out-group, and that these can be reduced by informing people that their beliefs about polarization are inaccurate.

24. "Partisanship and Political Animosity in 2016," Pew Research Center, updated June 26, 2016, https://www.people-press.org/2016/06/22/partisanship-and-political -animosity-in-2016. See also Mark J. Brandt, Geoffrey Wetherell, and Jarret T. Crawford, "Moralization and Intolerance of Ideological Outgroups," in *The Social Psychology of Morality*, ed. Joseph P. Forgas, Lee Jussim, Paul A. M. van Lange (New York: Routledge, 2016), 239–56.

25. Lilliana Mason, "'I Disrespectfully Agree': The Differential Effects of Partisan Sorting on Social and Issue Polarization," *American Journal of Political Science*, 59, no. 1 (2015): 128–45.

26. Cass Sunstein, *Going to Extremes: How Like Minds Unite and Divide* (Oxford: Oxford University Press, 2009). See also Robert Talisse, *Overdoing Democracy* (Oxford: Oxford University Press, 2019), on how this phenomenon is accelerated because of the contemporary tendency to ascribe political value to mundane activities such as brand preference and hobbies, which further sorts people into distinct political camps.

27. Kevin Vallier, *Trust in a Polarized Age* (Oxford: Oxford University Press, 2021), 9.

28. Pippa Norris and Robert Inglehart, *Cultural Backlash: Trump, Brexit, and Authoritarian Populism* (Cambridge, UK: Cambridge University Press, 2019).

29. For a theoretical framing of this media phenomenon in the current age, and a large-scale data analysis of traditional and new media that shows how they operate, see Yochai Benkler, Robert Farris, and Hai Roberts, *Propaganda Network, Manipulation, Disinformation, and Radicalization in American Politics* (Oxford: Oxford University Press, 2018).

30. Recently, Matthew Graham and Milan Svolik found voters with strong partisan identities were willing to vote for party-aligned candidates even when they promoted anti-democratic values. Matthew H. Graham and Milan W. Svolik, "Democracy in America? Partisanship, Polarization, and the Robustness of Support for Democracy in the United States," *American Political Science Review* 114, no. 2 (2020): 392–409. In addition, many young voters in the United States today do not see democracy as important to them. See R. S. Foa, A. Klassen, D. Wenger, A. Rand, and M. Slade, "Youth and Satisfaction with Democracy: Reversing the Democratic Discontent?" (Cambridge, UK: Centre for the Future of Democracy, October 2020), https://www.bennettinstitute.cam.ac.uk /publications/youth-and-satisfaction-democracy.

31. Vallier, *Trust*, 6.

32. Allen, *Talking to Strangers*, xvi.

33. Robert D. Putnam and Shaylyn Romney Garrett, *Upswing: How America Came Together a Century Ago and How It Can Do It Again* (New York: Simon & Schuster, 2020).

34. Allen, *Talking to Strangers*, 155.

35. "In Changing U.S. Electorate, Race and Education Remain Stark Dividing Lines," Pew Research Center, updated June 2, 2020, https://www.pewresearch.org/politics /2020/06/02/in-changing-u-s-electorate-race-and-education-remain-stark-dividing -lines.

36. See the influence of religiosity on news interpretation in Francesca Tripodi, *Searching for Alternative Facts: Analyzing Scriptural Inference in Conservative News Practices* (New York: Data & Society Research Institute, 2018), https://datasociety.net/wp -content/uploads/2018/05/Data_Society_Searching-for-Alternative-Facts.pdf.

37. See Richard Rothstein, *The Color of Law: A Forgotten History of How Our Government Segregated America* (New York: Liveright, 2017).

38. Nolan M. McCarty, Keith T. Poole, Howard Rosenthal, *Polarized America: The Dance of Ideology and Unequal Riches* (Cambridge, MA: MIT Press, 2006).

39. Matt Motyl, Ravi Iyer, Shigehiro Oishi, Sophie Trawalter, and Brian A. Nosek, "How Ideological Migration Geographically Segregates Groups," *Journal of Experimental Social Psychology* 51 (2014): 1–14.

40. Shanto Iyengar, Gaurav Sood, and Yphtach Lelkes, "Affect, Not Ideology: A Social Identity Perspective on Polarization," *Public Opinion Quarterly* 76, no. 3 (Fall 2012): 405–31.

41. Jamie Settle, *Frenemies* (Cambridge, UK: Cambridge University Press, 2021).

42. See, for example, the poll conducted in September 2020 by Ipsos on behalf of FixUS: Committee for a Responsible Federal Budget, "FixUS-Ipsos: America's Values, Goals, and Aspirations," 2021, https://fixusnow.org/americas-values-poll.

43. See this Pew poll documenting partisan divide in attitudes toward higher education: Kim Parker, "The Growing Partisan Divide in Views of Higher Education," Pew Research Center, August 19, 2019, https://www.pewsocialtrends.org/essay/the-growing -partisan-divide-in-views-of-higher-education.

44. Nancy Rosenblum, *On the Side of the Angels: An Appreciation of Parties and Partisanship* (Princeton, NJ: Princeton University Press, 2008), 371.

45. J. M. Berger, *Extremism* (Cambridge, MA: MIT Press, 2018).

46. David E. Broockman, Joshua L. Kalla, and Sean J. Westwood, "Does Affective Polarization Undermine Democratic Norms or Accountability? Maybe Not," *American Journal of Political Science* (forthcoming), published ahead of print, December 21, 2020, https://doi.org/10.31219/osf.io/9btsq.

47. Eli J. Finkel, Christopher A. Bail, Mina Cikara, Peter H. Ditto, Shanto Iyengar, Samara Klar, Lilliana Mason, Mary C. McGrath, Brendan Nyhan, David G. Rand, Linda J. Skitka, Joshua A. Tucker, Jay J. Van Bavel, Cynthia S. Wang, and James N. Druckman, "Political Sectarianism in America," *Science* 370, no. 6516 (2020): 533–36, https://doi.org /10.1126/science.abe1715.

48. Annette Baier, "Trust and Antitrust," *Ethics* 96, no. 2 (January 1986): 235.

49. Baier, "Trust and Antitrust," 236.

50. See Zeynep Tufekci, "How Social Media Took Us from Tahrir Square to Donald Trump," *MIT Technology Review*, updated August 14, 2018, https://www.technologyreview .com/2018/08/14/240325/how-social-media-took-us-from-tahrir-square-to-donald -trump.

51. Camila Domonoske, "Storming the Capitol Didn't Change the Election, Some Trump Backers Realize," *NPR*, updated January 7, 2021, https://www.npr.org/sections /congress-electoral-college-tally-live-updates/2021/01/07/954257324/storming-the -capitol-didnt-change-the-election-some-trump-backers-realize.

52. Sophia Rosenfeld, *Democracy and Truth* (Philadelphia: University of Pennsylvania, 2018). See chapter 2 in particular.

53. Allen, *Talking to Strangers*, 87.

54. Fights over public health measures, like mask mandates, during the COVID-19 crisis brought into sharp relief the consequences of losing trust in shared public institutions, such as public health experts and departments, and elected officials.

55. Troy Closson, "Amy Cooper Falsely Accused Black Bird-Watcher in 2nd 911 Conversation," *New York Times*, updated May 26, 2021, https://www.nytimes.com/2020/10/14/nyregion/amy-cooper-false-report-charge.html.

56. As is clear in the analysis of civic distrust across the Black-white racial divide in Allen, *Talking to Strangers*.

57. This analysis is summarized by Ezra Klein in *Why We're Polarized* (New York: Simon & Schuster, 2020).

58. Gavan Titley, *Is Free Speech Racist?* (Cambridge, UK: Wiley, 2020).

59. C. Thi Nguyen, "Echo Chambers and Epistemic Bubbles," *Episteme* 17, no. 2 (June 2020): 141–61. Nguyen differentiates between epistemic bubbles, whose participants lack exposure to opposing ideas, and echo chambers, in which people actively avoid and reject alternative views. Echo chambers are not unique to virtual connections, and are reflective of the willful ignorance which I discuss in the next chapter.

60. Stuart A. Thompson and Charlie Warzel, "They Used to Post Selfies. Now They're Trying to Reverse the Election," *New York Times*, January 14, 2021, https://www.nytimes.com/2021/01/14/opinion/facebook-far-right.html.

61. See Yochay Benkler, Robert Faris, and Hal Roberts, *Network Propaganda: Manipulation, Disinformation, and Radicalization in American Politics* (Oxford: Oxford University Press, 2018).

62. Richard I. Hasen, *Cheap Speech: How Disinformation Poisons Our Politics—and How to Cure It* (New Haven, CT: Yale University Press, 2022).

63. Shoshana Zuboff documents many of these concerns in *The Age of Surveillance Capitalism* (New York: PublicAffairs, 2019).

64. For an analysis of the existing interpretation of the First Amendment and a suggestion that this interpretation does not stand the test of our current time, see Tim Wu, "Is the First Amendment Obsolete?," Knight First Amendment Institute at Columbia University, September 1, 2017, https://knightcolumbia.org/content/tim-wu-first-amendment-obsolete.

65. That older users are more likely to spread misinformation is an encouraging sign for those who advocate for the use of educational programs as a means of improving users' skills in addressing these issues. This is further discussed in chapter 4. For more about age and spearing misinformation see Andrew Guess, Jonathan Nagler and Joshua Tucker, "Less Than You Think: Prevalence and Predictors of Fake News Dissemination of Facebook," *Science Advances* 5, no. 1 (January 9, 2019): eaau4586.

66. Ethan Zuckerman, *Mistrust: Why Losing Faith in Institutions Provides the Tools to Transform Them* (New York: Norton, 2021).

67. Jennifer Forestal, "Beyond Gatekeeping: Propaganda, Democracy, and the Organization of Digital Public" *Journal of Politics* 83, no. 1 (January 2021): 306–19.

CHAPTER 2

1. For background on this controversy, see Daniel Clery, "New Front Emerges in Battle to Build Giant Telescope in Hawaii," *Science Magazine*, January 14, 2020, https://www.sciencemag.org/news/2020/01/new-front-emerges-battle-build-giant-telescope -hawaii.

2. See John Laloggia, "Republicans and Democrats agree: They can't agree on basic facts," Pew Research Center, August 23, 2018, https://www.pewresearch.org/fact-tank /2018/08/23/republicans-and-democrats-agree-they-cant-agree-on-basic-facts.

3. For a comprehensive analysis of the state of truth in the current era, see Lee McIntyre, *Post-Truth* (Cambridge, MA: MIT Press, 2018); Cailin O'Connor and James Owen Weatherall, *The Misinformation Age: How False Beliefs Spread* (New Haven, CT: Yale University Press, 2018).

4. Hannah Arendt, *Origins of Totalitarianism* (New York: Harcourt Brace, 1951), 353.

5. For an argument in favor of stronger regulation of lies, see Seana Valentine Shiffrin, *Speech Matters: On Lying, Morality, and the Law* (Princeton, NJ: Princeton University Press, 2014).

6. Jeremy Waldron, "Damned Lies" (Public Law Research Paper No. 21-11, NYU School of Law, March 3, 2021), http://dx.doi.org.proxy.library.upenn.edu/10.2139/ssrn .3797216; Catherine J. Ross, *A Right to Lie? Presidents, Other Liars, and the First Amendment* (Philadelphia: University of Pennsylvania Press, 2021).

7. Bruno Latour, *Down to Earth: Politics in the New Climatic Regime* (Cambridge, UK: Polity, 2018), 23.

8. Sophia Rosenfeld, *Common Sense: A Political History* (Cambridge, MA: Harvard University Press, 2014).

9. See discussion on C. Thi Nguyen's work on echo chambers later in this chapter.

10. For the factual basis of the instructor's claim, leaving aside the way in which they were expressed, see, for example, R. Oza-Frank, and S. A. Cunningham, "The Weight of US Residence Among Immigrants: A Systematic Review," *Obesity Reviews* 11, no. 4 (April 2010): 271–80, https://doi-org.proxy.library.upenn.edu/10.1111/j.1467-789X .2009.00610.x.

11. In the 2018 PISA, only 13.5 percent of students correctly labeled facts and opinions. See "PISA 2018 Results," OECD Programme for International Assessment (2018), https://www.oecd.org/pisa/publications/pisa-2018-resultshtm.htm.

12. A 2018 survey suggests that most Americans cannot distinguish between factual statements and statements of opinion. See Amy Mitchell, Jeffrey Gottfried, Michael Bartel, and Nami Sumida, "Distinguishing Between Factual and Opinion Statements in the News," Pew Research Center, June 18, 2018, https://www.journalism.org/2018/06/18 /distinguishing-between-factual-and-opinion-statements-in-the-news.

13. See Waldron's discussion of group libel in *The Harm in Hate Speech* (Cambridge, MA: Harvard University Press, 2013), as well as Gavan Titley, *Is Free Speech Racist?* (Cambridge, UK: Wiley, 2020).

14. John Stuart Mill, *On Liberty* (London: Walter Scott, 1859; Project Gutenberg, 2011), https://www.gutenberg.org/files/34901/34901-h/34901-h.htm. For a contem-

porary argument based in liberal ideas about teaching historical facts, see Harry Brighouse, "Should We Teach Patriotic History?," in *Citizenship and Education in Liberal-Democratic Societies: Teaching for Cosmopolitan Values and Collective Identities*, ed. Kevin McDonough and Walter Feinberg (Oxford: Oxford University Press, 2003).

15. See fifteen recent studies summarized in Emily Kubin, Curtis Puryear, Chelsea Schein, and Kurt Gray, "Personal Experiences Bridge Moral and Political Divides Better than Facts," *Proceedings of the National Academy of Sciences* 118, no. 6 (February 2021), https://doi.org/10.1073/pnas.2008389118. I return to the findings in this article later, as they indicate the importance of sharing personal experiences, particularly around harm, to help bridge differences.

16. See Richard Rorty's last, controversial book *What's the Use of Truth?* (New York: Columbia University Press, 2007), as well as Bernard E. Harcourt, "The Last Refuge of Scoundrels: The Problem of Truth in a Time of Lying" (Columbia Public Law Research Paper No. 14-628, 2019).

17. Russell Muirhead and Nancy L. Rosenblum, *A Lot of People Are Saying* (Princeton, NJ: Princeton University Press, 2020), 118.

18. Sophia Rosenfeld, *Democracy and Truth* (Philadelphia: University of Pennsylvania Press, 2018).

19. Tom Nichols, *The Death of Expertise* (Oxford: Oxford University Press, 2017), 20.

20. Gil Eyal, *The Crisis of Expertise* (Cambridge, UK: Polity, 2019), 20.

21. This is the essential argument in Bruno Latour, "Why Has Critique Run Out of Steam? From Matters of Fact to Matters of Concern," *Critical Inquiry* 30, no. 2 (Winter 2004), https://doi.org/10.1086/421123. Latour observes with concern the weaponization of a democratized vision of knowledge and the prioritization of skepticism for acquiring knowledge by climate deniers and others.

22. Noam Chomsky, "The Responsibility of Intellectuals," in *The Chomsky Reader*, ed. James Peck (New York: Pantheon Books, 1987), 60.

23. Jonathan Rauch, *The Constitution of Knowledge* (Washington, DC: Brookings Institution Press, 2021).

24. Nadia Urbinati, *Democracy Disfigured: Opinion, Truth, and the People* (Cambridge, MA: Harvard University Press, 2014).

25. Rosenfeld, *Democracy and Truth*, 75.

26. Gordon Pennycook, Tyrone D. Cannon, and David G. Rand, "Prior Exposure Increases Perceived Accuracy of Fake News," *Journal of Experimental Psychology: General* 147, no. 12 (December 2018): 1865–80.

27. Jay J. Van Bavel and Andrea Pereira, "The Partisan Brain: An Identity-Based Model of Political Belief," *Trends in Cognitive Sciences* 22, no. 3 (March 2018): 213–24.

28. As suggested in Ethan Zuckerman, "What Is Digital Public Infrastructure?," Center For Journalism and Liberty, November 17, 2020, https://www.journalismliberty.org/publications/what-is-digital-public-infrastructure.

29. Other historical eras that saw the rise of media such as mass-produced newspapers, radio, and television have experienced similarly blurred lines between fact and opinion, fact and fiction, until new norms evolved. See Jennifer Kavanagh and Michael D. Rich, *Truth Decay: An Initial Exploration of the Diminishing Role of Facts and Analysis in American*

Public Life (Santa Monica, CA: Rand Corporation, 2018). New norms, practices, and expertise on the part of consumers have slowly developed in these eras, including our own.

30. Daniel A. Effron, "It Could Have Been True: How Counterfactual Thoughts Reduce Condemnation of Falsehoods and Increase Political Polarization," *Personality and Social Psychology Bulletin* 44, no. 5 (May 2018): 729-45.

31. Erik Peterson and Shanto Iyengar, "Partisan Gaps in Political Information and Information-Seeking Behavior: Motivated Reasoning or Cheerleading?," *American Journal of Political Science* 65, no. 1 (2021): 133-47, https://doi.org/10.1111/ajps.12535.

32. Daniel Goldstein and Johannes Wiedemann, "Who Do You Trust? The Consequences of Partisanship and Trust for Public Responsiveness to COVID-19 Orders," *Perspectives on Politics*, FirstView (April 2021): 1-27.

33. Charles Mills, "White Ignorance," in *Race and Epistemologies of Ignorance*, ed. Shannon Sullivan and Nancy Tuana (Albany, NY: SUNY Press, 2007), 13.

34. For a recent philosophical and psychological analysis, see Trip Glazer and Nabina Liebow "Confronting White Ignorance: White Psychology and Rational Self-Regulation," *Journal of Social Philosophy* 52, no. 1 (Spring 2020): 50-71.

35. Kristie Dotson, "Tracking Epistemic Violence, Tracking Practices of Silencing," *Hypatia* 26, no. 2 (Spring 2011): 238.

36. See, for example, Daniel Solorzano, Miguel Ceja, and Tara Yosso, "Critical Race Theory, Racial Microaggressions, and Campus Racial Climate: The Experiences of African American College Students," *Journal of Negro Education* 69, no. 1/2 (Spring 2000): 60-73.

37. Clarissa Hayward, "Disruption: What is it Good For?," *Journal of Politics* 82, no. 2 (April 2020): 453.

38. Josh Pasek, "It's Not My Consensus: Motivated Reasoning and the Sources of Scientific Illiteracy," *Public Understanding of Science* 27, no. 7 (October 2018): 787-806. https://doi.org/10.1177/0963662517733681.

39. Dan M. Kahan, David A. Hoffman, Donald Braman, Danieli Evans, and Jeffrey J. Rachlinski, "'They Saw a Protest': Cognitive Illiberalism and the Speech/Conduct Distinction." *Stanford Law Review* 64, no. 4 (April 2012): 851-906.

40. Kavanagh and Rich, *Truth Decay*.

41. See Jennifer Mercieca, *Demagogue for President: The Rhetorical Genius of Donald Trump* (College Station: Texas A&M University Press, 2020).

42. For a recent analysis, see Jennifer Lackey, *The Epistemology of Groups* (Oxford: Oxford University Press, 2021). For earlier notable treatments of this issue, see Mills, "White Ignorance"; Linda Alcoff, "Epistemologies of Ignorance: Three Types," in *Race and Epistemologies of Ignorance*, ed. Shannon Sullivan and Nancy Tuana (Albany, NY: SUNY Press, 2007).

43. Elizabeth Anderson, "Can We Talk?," Oxford Uehiro lecture series, December 2019, https://www.practicalethics.ox.ac.uk/uehiro-lectures-2019.

44. Kathleen Hall Jamieson and Joseph N. Cappella, *Echo Chamber: Rush Limbaugh and the Conservative Media Establishment* (Oxford: Oxford University Press 2008).

45. C. Thi Nguyen, "Echo Chambers and Epistemic Bubbles," *Episteme* 17, no. 2 (June 2020): 146.

46. For an example of the spread of belief in groundless and bizarre claims in 2020, see: Mallory Newall, "More Than 1 in 3 Americans Believe a 'Deep State' Is Working to Undermine Trump," Ipsos (News), December 30, 2020, https://www.ipsos.com/en-us/news-polls/npr-misinformation-123020.

47. Christopher H. Achen and Larry M. Bartels, *Democracy for Realists* (Princeton, NJ: Princeton University Press 2016), 268.

48. Matthew J. Hornsey, Emily A. Harris, and Kelly S. Fielding, "The Psychological Roots of Anti-vaccination Attitudes: A 24-Nation Investigation," *Health Psychology* 37, no. 4 (April 2018): 307–15.

49. David P. Redlawsk, Andrew J. W. Civettini, and Karen M. Emmerson, "The Affective Tipping Point: Do Motivated Reasoners Ever 'Get It'?," *Political Psychology* 31, no. 4 (2010): 563–93, http://www.jstor.org/stable/20779584.

50. McIntyre, *Post-Truth*, 155.

51. Zakary L. Tormala and Richard E. Petty, "What Doesn't Kill Me Makes Me Stronger: The Effects of Resisting Persuasion on Attitude Certainty," *Journal of Personality and Social Psychology* 83, no. 6 (2002): 1298–313, https://doi.org/10.1037/0022-3514.83.6.1298.

52. McIntyre, *Post-Truth*, 157.

53. Many studies that discuss the psychological phenomenon of politically motivated reasoning focus on social and individual psychology as the domains where a response can be found. This is dubbed "contact theory" by Gordon W. Allport in *The Nature of Prejudice* (Cambridge, MA: Perseus Books, 1954), and more recently by Elizabeth Levy Paluck, Seth A. Green, and Donald Green, "The Contact Hypothesis Re-evaluated," *Behavioural Public Policy* 3, no. 2 (2019): 129–58, https://doi.org/10.1017/bpp.2018.25.

54. Uehiro lectures, as well as Elizabeth Anderson, "Democracy: Instrumental vs. Non-instrumental Value" in *Contemporary Debates in Political Philosophy*, ed. Thomas Christiano and John Philip Christman (Oxford: Wiley-Blackwell, 2009), 213–27.

55. Michael Patrick Lynch, "The Value of Truth," *Boston Review*, February 26, 2021, https://bostonreview.net/articles/michael-patrick-lynch-epistemology-tk/.

56. Logan Strother, Spencer Piston, Ezra Oberstein, Sarah E. Gollust, and Daniel Eisenberg, "College Roommates Have a Modest but Significant Influence on Each Other's Political Ideology," *Proceedings of the National Academy of Sciences* 118, no. 2 (January 2021), https://doi.org/10.1073/pnas.2015514117.

57. This description is obviously idealized, and its application faces many critiques. I do not address these justified critiques here, as I instead focus in this chapter on the epistemic role of higher education institutions in a democracy. For a recent discussion of such critiques see Michael Sandel, *The Tyranny of Merit: What's Become of the Common Good?* (New York: Farrar, Strauss & Giroux, 2020).

58. Conservatives' views of higher education have been increasingly unfavorable since 2016, and cost is a concern across the political spectrum. See A. W. Geiger, "From Universities to Churches, Republicans and Democrats Differ in Views of Major Institutions," Pew Research Center, September 26, 2016, https://www.pewresearch.org/fact-tank/2016/09/26/from-universities-to-churches-republicans-and-democrats-differ-in-views-of-major-institutions.

59. Joan Wallach Scott, *Knowledge, Power, and Academic Freedom* (New York: Columbia University Press, 2019); Joan Wallach Scott, "How the Right Has Weaponized Free Speech," *Chronicle of Higher Education,* January 7, 2018, https://www.chronicle.com /article/how-the-right-weaponized-free-speech/. Some of these tensions are longstanding, as documented in, for example, Elizabeth Anderson, "The Democratic University: The Role of Justice in the Production of Knowledge," *Social Philosophy and Policy* 12, no. 2 (1995): 186–219.

60. Ronald J. Daniels, *What Universities Owe Democracy* (Baltimore: Johns Hopkins University Press, 2021), 180–81.

61. Robert D. Putnam, *Bowling Alone: The Collapse and Revival of American Community* (New York: Simon & Schuster, 2000).

62. Danielle S. Allen, *Talking to Strangers: Anxieties of Citizenship Since Brown v. Board of Education* (Chicago: University of Chicago Press, 2004), 101.

63. Catherine Z. Elgin, *True Enough* (Cambridge, MA: MIT Press, 2017), 172.

64. Broadly, searching for truth requires that knowledge would be a shared aim. See Jonathan E. Adler, "Knowledge, Truth, and Learning," in *A Companion to the Philosophy of Education,* ed. Randall Curren (Malden, MA: Blackwell, 2003), 285–304.

65. I develop this point further in Sigal R. Ben-Porath, *Free Speech on Campus* (Philadelphia: University of Pennsylvania Press, 2017).

66. This does not mean that shutting down a conversation is never the right move, as I discuss elsewhere in this book, and as suggested in Eamonn Callan, "When to Shut Students Up: Civility, Silencing, and Free Speech," *Theory and Research in Education* 9, no. 1 (2011): 3–22, https://doi.org/10.1177/1477878510394352.

67. Eyal, *Crisis of Expertise,* 37.

68. See Achen and Bartels, *Democracy for Realists.*

69. Achen and Bartels, *Democracy for Realists,* 267.

70. Lilliana Mason, *Uncivil Agreement: How Politics Became Our Identity* (Chicago: University of Chicago Press, 2020).

71. "Why Americans Don't Fully Trust Many Who Hold Positions of Power and Responsibility," Pew Research Center, September 19, 2019, https://www.pewresearch.org /politics/2019/09/19/why-americans-dont-fully-trust-many-who-hold-positions-of -power-and-responsibility.

72. Margaret Sullivan, *Ghosting the News: Local Journalism and the Crisis of American Democracy* (New York: Columbia Global Reports, 2020); Lee Shaker, "Dead Newspapers and Citizens' Civic Engagement" *Political Communication* 31, no. 1 (2014): 131–48.

73. For more about the life of Derek Black, see Eli Saslow, *Rising out of Hatred: The Awakening of a White Nationalist* (New York: Anchor Press, 2018).

74. Eric Beerbohm, "Ethics of Polarization" (unpublished manuscript), Microsoft Word file.

CHAPTER 3

1. The order itself was removed from the White House page. For a report about the effect of the order on colleges, see Katherine Mangan, "Colleges Comb Diversity

Programs for Content That Could Trigger Feds," *Chronicle of Higher Education*, October 7, 2020, https://www.chronicle.com/article/colleges-comb-diversity-programs-for-content-that-could-trigger-feds.

2. Elizabeth Anderson, "Epistemic Justice as a Virtue of Social Institutions," *Social Epistemology* 26, no. 2 (2012): 172.

3. Eamonn Callan, "Education in Safe and Unsafe Spaces," *Philosophical Inquiry in Education* 24, no. 1 (November 2016): 64–78. Also see Sigal R. Ben-Porath, *Free Speech on Campus* (Philadelphia: University of Pennsylvania Press, 2017).

4. On the centrality of reducing competition to allow social solidarity, and its importance for sustainable democratic institutions, see Waheed Hussain, "Pitting People Against Each Other," *Philosophy and Public Affairs* 48, no. 1 (Winter 2020): 79–113, https://doi.org/10.1111/papa.12158.

5. Chelsea Schein and Kurt Gray, "The Theory of Dyadic Morality: Reinventing Moral Judgment by Redefining Harm," *Personality and Social Psychology Review* 22, no. 1 (2018): 32–70.

6. Dax D'Orazio, "Expressive Freedom on Campus and the Conceptual Elasticity of Harm" *Canadian Journal of Political Science* 53, no. 4 (September 2020).

7. *Whitney v. California*, 274 U.S. 357 (1927).

8. John Keane, *Violence and Democracy* (Cambridge, UK: Cambridge University Press, 2004), 34–35.

9. Sarah Schulman, *Conflict Is Not Abuse: Overstating Harm, Community Responsibility, and the Duty of Repair* (Vancouver, BC: Arsenal Pulp Press, 2016), 92. I am grateful to Matthew Shafer for conversations about this topic and for clarifying this point for me in his work on epistemic violence.

10. Miranda Fricker, *Epistemic Injustice: Power and the Ethics of Knowing* (Oxford: Oxford University Press, 2007), 32.

11. Kevin L. Nadal, *Microaggressions and Traumatic Stress: Theory, Research, and Clinical Treatment* (Washington, DC: American Psychological Association, 2018), https://doi.org/10.1037/0000073-000.

12. Rae Langton "Hate Speech and the Epistemology of Justice," *Criminal Law and Philosophy* 10 (2016): 868.

13. Fricker, *Epistemic Injustice*, 43.

14. For a discussion on preventing hate speech, which generated a broad legal discussion, see Jeremy Waldron, *The Harm in Hate Speech* (Cambridge, MA: Harvard University Press, 2014).

15. Corey Brettschneider, *When the State Speaks, What Should it Say?* (Princeton, NJ: Princeton University Press, 2012).

16. Seana Valentine Shiffrin, "A Thinker-Based Approach to Freedom of Speech," *Constitutional Commentary* 27, no. 2 (Fall 2011): 287, https://hdl.handle.net/11299/163435.

17. *Speech First, Inc. v. Schlissel*, 939 F.3d 756, 766 (6th Cir. 2019).

18. I am grateful to Monika Greco for a clarifying conversation about this distinction.

19. See, for example, the case of a professor who posted a blog in which he spoke pejoratively about a student in her teaching role. Shawn Johnson, "State Supreme

Court Hears Arguments over Suspension of Marquette Professor," *Wisconsin Public Radio*, April 19, 2018, https://www.wpr.org/state-supreme-court-hears-arguments-over-suspension-marquette-professor. He was correctly punished, though the court ruled against the university, indicating that the punishment was disproportionate to the transgression (among other reasons).

20. See, for example, the case of a Boise State University political science professor who expressed his view that women are not suitable for professions such as engineering and law, and should support their children and families instead. Jenn Selva and Amy Simonson, "Protests Held at Boise State After Professor Says at Conference That Men, Not Women, Should Be Recruited into Fields Like Medicine and Law," *CNN*, December 8, 2021, https://www.cnn.com/2021/12/08/us/boise-state-professor-men-women-studies/index.html.

21. Pippa Norris, "Cancel Culture: Myth or Reality?," *Political Studies* (August 2021): 4, https://doi.org/10.1177/00323217211037023.

22. D'Orazio, "Expressive Freedom," 755–76, 2. D'Orazio is discussing this claim rather than making it.

23. Erec Smith, *A Critique of Anti-Racism in Rhetoric and Composition* (Lanham, MD: Lexington Books, 2020), 11.

24. Christopher L. Eisgruber, "Contested Civility: Free Speech & Inclusivity on Campus" (Inaugural Arlin M. Adams Lecture on Law, Religion, and the First Amendment at the University of Pennsylvania Law School, Philadelphia, PA, November 12, 2019) https://president.princeton.edu/blogs/contested-civility-free-speech-inclusivity-campus.

25. Words are often types of action: for example, think of a sign that reads "Italians need not apply." For a legal discussion of these issues, see Jeremy Waldron, *The Harm in Hate Speech* (Cambridge, MA: Harvard University Press, 2012); for a philosophical analysis, see Rae Langton, "The Authority of Hate Speech," in *Oxford Studies in Philosophy of Law, Volume 3*, ed. John Gardner, Leslie Green, and Brian Leiter (Oxford: Oxford University Press, 2018), 123–52.

26. The United States Court of Appeals for the Sixth Circuit rejected this argument in *Meriwether v. Hartop*, suggesting that the professor cannot be compelled to use speech he does not believe in or speech that stands in opposition to his religious views. I see this as a mistaken decision for reasons that go beyond the current scope of the discussion, particularly as the university provided the professor with good alternatives. See Andrew Koppelman, "Abuse as a Constitutional Right: The Meriwether Case," *The Hill*, April 5, 2021, https://thehill.com/opinion/judiciary/546444-abuse-as-a-constitutional-right-the-meriwether-case.

27. For details about this case at Harvard, see Hannah Natanson, "Harvard Rescinds Acceptances for at Least Ten Students for Obscene Memes," *Harvard Crimson*, June 5, 2017, https://www.thecrimson.com/article/2017/6/5/2021-offers-rescinded-memes/; as well as at Xavier, see Walter Smith-Randolph, "Xavier Revokes Student Athlete's Admission after Racist Social Media Posts," *Local 12*, June 3, 2020, https://local12.com/news/local/xavier-revokes-student-athletes-admission-after-racist-social-media-posts-cincinnati.

28. Elizabeth Anderson, "Can We Talk? Communicating Moral Concern in an Era of Polarized Politics," Oxford Uehiro lecture, December 2019, https://www.practicalethics .ox.ac.uk/uehiro-lectures-2019#tab-1306611, see esp. part 3.

29. Kevin Vallier, *Trust in a Polarized Age* (Oxford: Oxford University Press, 2021), 14.

30. Margaret Levi and Laura Stoker, "Political Trust and Trustworthiness," *Annual Review of Political Science* 3 (June 2000): 475–507. See also Amy E. Lerman, *Good Enough for Government Work: The Public Reputation Crisis in America (And What We Can Do to Fix It)* (Chicago: University of Chicago Press, 2019).

31. Vallier, *Trust*, 6.

32. Tom Bartlett, "A Professor Has Long Used a Racial Slur in Class to Teach Free Speech Law. No More, He Says," *Chronicle of Higher Education*, March 7, 2019, https:// www.chronicle.com/article/a-professor-has-long-used-a-racial-slur-in-class-to-teach -free-speech-law-no-more-he-says/.

33. Geoffrey R. Stone, Marianne Bertrand, Angela Olinto, Mark Siegler, David A. Strauss, Kenneth Warren, and Amanda Woodward, "Report of the Committee on Freedom of Expression" (Chicago: The University of Chicago, 2014), https://provost .uchicago.edu/sites/default/files/documents/reports/FOECommitteeReport.pdf. This report was later widely disseminated under the title 'Chicago Statement' or 'Chicago Principles,' and was adopted by organizations devoted to the protection of campus free speech, such as the Foundation for Individual Rights in Education, as well as dozens of universities in the United States and in other countries.

34. Randall L. Kennedy and Eugene Volokh, "Quoting Epithets in the Classroom and Beyond" (Harvard Public Law Working Paper No. 20-38, August 29, 2020, draft), http:// dx.doi.org./10.2139/ssrn.3683139.

35. Kathryn Rubino, "Law School N-Word Controversy Is More Complicated Than It Appears at First Glance," *Above the Law*, January 13, 2021, https://abovethelaw.com /2021/01/law-school-n-word-controversy-is-more-complicated-than-it-appears-at -first-glance; for some additional details, see Andrew Koppelman, "Is This Law Profes- sor Really a Homicidal Threat?," *Chronicle of Higher Education*, January 19, 2021, https:// www.chronicle.com/article/is-this-law-professor-really-a-homicidal-threat.

36. For a summary of the events, see Greta Anderson, "Student Strike at Bryn Mawr College Ends," *Inside Higher Ed*, November 24, 2020, https://www.insidehighered.com /quicktakes/2020/11/24/student-strike-bryn-mawr-college-ends. See also Adrian Velonis, "Bryn Mawr Students Issue Demands for Administration, Initiate Strike," *Bi- College News*, November 5, 2020, https://bicollegenews.com/2020/11/05/bryn-mawr -students-issue-demands-for-administration-initiate-strike.

37. Jennifer Morton discusses the social, ethical, and epistemic challenges in *Moving Up Without Losing Your Way* (Princeton, NJ: Princeton University Press, 2019).

38. Derek Anderson, "An Epistemological Conception of Safe Spaces," *Social Episte- mology* 35, no. 3 (2021): 308, https://doi.org/10.1080/02691728.2020.1855485.

39. For a discussion on the growing role of administrators, see Jonathan Zimmer- man, *Campus Politics: What Everyone Needs to Know* (New York: Oxford University Press, 2016).

40. Kennedy and Volokh, "Quoting Epithets," 14.

41. Herman Cappelen, Ernest Lepore, and Matthew McKeever, "Quotation," in *The Stanford Encyclopedia of Philosophy*, ed. Edward N. Zalta (Summer 2020 Edition), https://plato.stanford.edu/entries/quotation.

42. Luvell Anderson, "Why So Serious? An Inquiry on Racist Jokes," *Journal of Social Philosophy* (published ahead of print, November 3, 2020), https://doi.org/10.1111/josp .12384.

43. Kennedy and Volokh, "Quoting Epithets," 12.

44. I offered some of the arguments in this section in *Free Speech on Campus* (2017), and briefly reassert and develop them here, to situate them within the broader democratic context.

45. Geoffrey R. Stone et al., "Report of the Committee on Freedom of Expression."

46. Bruce Ackerman, "Why Dialogue?," *Journal of Philosophy* 86, no. 1 (1989): 5–22.

47. Candice Delmas, *The Duty to Resist: When Disobedience Should Be Uncivil* (Oxford: Oxford University Press, 2018).

48. Waheed Hussain, "The Common Good," *Stanford Encyclopedia of Philosophy*, February 16, 2018, https://plato.stanford.edu/archives/spr2018/entries/common-good.

49. Matthew S. Levendusky "Americans, Not Partisans: Can Priming American National Identity Reduce Affective Polarization?," *Journal of Politics* 80, no. 1 (2018): 59–70.

50. Sigal R. Ben-Porath, "Citizenship as Shared Fate," *Educational Theory* 62, no. 4 (August 2012): 381–95.

51. Mansur Lalljee, Geoffrey Evans, Shreya Sarawgi, and Katrin Voltmer. "Respect Your Enemies: Orientations Towards Political Opponents and Political Involvement in Britain," *International Journal of Public Opinion Research* 25, no. 1 (2013): 119–31; Sonya Dal Cin, Mark P. Zanna, and Geoffrey T. Fong, "Narrative Persuasion and Overcoming Resistance," in *Resistance and Persuasion*, ed. Eric S. Knowles and Jay A. Linn (University of Arkansas Press, 2004), 175–91.

52. Danielle Allen, *Our Declaration: A Reading of the Declaration of Independence* (New York: Norton, 2014), 188.

53. Morton, *Moving Up*; see also Anthony Laden, "Teaching, Indoctrination and Trust" (unpublished manuscript), Microsoft Word file.

54. Many such programs have been developed in recent years. For example, Braver Angels (see study on its effects in the next endnote); ICDP; PEN America; Center for Free Speech and Civic Engagement (multiple programs); Paideia; National Coalition Against Censorship; ACLU; University of Richmond workshops. I discuss these again in chapter 5.

55. Hannah Baron, Robert Blair, Donghyun D. Choi, Laura Gamboa, Jessica Gottlieb, Amanda L. Robinson, Steven Rosenzweig, Megan Turnbull, and Emily West, "Can Americans Depolarize? Assessing the Effects of Reciprocal Group Reflection on Partisan Polarization," OSF Preprints, May 10, 2021, https://doi.org/10.31219/osf.io/3x7z8.

56. Joshua Kalla and David Broockman, "Voter Outreach Campaigns Can Reduce Affective Polarization Among Implementing Political Activists," OSF Preprints, June 18, 2021, https://doi.org/10.31219/osf.io/5yahr.

57. See Eli Saslow, *Rising out of Hatred: The Awakening of a White Nationalist* (New York: Anchor, 2018).

58. Joshua Kalla and David Broockman, "Reducing Exclusionary Attitudes through Interpersonal Conversation: Evidence from Three Field Experiments," *American Political Science Review* 114, no. 2 (2020): 410–25, https://doi.org/10.1017/S0003055419000923.

59. Matthew Levendusky, *We Need to Talk: How Cross-Party Dialogue Reduces Affective Polarization* (Cambridge, UK: Cambridge University Press, 2021).

60. Anthony Laden, *Reasoning: A Social Picture* (Oxford: Oxford University Press, 2012).

61. Eric Beerbohm and Ryan W. Davis, "The Buck-Passing Account of the Common Good," *Journal of Political Philosophy* 25, no. 4 (2017), 12.

62. See Alexander Dietz, "What We Together Ought to Do," *Ethics* 126, no. 1 (2016): 955–82.

63. People experiencing this disconnection include seniors but are common across other age groups as well, in the United States and other countries. See "The 'Loneliness Epidemic,'" Health Resources Services Administration, January 2019, https://www.hrsa.gov/enews/past-issues/2019/january-17/loneliness-epidemic; Bianca DiJulio, Liz Hamel, Cailey Muñana, and Mollyann Brodie, "Loneliness and Social Isolation in the United States, the United Kingdom, and Japan: An International Survey," Kaiser Family Foundation, August 30, 2018, https://www.kff.org/report-section/loneliness-and-social-isolation-in-the-united-states-the-united-kingdom-and-japan-an-international-survey-introduction.

64. Vivek Murthy, *Together: The Healing Power of Social Connection in a Sometimes Lonely World* (New York: Harper Collins, 2020).

65. See, for example, Living Room Conversations (https://livingroomconversations.org/); Braver Angels (https://braverangels.org); and Bridge USA (https://www.bridgeusa.org).

66. For an example, see H.B. 1218, 93rd Gen. Assemb., Reg. Sess. (Ark. 2021). Arkansas's house bill was proposed, but it failed to pass. Similar "divisive topics" bills were proposed or passed in twenty states in 2020 and 2021.

67. H.B. 1218, 93rd Gen. Assemb., Reg. Sess. (Ark. 2021).

68. Allen, *Talking to Strangers*, xix.

CHAPTER 4

1. I am grateful to Adrienne Stang for reading an early draft of this chapter and for providing many insightful suggestions that have helped improve it.

2. See, for example, the growing Campus Compact network: "A national coalition of colleges and universities committed to the public purposes of higher education. We build democracy through civic education and community development," (mission statement) "Who We Are," Campus Compact, https://compact.org/who-we-are/.

3. See, for example, a recent effort to revitalize civic education in schools, which includes curricular materials and implementation guidance, recognizing the need for a more robust education for democracy, as well as for assessment that is aligned with state standards, "Roadmap to Educating for American Democracy," Educating for American Democracy, 2021, https://www.educatingforamericandemocracy.org.

4. Ronald J. Daniels, *What Universities Owe Democracy* (Baltimore: Johns Hopkins University Press, 2021), 96.

5. Aaron C. Weinschenk and Christopher T. Dawes, "Civic Education in High School and Voter Turnout in Adulthood," *British Journal of Political Science* (2021): 1–15, https://doi.org/10.1017/S0007123420000435.

6. See one such effort in Frederick M. Hess and Pedro A. Noguera, *A Search for Common Ground: Conversations about the Toughest Questions in K–12 Education* (New York: Teachers College Press, 2021).

7. Catherine J. Ross, *Lessons in Censorship* (Cambridge, MA: Harvard University Press, 2005).

8. Bruce Maxwell, Kevin McDonough, and David I. Waddington, "Broaching the Subject: Developing Law-Based Principles for Teacher Free Speech in the Classroom," *Teaching and Teacher Education* 70 (2018): 196–203.

9. Diana Hess and Paula McAvoy, *The Political Classroom: Evidence and Ethics in Democratic Education* (London: Routledge, 2014).

10. The majority of states require just one semester of civics (or similar) course, though some are passing bills, especially since 2020, that require a greater investment in civic education.

11. *Tinker v. Des Moines Independent Community School District*, 393 U.S. 503 (1969).

12. *Morse v. Frederick*, 551 U.S. 393 (2007).

13. Elizabeth Anderson, *Private Government: How Employers Rule Our Lives (and Why We Don't Talk about It)* (Princeton, NJ: Princeton University Press, 2017).

14. Justin Driver, *The Schoolhouse Gate: Public Education, The Supreme Court and the Battle for the American Mind* (New York: Penguin Random House, 2018), 72.

15. Catherine J. Ross, *Lessons in Censorship* (Cambridge, MA: Harvard University Press, 2015).

16. *Tinker v. Des Moines Independent Community School District*, 393 U.S. 503 (1969).

17. Frank LoMonte and Ann Marie Tamburro, "From After-School Detention to the Detention Center: How Unconstitutional School-Disruption Laws Place Children at Risk of Prosecution for 'Speech Crimes,'" *Lewis and Clark Law Review* 25, no. 1 (2021): 1–64, https://law.lclark.edu/live/files/31603-5-lomonte-tamburro-article-251pdf.

18. Linda Greenhouse, "Vote Against Banner Shows Divide on Speech in Schools," *New York Times*, June 26, 2007, https://www.nytimes.com/2007/06/26/washington/26speech.html.

19. "Rhode Island District Court Applauds but Dismisses a Suit Seeking to Establish a Federal Constitutional Right to a Civic Education," *Teachers College Newsroom*, Columbia University, October 16, 2020, https://www.tc.columbia.edu/articles/2020/october/ri-court-dismisses-suit-to-establish-constitutional-right-to-a-civic-education.

20. As sociologist Richard Arum has noted, school discipline over the past fifty years has suffered from an increase in court supervision and the attendant rise of bureaucratic formalism, robbing schools of their autonomy and moral authority. Richard Arum, *Judging School Discipline: The Crisis of Moral Authority* (Cambridge, MA: Harvard University Press, 2005). For a discussion in the context of school discipline, see Campbell F. Scrib-

ner and Bryan R. Warnick, *Spare the Rod: Punishment and the Moral Community of Schools* (Chicago: University of Chicago Press, 2021).

21. *The First Amendment on Campus 2020 Report: College Students' Views of Free Expression* (Miami: Knight Foundation, 2020), https://knightfoundation.org/wp-content /uploads/2020/05/First-Amendment-on-Campus-2020.pdf.

22. *Hazelwood School District v. Kuhlmeier*, 484 U.S. 260 (1988).

23. Daniel Hart and James Youniss, *Renewing Democracy in Young America* (New York: Oxford University Press, 2018), 57.

24. See, for example, reports and resources on the breadth of learning that is required for a robust civic education at the Democracy Knowledge Project, https://www .democraticknowledgeproject.org/.

25. *Our Common Purpose: Reinventing American Democracy for the 21st Century* (report of the Commission on the Practice of Democratic Citizenship, Cambridge, MA: American Academy of Arts and Sciences, 2020), https://www.amacad.org/sites/default/files /publication/downloads/2020-Democratic-Citizenship_Our-Common-Purpose_0.pdf.

26. An annual poll traces public school attendance and the attitudes of the public, including both parents and others, toward public schools; it shows high general levels of trust, though those are lower for minority groups, and have fluctuated during the COVID-19 pandemic. See most recently, "53rd Annual PDK Poll of the Public's Attitudes Toward the Public Schools," (Arlington, VA: Phi Delta Kappan, 2021), as well as prior years' polls, all available at https://pdkpoll.org/.

27. Stephen Sawchuk, "$1 Billion for Civics Education? Bipartisan Bill Eyes Dramatic Federal Investment," *Education Week*, September 17, 2020, https://www.edweek .org/education/1-billion-for-civics-education-bipartisan-bill-eyes-dramatic-federal -investment/2020/09.

28. See Harry Brighouse, "Civic Education and Liberal Legitimacy," *Ethics* 108, no. 4 (July 1998): 719–45.

29. Amy Gutmann, *Democratic Education* (Princeton, NJ: Princeton University Press, 1999).

30. For policy suggestions, see "Policy Roadmap," 50x2026, https://www.50x2026 .org. For more on curricular advocacy, see Generation Citizen (website), https:// generationcitizen.org.

31. Quassim Cassam, *Conspiracy Theories* (Cambridge, UK: Polity, 2019), chap. 4.

32. This vignette is a lightly edited version of a longer story reported by Sarah Schwartz, "Disinformation Is Rampant. Here's How Teachers Are Combatting It," *Education Week*, November 25, 2020, https://www.edweek.org/teaching-learning /disinformation-is-rampant-heres-how-teachers-are-combatting-it/2020/11.

33. "U.S. Media Literacy Policy Report 2020" (Watertown, MA: Media Literacy Now, 2020), https://medialiteracynow.org/u-s-media-literacy-policy-report-2020.

34. Jon Henley, "How Finland Starts Its Fight against Fake News in Primary Schools," *Guardian*, January 29, 2020, https://www.theguardian.com/world/2020/jan/28/fact -from-fiction-finlands-new-lessons-in-combating-fake-news.

35. "Fake News and Information Literacy," University of Oregon Libraries, December 9, 2021, https://researchguides.uoregon.edu/fakenews/sift.

36. Nicole M. Lee, "Fake News, Phishing, and Fraud: A Call for Research on Digital Media Literacy Education beyond the Classroom," *Communication Education* 67, no. 4 (2018): 460–66, https://doi.org/10.1080/03634523.2018.1503313.

37. Joel Breakstone, Mark Smith, and Sam Wineburg, *Students' Civic Online Reasoning: A National Portrait* (Stanford, CA: Stanford History Education Groups, 2019).

38. Renee Hobbs, *Mind over Media: Propaganda Education for the Digital Age* (New York: Norton, 2020).

39. For more about SIFT, see Mike Caulfield, "SIFT: The Four Moves," *Hapgood*, June 19, 2019, https://hapgood.us/2019/06/19/sift-the-four-moves. Also see NJIT Library, "How to Evaluate Information Sources: CRAAP Test," New Jersey Institute of Technology, updated August 5, 2021, https://researchguides.njit.edu/evaluate/CRAAP.

40. Nicole A. Cooke, "Posttruth, Truthiness, and Alternative Facts: Information Behavior and Critical Information Consumption for a New Age," *Library Quarterly* 87, no. 3 (2017): 211–21.

41. For an example of how efforts to debunk vaccine myths backfire, see Cornelia Betsch and Katharina Sachse, "Debunking Vaccination Myths: Strong Risk Negations Can Increase Perceived Vaccination Risks," *Health Psychology* 32, no. 2 (2013): 146–55, https://doi.org/10.1037/a0027387.

42. See, for example, *The College, Career, and Civic Life (C3) Framework for Social Studies State Standards: Guidance for Enhancing the Rigor of K–12 Civics, Economics, Geography, and History* (Silver Spring, MD: National Council for the Social Studies [NCSS], 2013).

43. Joel Breakstone, Mark Smith, Sam Wineburg, Amie Rapaport, Jill Carle, Marshall Garland, and Anna Saavedra, "Students' Civic Online Reasoning: A National Portrait" (Palo Alto, CA: Stanford History Education Group & Gibson Consulting, November 14, 2019), https://sheg.stanford.edu/students-civic-online-reasoning.

44. Paul Mihailidis and Benjamin Thevenin, "Media Literacy as a Core Competency for Engaged Citizenship in Participatory Democracy," *American Behavioral Scientist* 57 (2013): 1611–22, https://doi.org/10.1177/0002764213489015.

45. See, for example, Sarah McGrew, "Learning to Evaluate: An Intervention in Civic Online Reasoning," *Computers & Education* 145 (February 2020), https://doi.org/10.1016/j.compedu.2019.103711.

46. "NCTE Annual Reports," National Council of Teachers of English, 2019, https://ncte.org/wp-content/uploads/2020/01/2019_Annual_Reports-1.pdf.

47. See Adam Laats and Harvey Siegel, *Teaching Evolution in a Creation Nation* (Chicago: University of Chicago Press, 2016).

48. Joseph Kahne and Benjamin Bowyer, "Educating for Democracy in a Partisan Age: Confronting the Challenges of Motivated Reasoning and Misinformation," *American Educational Research Journal* 54, no. 1 (February 2017): 3–34.

49. Hans Martens and Renee Hobbs, "How Media Literacy Supports Civic Engagement in a Digital Age," *Atlantic Journal of Communication* 23, no. 2 (2015): 120–37, https://doi.org/10.1080/15456870.2014.961636.

50. Monica Bulger and Patrick Davison, "The Promises, Challenges, and Futures of Media Literacy," Data and Society, February 21, 2018, https://datasociety.net/library/the-promises-challenges-and-futures-of-media-literacy.

51. David Fleming, "Fear of Persuasion in the English Language Arts," *College English* 81, no. 6 (2019): 508–41.

52. Joseph Kahne and Benjamin Bowyer, "Can Media Literacy Education Increase Digital Engagement in Politics?," *Learning, Media and Technology* 44 no. 2 (2019): 211–24, https://doi.org/1080/17439884.2019.1601108.

53. Mihailidis and Thevenin, "Media Literacy as a Core Competency," 1619.

54. This is an edited version (for length) of an incident reported, based on a classroom video, and discussed in Abby Reisman, Lisette Enumah, and Lightning Jay, "Interpretive Frames for Responding to Racially Stressful Moments in History Discussions," *Theory & Research in Social Education* 48, no. 3 (2020), 321–45, https://doi.org/10.1080 /00933104.2020.1718569.

55. Amy Gutmann, Dennis Thompson, and Sigal Ben-Porath, "Teaching Competition and Cooperation" (paper presented at the NOMOS 2021 conference on Civic Education in Polarized Times, October 29, 2021).

56. See Rachel Wahl, "Just Talk? Learning across Political Divides on College Campuses," *Theory and Research in Education* 17, no. 2 (2019): 139–64.

57. Paula McAvoy, "Can Schools Combat Partisan Belligerency?," *Dewey Studies* 4, no. 1 (2020): 128. In this article, McAvoy discusses an approach to citizenship education during wartime, which I developed in Sigal R. Ben-Porath, *Citizenship under Fire: Democratic Education in Times of Conflict* (Princeton, NJ: Princeton University Press, 2006).

58. Scribner and Warnick, *Spare the Rod*, 105.

59. There are various pedagogical approaches to facilitating hard conversations in class. See one useful example in Walter C. Parker, "Structured Academic Controversy: What It Can Be," in *Making Discussions Work*, ed. Jane Lo (New York: Teachers College Press, 2021).

60. For a broad discussion of curricular as well as pedagogical approaches to teaching hard histories, see Abby Reisman, "Entering the Historical Problem Space: Whole-Class Text-Based Discussion in History Class," *Teachers College Record* 117, no. 2 (2015): 1–44.

61. McAvoy, "Can Schools Combat Partisan Belligerency?," 128. See also Paula McAvoy and Gregory E. McAvoy, "Can Debate and Deliberation Reduce Partisan Divisions? Evidence from a Study of High School Students," *Peabody Journal of Education* 96, no. 3 (2021): 275–84.

62. Will Kymlicka, "Education for Citizenship," in *Politics in the Vernacular: Nationalism, Multiculturalism, and Citizenship* (Oxford: Oxford University Press, 2001), 296.

63. Diana E. Hess, *Controversy in the Classroom: The Democratic Power of Discussion* (New York: Routledge, 2009), 14.

64. Hess and McAvoy, *The Political Classroom*, 46–51.

65. For more on teachers' speech rights in class, including the need for them to be secure in their jobs as well as their need to feel secure in their ability to lead classroom discussion, see Maxwell, McDonough, and Waddington, "Broaching the Subject."

66. Hess, *Controversy in the Classroom*, 162.

67. Hess and McAvoy, *The Political Classroom*, 8.

68. Civic capacity tracks economic resources and educational achievement. In comparing measures of success in these domains, income and wealth correlate with mea-

sures of achievement on standardized tests, as well as educational attainment; both of these are strongly correlated with formal civic measures such as registering to vote and voting, contacting elected officials, and participating in campaigns. The civic empowerment gap demonstrates the importance of developing young people's ability to communicate across these and other divides, and to be able to participate effectively in both the competition for power and influence and in the cooperative venture that makes daily democratic life possible. See Meira Levinson, "The Civic Empowerment Gap: Defining the Problem and Locating Solutions," in *Handbook of Research on Civic Engagement*, ed. Lonnie Sherrod, Judith Torney-Purta, and Constance A. Flanagan (Hoboken, NJ: John Wiley & Sons, 2010), 331–61.

CHAPTER 5

1. Julia A. Minson and Frances S. Chen, "Receptiveness to Opposing Views: Conceptualization and Integrative Review," *Personality and Social Psychology Review*, published ahead of print December 29, 2021.

2. Annette C. Baier, "Trust," in *The Tanner Lectures* (Princeton University, March 6–8, 1991), 168–69, https://tannerlectures.utah.edu/_resources/documents/a-to-z/b/baier92.pdf.

3. "Report of the Independent Review of Freedom of Speech in Australian Higher Education Providers," (Australia: Department of Education and Training, 2019), https://www.education.gov.au/independent-review-freedom-speech-australian-higher-education-providers.

4. Some regional governments in Canada, particularly conservative ones, have required that universities adopt free speech policies similar to the Chicago Statement. Also see a statement from Wilfrid Laurier University following some public controversies: "Statement on Freedom of Expression," Senate of Wilfrid Laurier University, 2018, https://www.wlu.ca/about/discover-laurier/freedom-of-expression/statement.html.

5. See report on disagreements over a "pro-colonialism" professor at Oxford, in James McDougall, "The History of Empire Isn't about Pride—Or Guilt," *Guardian*, January 3, 2018, https://www.theguardian.com/commentisfree/2018/jan/03/history-empire-pride-guilt-truth-oxford-nigel-biggar.

6. Civic culture is the relationship among compatriots, which is less intimate than the relationships we have with family or friends, but are still interpersonal—they relate to people, real and imagined, rather than to institutions or constructs such as "the nation."

7. See summary of research in T. S. Dee, "Education and Civic Engagement," in *The Economics of Education*, 2nd ed., ed. Steve Bradley and Colin Green (London: Academic Press, 2020), 103–8.

8. See Amy E. Lerman, *Good Enough for Government Work: The Public Reputation Crisis in America (And What We Can Do to Fix It)* (Chicago: University of Chicago Press, 2019).

9. "53rd Annual PDK Poll of the Public's Attitudes Toward the Public Schools," (Arlington, VA: Phi Delta Kappan, 2021), https://pdkpoll.org.

10. "State of Public Trust in Local News," Knight Foundation and Gallup, October 29, 2019, https://knightfoundation.org/reports/state-of-public-trust-in-local-news.

11. John Stuart Mill, *On Liberty* (London: Walter Scott, 1859; Project Gutenberg, 2011), 28, https://www.gutenberg.org/files/34901/34901-h/34901-h.htm.

12. For far more detailed accounts of free speech as a democratic value, see Seana Valentine Shiffrin, *Speech Matters: On Lying, Morality, and the Law* (Princeton, NJ: Princeton University Press, 2014); Corey Brettschneider, *When the State Speaks, What Should It Say? How Democracies Can Protect Expression and Promote Equality* (Princeton, NJ: Princeton University Press, 2012).

13. Shiffrin, *Speech Matters*, 182.

14. This is the subject of Shiffrin's chapter on "Sincerity and Institutional Values," in which she argues that within the reasonable institutional expectations from researchers, transparency and sincerity are paramount; and even with regard to anodyne lies, "their use in academic research stands in problematic tension with the values the university is supposed to embody and champion." Shiffrin, *Speech Matters*, 183.

15. As discussed in chapter 3. See a detailed and thoughtful account in Nadine Strossen, *Hate: Why We Should Resist It with Free Speech, Not Censorship* (Oxford: Oxford University Press, 2018).

16. As is the case with instructors who fail to teach relevant and accurate content. A striking recent example was an archaeology professor who during a virtual panel, when his unrelated point of order was not accepted, used Nazi rhetoric and a Nazi salute to express his dissatisfaction. See Hannah Gross, "Penn Professor Uses Nazi Phrase and Salute at Archaeology Conference, Sparking Outrage," *Daily Pennsylvanian*, January 10, 2021, https://www.thedp.com/article/2021/01/nazi-salute-phrase-archaeology-conference-penn-professor-robert-schuyler.

17. For some recent state-level legislative efforts to regulate classroom speech and syllabus content, see Lindsay Ellis, "No 'Social Justice' in the Classroom: Statehouses Renew Scrutiny of Speech at Public Colleges," *Chronicle of Higher Education*, February 3, 2021, https://www.chronicle.com/article/no-social-justice-in-the-classroom-new-state-scrutiny-of-speech-at-public-colleges.

18. Keith Whittington, *Speak Freely: Why Universities Should Defend Free Speech* (Princeton, NJ: Princeton University Press, 2018).

19. Elizabeth Anderson, "What Is the Point of Equality?," *Ethics* 109, no. 2 (January 1999): 287–337.

20. For a discussion of a broad model for revitalizing democracy, including both institutional and civic dimensions, see Our Common Purpose, *Reinventing American Democracy for the 21st Century* (Cambridge, MA: American Academy of Arts & Sciences, June 2020), https://www.amacad.org/ourcommonpurpose.

21. Kevin Vallier, *Trust in a Polarized Age* (Oxford: Oxford University Press, 2021), 6.

22. Erwin Chemerinsky, "Tobriner Memorial Lecture: Free Speech on Campus," *Hastings Law Journal* 69, no. 5 (2018): 1347. Also see critical legal discussion of this leading vision and related views in Chris Demaske, *Free Speech and Hate Speech in the United States: The Limits of Toleration* (New York: Routledge, 2020). See chapter 8 in particular.

23. Strossen, *Hate*, 182.

24. Suzanne Nossel, *Dare to Speak* (New York: Harper Collins, 2020).

25. Suzanne B. Goldberg, "Free Expression on Campus: Mitigating the Costs of Contentious Speakers," *Harvard Journal of Law & Public Policy* 41, no. 1 (2018): 163.

26. Matthew W. Finkin and Robert C. Post, *For the Common Good: Principles of American Academic Freedom* (New Haven, CT: Yale University Press, 2009), 2.

27. Finkin and Post, *For the Common Good*, 2.

28. David Folkenflik, "UNC Journalism School Tried to Give Nikole Hannah-Jones Tenure. A Top Donor Objected," *NPR*, June 21, 2021, https://www.npr.org/2021/06/21/1007778651/journalism-race-and-the-fight-over-nikole-hannah-jones-tenure-at-unc.

29. Jennifer Larson, Mark McNeilly, and Timothy J. Ryan, "Free Expression and Constructive Dialogue at the University of North Carolina at Chapel Hill" (report, The University of North Carolina at Chapel Hill, March 2, 2020), https://fecdsurveyreport.web.unc.edu/files/2020/02/UNC-Free-Expression-Report.pdf.

30. Michael Sandel, *The Tyranny of Merit* (Cambridge, MA: Harvard University Press, 2020), 211.

31. John Gramlich, "Young Americans Are Less Trusting of Other People—and Key Institutions—Than Their Elders," Pew Research Center, August 6, 2019, https://www.pewresearch.org/fact-tank/2019/08/06/young-americans-are-less-trusting-of-other-people-and-key-institutions-than-their-elders.

32. Hans Pitnik and Martin Rode, "Radical Distrust: Are Economic Policy Attitudes Tempered by Social Trust?," WIFO Working Papers, no. 594 (December 18, 2019), http://www.wifo.ac.at/wwa/pubid/62259.

33. Mark Warren, "Trust and Democracy," in *The Oxford Handbook of Social and Political Trust*, ed. Eric Uslaner (Oxford: Oxford University Press, 2018), 75–94. See discussion in Vallier, *Trust in a Polarized Age*, 240.

34. Danielle S. Allen, *Talking to Strangers: Anxieties of Citizenship Since Brown v. Board of Education* (Chicago: University of Chicago Press, 2004); Nancy L. Rosenblum, *Good Neighbors: The Democracy of Everyday Life in America* (Princeton, NJ: Princeton University Press, 2016).

35. Ronald J. Daniels, *What Universities Owe Democracy* (Baltimore: Johns Hopkins University Press, 2021), 190.

36. Elizabeth Anderson, "John Stuart Mill and Experiments in Living" *Ethics* 102, no. 1 (1991): 4–26.

37. Michael Sandel, *The Tyranny of Merit: What's Become of the Common Good?* (New York: Farrar, Strauss & Giroux, 2020).

38. Sandel, *The Tyranny of Merit*.

39. One exception is a module I helped to develop that is presented online to new University of Pennsylvania students prior to their arrival on campus. A few other examples are the civic engagement and free speech module that is part of the new student orientations at Purdue and Princeton, as well as the Johns Hopkins one described by Ronald Daniels in *What Universities Owe Democracy*. There have been other sporadic efforts, such as the Chicago letter, which I discuss below. There may be a few others, but it is decidedly not a common focus in new student orientations.

40. For the results of this survey, see Sarah Hurtado, Allison BrckaLorenz, Lesley Sisaket, and Sylvia Washington, "Difficult Discourse and Critical Pedagogies: A Large-Scale Mixed-Methods Exploration of Faculty Practice," (virtual paper presentation, Annual Meeting for the Association for the Study of Higher Education, 2020) https://scholarworks.iu.edu/dspace/handle/2022/25957; also see https://www.chronicle.com/article/teaching-in-the-age-of-disinformation.

41. For a discussion of the current landscape in the United Kingdom, see Alison Scott-Baumann and Simon Perfect, *Freedom of Speech in Universities: Islam, Charities and Counter-terrorism* (London: Routledge, 2021), https://doi.org/10.4324/9780429289835.

42. Sigal R. Ben-Porath, *Free Speech on Campus* (Philadelphia: University of Pennsylvania Press, 2017).

43. The history of the legal and social struggle over affirmative action goes well beyond the scope of the current discussion. While much of it has focused on Black and white students, the focus of legal cases in recent years has been Asian students, especially in regard to the argument that they are discriminated against by Harvard and other elite institutions. For their arguments and legal steps taken, see "Help Us Eliminate Race and Ethnicity from College Admissions," Students for Fair Admissions, 2022, https://studentsforfairadmissions.org/.

44. See Masha Gessen, "Does the Far Right Have a Place at Academic Conferences?," *New Yorker*, October 26, 2017, https://www.newyorker.com/news/our-columnists/does-the-far-right-have-a-place-at-academic-conferences.

45. Private institutions have greater autonomy in this domain than public ones, as the latter are limited by the First Amendment's demand for neutrality by governmental actors (among which public universities are counted). See Erwin Chemerinsky and Howard Gillman, *Free Speech on Campus* (New Haven, CT: Yale University Press, 2017).

46. Michael Powell, "Inside a Battle Over Race, Class and Power at Smith College," *New York Times*, February 24, 2021, https://www.nytimes.com/2021/02/24/us/smith-college-race.html.

47. I benefitted from public discussions about this matter with Cerri Banks, as well as another public conversation with Henry Reichman and Brian Soucek, under the auspices of the Center for Free Speech and Civic Engagement. The events were organized and expertly led by Michelle Deutchman, and their recordings are available at the center's website: https://freespeechcenter.universityofcalifornia.edu.

48. Corey Brettschneider, *When the State Speaks, What Should it Say?* (Princeton, NJ: Princeton University Press 2012), 71.

49. See an extended statement about the State of the University from Princeton's president Christopher Eisgruber, who makes the case for this dual-layer commitment in his 2021 letter to members of Princeton's community: Christopher Eisgruber, "The University's Role in a Time of Crisis," State of the University Letter, Princeton University, February 2021, https://president.princeton.edu/sites/president/files/state_of_the_university_letter_2021.pdf.

50. "An Update and Overview of Princeton University's Ongoing Efforts to Combat Systemic Racism," Office of Communications, Princeton University, September 2,

2020, https://www.princeton.edu/news/2020/09/02/update-and-overview-princeton -universitys-ongoing-efforts-combat-systemic-racism. This statement prompted an investigation by the Department of Education, which was seen as a political retaliatory move and was dropped at the start of the Biden administration. Granted, a private and well-resourced institution like Princeton has an easier time taking on such a significant response to systemic racism and the political ire it raised at the time.

51. Diana Hess, "Teaching in the Tip: Controversies about What Is Controversial," in *Controversy in the Classroom: The Democratic Power of Discussion* (New York: Routledge, 2009), 113–30.

52. See Deborah Lipstadt, *Denial: Holocaust History on Trial* (New York: Ecco, 2016).

53. This technique is described along with some similar inclusive pedagogical practices in "Race, Class, Culture," chap. 3 in *A Handbook for Engaging Difficult Dialogues in the Classroom*, ed. Kay Landis (Anchorage: University of Alaska Anchorage and Alaska Pacific University, 2008), https://www.uaa.alaska.edu/academics/institutional -effectiveness/_documents/3-race-class-culture.pdf.

54. Loretta Ross, "I'm a Black Feminist. I Think Call-Out Culture Is Toxic," *New York Times*, August 17, 2019, https://www.nytimes.com/2019/08/17/opinion/sunday/cancel -culture-call-out.html. Also see Loretta Ross's forthcoming book, *Calling in the Calling Out Culture: Detoxing Our Movement* (New York: Simon & Schuster).

55. "Engaged Listening Project," Middlebury College, 2018, https://engagedlistening .middcreate.net. I discuss this case in detail in my 2017 book *Free Speech on Campus*.

56. Similarly, in 2017, the Association of Governing Boards circulated a primer for its members on current tensions and ways to support free expression on campus: "Freedom of Speech on Campus: Guidelines for Governing Boards and Institutional Leaders" (Washington, DC: AGB Press, 2017), https://www.agb.org/sites/default/files/u27335 /report_2017_free_speech.pdf.

57. "Board of Regents Policy Manual: Freedom of Expression," University System of Georgia, updated January 2018, https://www.usg.edu/policymanual/section6/C2653.

58. Vanessa Miller, "After Recent Free Speech Controversies, Iowa Board of Regents Instigates Review of University Policies," *Gazette*, November 20, 2020, https://www .thegazette.com/subject/news/education/after-recent-free-speech-controversies-iowa -board-of-regents-instigates-review-of-university-policies-20201120.

59. For more on limiting student expression, see the section below on disruption. For more on limiting faculty speech, refer to recent cases in which policy-makers worked to collect syllabi about specific topics or forbid the teaching of specific views on race (such as critical race theory, or the 1619 Project).

60. Daniels, *What Universities Owe Democracy*, 227.

61. Cass Sunstein, "The Law of Group Polarization," *Journal of Political Philosophy* 10, no. 2 (2002): 175–95.

62. Corrado Fumagalli, "Counterspeech and Ordinary Citizens: How? When?," *Political Theory* 49, no. 6 (December 2021): 1021–47, https://doi.org/10.1177 /0090591720984724.

63. Rae Langton, "Blocking as Counter-Speech," in *New Work on Speech Acts*, ed. Daniel Harris, Daniel Fogal, and Matt Moss (New York: Oxford University Press 2017), 10.

64. The Chicago guidance on disruption is provided in a detailed report: "Revised Final Report of the Committee on University Discipline for Disruptive Conduct" (Chicago: University of Chicago, 2017), https://provost.uchicago.edu.

65. "Sec. 900-23: UCI Guidance Concerning Disruption of University Activities," UC Irvine Vice Chancellor for Student Affairs, September 2019, http://www.policies.uci.edu/policies/procs/900-23.php.

66. Pia Singh, "Before Former ICE Director Speaks, Penn Shuts the Event Down Citing Loud Student Chants," *Daily Pennsylvanian*, October 23, 2019, https://www.thedp.com/article/2019/10/ice-protest-perry-world-house-immigration-customs.

67. Regent Policy Document 4-21, "Commitment to Academic Freedom and Freedom of Expression," University of Wisconsin Board of Regents, October 2017, https://www.wisconsin.edu/regents/policies/commitment-to-academic-freedom-and-freedom-of-expression.

68. H.B. 3409, 102nd Gen. Assemb., Reg. Sess. (Ill. 2021).

69. Natalie Allison, "Republican Senators to Tennessee's Public Colleges: Stop Athletes from Kneeling During National Anthem," *Tennessean*, February 23, 2021, https://www.tennessean.com/story/news/politics/2021/02/23/republican-state-senators-tennessee-public-colleges-stop-athletes-kneeling-during-national-anthem/4556148001.

70. For an argument that "school disturbance laws are not only unnecessary for maintaining school discipline, but are unconstitutionally vague and overbroad," see Noelia Rivera Calderón, "Arrested at the Schoolhouse Gate: Criminal School Disturbance Laws and Children's Rights in Schools," *National Law Guild Review* 76, no. 1 (2019), 13.

71. For a summary of legislative efforts against protest, see Lee Rowland and Vera Eidelman, "Where Protests Flourish, Anti-Protest Bills Follow," ACLU blog, February 17, 2017, https://www.aclu.org/blog/free-speech/rights-protesters/where-protests-flourish-anti-protest-bills-follow?redirect=blog/speak-freely/where-protests-flourish-anti-protest-bills-follow.

72. Frank D. LoMonte and Clay Calvert, "The Open Mic, Unplugged: Challenges to Viewpoint-Based Constraints on Public-Comment Periods" *Case Western Reserve Law Review* 69, no. 1 (2018): 39.

73. For an argument advancing this view, see Jeremy Waldron, "Heckle: To Disconcert with Questions, Challenges, or Gibes," Public Law Research Paper No. 17-42, NYU School of Law, June 17, 2017, https://ssrn.com/abstract=3054555; http://dx.doi.org/10.2139/ssrn.3054555.

74. Again, I do not attempt to provide a comprehensive legal analysis here. For more on the legal considerations, see Chemerinsky and Gillman, *Free Speech on Campus*.

75. PEN America has developed a set of policy suggestions on these and related matters. See "Campus Free Speech Guide," PEN America, https://campusfreespeechguide.pen.org/.

76. "200 Protesters disrupt UNM event over pro-Donald Trump bridge sign" October 6, 2016, https://campus-climate.umn.edu/content/200-protesters-disrupt-umn-event-over-pro-donald-trump-bridge-sign.

77. In my 2017 book *Free Speech on Campus*.

78. For more on the Chicago letter, see Scott Jaschik, "The Chicago Letter and Its Aftermath," *Inside Higher Ed*, August 29, 2016, https://www.insidehighered.com/news/2016/08/29/u-chicago-letter-new-students-safe-spaces-sets-intense-debate. The letter is aligned with the Chicago Statement, now endorsed by many institutions, and which I find to be unhelpful overall, as I explain in Sigal R. Ben-Porath, "Against Endorsing the Chicago Principles," *Inside Higher Ed*, December 11, 2018, https://www.insidehighered.com/views/2018/12/11/what-chicago-principles-miss-when-it-comes-free-speech-and-academic-freedom-opinion.

79. David Gooblar, *The Missing Course: Everything They Never Taught You about College Teaching* (Cambridge, MA: Harvard University Press, 2021). See also Jonathan Zimmerman, *Amateur Hour* (Baltimore: Johns Hopkins Press, 2020).

80. I thank Kenneth Elmore for telling me about the success of such programs at Boston College.

A FINAL WORD

1. Daniels, *What Universities Owe Democracy*, 238.

2. "Scholars Under Fire Database," Foundation for Individual Rights in Education, continuously updated, https://www.thefire.org/research/scholars-under-fire-database/.

Index

global warming. *See* climate change
Goldberg, Suzanne, 117
governance, shared, 27, 39, 111
Graham, Matthew, 163n30

Hannah-Jones, Nikole, 118, 137
hate speech, 4, 24, 64–65, 75, 77, 95,
116, 127–28, 132, 134, 140–41, 171n14,
172n25
hatred: and campus speech, 132–34; and
disinformation/misinformation, 23–25,
133; and exclusion/inclusion, 88–89;
and lies/lying, 24, 88–89; and polarization, 23–25
Hayward, Clarissa, 41
Hess, Diana, 108–10
higher education: and civic culture/life,
50–54; and civic education, 175n2;
and civic trust, 4, 112; conservatives'
views of, 169n58; and democracy, 1–2,
5–6, 91–92, 136–37, 157, 169n57; and
diversity, 48, 119; epistemic role of, in
democracy, 169n57; and epistemology,
shared, 48; and First Amendment,
114–15, 123; and free speech, 5–6, 57,
119, 154–55; and inclusion, 64; and
knowledge, 48–49; and open expression, 10, 128, 159, and partisanship,
164n43; politicization of, 48–49, 129,
136, 153–54; and truth, 46–48, 53. *See
also* campus speech
Hillsdale College, 123–24
Holocaust denial, 29, 133
Hussain, Waheed, 85, 171n4

I Am Not Your Negro (Baldwin), 77
ideas: and arguments, 51; and beliefs,
108–9; and campus speech, 128, 143;
and counterevidence, 23; diverse,
23; and knowledge, 108–9; and new
avenues for investigation, 49; and
opinions, 73; and values, 51
identity: and campus speech, collaboration, 151–52; and group affiliation/
connections, 43; and ideology, 86;
mega, and extremism, 13; national,
and inclusion, 86–87; and polarization,

12–16, 107; and political reasoning,
43; and politics, 107. *See also* social
identities
ideology: and biases, 124; and class differences, 121; and democracy, 31, 46;
and diversity, 46–48, 137, 146, 155; and
epistemology, shared, 87; and free
speech, 9, 157; and identity, 86; and
media, 13–14; and mistrust, 13–14; and
open expression, 99; and polarization,
3, 15–17, 21, 40, 146; and truth, 40;
and values, 26, 40. *See also* political
ideology
ignorance, willful. *See* willful ignorance
inclusion: and academic freedom, 71–
73, 75–76, 90; and activism, 70; and
alienation, 62–63; and attitudes, 87,
96; and campus speech, 1–2, 60, 116–
17, 136; and cancel culture, 2, 4–5, 60,
68–72; and censorship, 72–73, 131; and
civic culture/life, 60, 88; and civility,
61–68, 83–84, 111; defined, 59; and
democracy, 5, 91; and dignitary safety,
51, 60; and dignity, 65; and disinformation, 23–24, 68, 154; and distrust/
mistrust, 91; and diversity, 59, 65, 69,
77, 86, 89, 91, 114, 125; and epistemology, shared, 156–57; and ethics, 65; and
First Amendment, 65–66, 72–73; and
free inquiry, 60; and free speech, 62,
77; and generational differences, 5–6;
and harm, 4–5, 59–91; and harm, subjective, 61–68; and hatred, 88–89; and
higher education, 64; and isolation,
88; and lies/lying, 61–68, 88–89; and
marginalization, 61, 65–70, 90; and
media, 77; and misinformation, 154;
and national identity, 86–87; and open
expression, 2, 5, 77, 90–91, 117, 121, 145,
159; and perilous spaces, 72–83; and
pluralism, 76, 154; and polarization,
85–91; promoting, 1–6, 153–57; and safe
spaces, 72–83, 90; significance of, 4;
and social conditions, 60; training, 59,
114; and trust, 85–91; and truth, 1–2, 5,
23–24, 70, 130–31; and values, 126. *See
also* exclusion